JOURNEY OUT OF

SILENCE

BY WILLIAM L. RUSH

MEDIA PRODUCTIONS & MARKETING

COVER DESIGN: TONY SCHAPPAUGH
BOOK DESIGN: TONY SCHAPPAUGH

ISBN: 0-939644-21-5
LIBRARY OF CONGRESS CATALOG CARD # 86-60700

FIRST EDITION, FIRST PRINTING
MADE IN U.S.A.

MEDIA PRODUCTIONS & MARKETING, INC.
2440 "O" STREET
LINCOLN, NEBRASKA 68510

Dedication:
To Deanne
who perceives me
as a
valid person,
not as an
invalid *person*

CONTENTS

William L. Rush
Lincoln, Nebraska
1986

Photo by John Butler

A FEW ACKNOWLEDGEMENTS

"Thank you" only has eight letters and is inadequate to express what I feel, but I must acknowledge a few of the many people that have helped me in my journey out of silence. So —

THANK YOU:
Mom and Dad for loving and accepting me—not aborting or institutionalizing me.

Brothers three—Jim, Don, Bob for fighting with and for me—not ignoring or patronizing me.

Grandma, grandpa, aunts, uncles, nieces, nephews, cousins. You showed me that I was, indeed, a part of a family. In doing so, you showed me that I belonged to the family of man.

THANK YOU:
Special teachers —

Jean Clanton for my first taste of success—the headstick—she simply expected me not to fail.

Joleen George for setting impossible goals and showing me how to reach them.

JoAnn Dickerson and Dick Streckfuss for wading through my pile of disjointed writings that eventually became this book, but more importantly, for welcoming me to their class as a fellow human being, not because of Section 504 of the Rehabilitation Act of 1973.
To the Journalism School of UNL for expecting excellence from me.

THANK YOU:
Westside High School Class of '73 for not waiting for Public Law 94-142.

x   Ed and Sally Henry for showing me I could survive and be happy away from home.

Roger Bacon for growing with me during our early days at UNL.

Mark Dahmke for giving me much more than a voice synthesizer.

Anne Fadiman for writing about me the way I am and being my friend.

Mark Caughey for understanding and being my friend.

And,

A special THANK YOU to Barbara Brennan Rueve, the first person to encourage me to write this book, for showing me how to get started on it.

A PERSONAL PREFACE

by Anne Fadiman
Staff Writer, Life Magazine

The first time I met Bill Rush, I thought he was having a seizure. I'd come to the University of Nebraska at Lincoln to write a story about him for *Life*, and we'd agreed to meet by the east side of the student union on the city campus. A tall skinny guy with a weird, unicorn-like metal rod attached to his forehead whirred up in an electric wheelchair to which his legs were tied with tattered white bandages. As I reached out my hand to shake his—I knew he couldn't shake mine, but I was full of idealistic notions about how to treat people with disabilities—Bill began to wiggle with such alarming energy that I thought if it weren't for those grimy bandages he might end up on the ground. Later, when I knew Bill better, it became clear to me that his "seizure" was in fact nothing of the sort. When he's excited, his athetoid cerebral palsy makes his body move in all sorts of uncontrollable ways, and though it was hardly deliberate, he was simply signalling that he was pleased to meet me.

I tell you this story because of one of the first things that Bill ever said to me. (When I say "said," I mean that he spelled out the words by pointing with that unicorn-like headstick to letters on an alphabet board placed across the arms of his wheelchair. Bill's comments are always so ironic, incisive, and generally on-target that in retrospect I tend to forget the laborious means by which they were conveyed.) "WHEN YOU WRITE ABOUT ME," he spelled, "PLEASE RE-MOVE MY HALO."

xii

What he meant was that he was tired of being promoted to angelic superstardom simply by virtue of his disability. He didn't want to be called "courageous" or "a hero." He wanted people to know that he drooled, that he made peculiar noises, that his arms flapped around as if, as he put it, "I AM CONDUCTING 'THE FLIGHT OF THE BUMBLEBEE.'" He was also annoyed at the popular image of wheelchair users as genderless children, and wanted people to know that he had all the usual sexual urges and felt frustrated by his lack of romantic experience. Once I asked him what his life's ambition was. I expected to hear that he hoped to win the Pulitzer Prize, because I knew he planned to be a journalist and obviously had considerable talent. Instead, he said, "MY GREATEST AMBITION IS TO HAVE MY OBITUARY READ: SURVIVED BY WIFE AND CHILDREN."

I've known Bill now for nearly seven years, and he's never stopped educating me. When I slip up and call a person with a disability a "victim," or use a negatively loaded phrase like "confined to a wheelchair," he invariably, and correctly, takes me to task. With all the power of his exceedingly strong character, he *forces* me to deal with him as the complete human being that he is. I will never forget one evening when he and his friend Mark Dahmke and I went to a movie together. As Mark and I were trying to shove his wheelchair into the tiny elevator, Bill indicated that he wanted to spell something to us. "Not right now," I said. "We're having problems with your chair. Wait till we get out of the elevator." It turned out that what he wanted to say was that the wheelchair wouldn't fit unless we removed its footrests, and he was furious that we didn't have the patience to let him communicate. After the movie, he spelled—and if Bill had a voice, I know it would have been icy—"ANNE, DON'T EVER DO THAT TO ME AGAIN."

Bill has plenty of anger in him, most of it justified, and most of it *helpful*—anyone who knows him will emerge, as I have, with raised consciousness. His anger is well balanced by his wit and compassion. He is one of the funniest people I know. Who else would observe, of a picture of him taking a bath in which his narrow chest was clearly visible, that the photograph was "overexposed but underdeveloped"? Bill is also one of the most thoughtful people I have ever met. Once, when he heard I was recovering from a minor operation at my parents' home in California, and knowing only my New York address, he motored his wheelchair to the local library and looked up

"Fadiman" in the Santa Barbara telephone book so he could send me a get-well card. It must have taken him at least a couple of hours. That is how he deals with all his friends: with complete attention, a kind of total *focus* that one rarely encounters in these days of casual acquaintanceship.

Bill's graduation from the UNL's College of Journalism with a 3.66 average, on a 4.0 scale, was an extremely moving occasion. He received his diploma from his wheelchair, looking handsomer than I'd ever seen him, wearing a black cap and gown and a gold medal suspended from his neck on a bright red ribbon, signifying that he was graduating with distinction. His intelligence and incredible stick-to-it-iveness had paid off. He'd been the first member of his family to go to college, and now, with his parents and brothers and friends watching, he was passing with honors into the real world. "Way to go, Bill," I said to myself. I'm glad I didn't have to talk, because I was completely choked-up. Bill may not have a halo, but at that moment I sure felt he had guts.

The book you are about to read is a testament to all of Bill's qualities—intelligence, anger, frustration, wit, sensitivity, and guts. As a journalist, I find it an impressively professional piece of work, one that I suspect will be widely read and remembered. Every word of it was typed with a headstick, which had no effect on the writing itself (Bill would be livid if I suggested that this difficult mode of composition should earn him any special deference), but may have some effect on the reader, as a simple lesson in patience. If you have a disability yourself, I hope that *Journey Out Of Silence* fires up your most extravagant ambitions, the ones our condescending culture has been telling you are out of reach. If you are able-bodied, I hope that Bill Rush will teach you, as he has taught me, to look at people in wheelchairs as neither better nor worse, neither more admirable nor more pitiable, neither nobler nor weaker, than the rest of us.

I'd like to say a word to you, Bill. You are one of the most interesting people I've ever met, and if you had not challenged me and taught me as you have these past seven years, my life would have been infinitely duller.

Anne Fadiman
New York
June, 1986

INTRODUCTION

This is an illustration of what one person with a disability experienced while struggling to be integrated into society.

Through the years people with impairments have been regarded as saints, as possessed by the devil, as children, as untouchables, as clowns, as tragedies, superhuman, or subhuman. Rarely, however, as human.

I have cerebral palsy—one of the most misunderstood disorders on the face of the earth. Cerebral palsy is simply damage to an infant brain. It is not inherited, terminal, or contagious.

Cerebral palsy has left me without the use of my arms, legs, or voice. It has, however, left me with the capacity to think, to remember, to hear, to see, and to feel skin sensations as well as emotions. In other words, I can (or have the potential to) understand anything in my social world.

For fifteen years I led a sheltered life. I was enrolled in a special school. Then I was enrolled in a homebound high school study program. Then I went to the University of Nebraska-Lincoln. I attended classes, lived in a dorm, burnt the midnight oil, fought with as well as learned from my professors, sweated finals, and loved just like any other college student.

My parents had a creed:
This is a baby. He needs what all babies need.
This is a child. He needs what all children need.
This is an adolescent. He needs what all adolescents need.
This is an adult. He needs what all adults need.
Oh, by the way, he has cerebral palsy.
I hope this collection of vignettes illustrates this creed in action.

PART ONE

JOURNEY WITH SILENCE

CHAPTER 1

CHILDHOOD YEARS

"The goal of this class is to tell the truth, the whole truth, and nothing but," said my English professor, who was wearing a neckbrace because of an automobile accident. "Now, next Tuesday I want you to write your first autobiographical story. Since Bill is obviously different from the rest of us and has already started on his autobiography, I want the class to write him questions that you would like to know about him or his disease, cerebral palsy."

I groaned since I couldn't talk. I wanted to say that cerebral palsy was not a "disease." Some would call it a disease, but it's not contagious. Some would call it a "handicap," but it doesn't handicap me. Stairs, curbs, narrow doorways, steep ramps, and an unaccepting or misinformed public are my handicaps. Some people would call CP a "disability." This is closer. A disability is a medically defined condition that manifests itself in a physical, emotional, and/or mental limitation. But I don't like that term. Basically, what cerebral palsy is to me is an inconvenience, like the professor's neckbrace was an inconvenience to him.

"Oh, I obviously said something wrong. How about if I use the word 'condition' instead of 'disease'? Is that better?" the professor asked, smiling.

I nodded. It would do, even though it did make me feel as if I were pregnant.

As the class wrote, I reflected on how they must have been seeing me. I was quite a sight, tied into a power chair that I operate by pushing against its control box with the back of my head. I have a stylus attached to my head via a band from a welder's helmet. Since I can't talk or use my hands, I point to a letter chart on my lap tray. A

4   kind classmate has to take off my mittens, take off my hat, and unzip my coat so I don't roast in class. Then, after class, he rebundles me so I can brave the Nebraska winters. The students hadn't any way of knowing that after the semester I would graduate from the University of Nebraska-Lincoln with a bachelor's degree in journalism. Nor could they have known that I was living in an apartment off campus. But I prayed that by the end of the semester my classmates would see that I was just like they were.

The professor collected the scraps of paper from the class and gave them to me. I glanced at them only for a second. But one note kept drumming in my mind. It asked me to recollect my earliest experiences.

I thought as I made my way to my other classes, "What were my earliest memories of my years in the world? Could I separate what I actually remembered from what was only told to me?" Sorting it out wasn't easy.

I remember being told that during my first year of life I had three expensive hernia operations. As a result, I cried a lot. Because I had no sucking reflex, I couldn't take a bottle until Grandma Rush devised a way of holding my lips around the nipple of my bottle.

I remember that my mother had told me that when I was about five months old an uncaring, cold pediatrician confirmed our family doctor's diagnosis of cerebral palsy:

"Your baby has cerebral palsy," he told my mom. "He might also be deaf, dumb, blind and mentally retarded."

According to my mom, he had stripped me, and laid me on the examining table. I was being treated as if I were of no value—as if I were invalid. The examining room was cold. So when the good doctor bent to examine my penis, I urinated in his face. My mother said that I always did have good instincts. She looked for another doctor because she knew I wasn't blind or mentally retarded and found a neurologist who specialized in cerebral palsy.

I remember being told that when I was nine months old I got my first set of braces. As my mom puts it, "They were heavy, expensive, confining and forever outgrown. But they did their job and kept your body straight."

I remember being told that although I was a demanding and expensive baby, I was loved. I remember somebody was always reading to me or holding me. I remember that I always felt love and acceptance.

I met my aide for lunch at a café on campus. I asked him to get the scraps of papers from my coat pocket and to arrange them so I could look at them. The top scrap asked two questions: "Where did you go to school before UNL?" and "If you can't walk how did you get there?" I pondered for a moment and read the next bit of paper. It had two questions: "How did you play?" and "Who did you play with?" I was about to read the third scrap of paper but my aide had returned with my lunch.

As I ate I thought about the questions and remembered my first days of kindergarten at Dr. J. P. Lord School, a school for students with orthopedic disabilities in Omaha (my hometown) and how miserable they were for me. At the age of five, I was a "Momma's Boy" and hadn't really been away from her.

For my mother, however, the first day of school was a blessing. "I knew that you were intelligent and your only chance for a life of value lay in your ability to use that intelligence," she told me years later. "For this, you needed an education."

School was to be the answer, the cure-all. As my mother explained to me when I was old enough to understand, she thought that everything was going to get better once I started school; I would learn to walk, talk, write my ABC's, and my family and I would live happily ever after. School offered some relief to her and to my father in raising a child with cerebral palsy but was definitely not the cure-all.

For five years they had been faced with a problem for which they hadn't been trained. As Mom has reminded me time and time again, I didn't come with an operating manual when I was born with cerebral palsy.

The first time the taxicab came to take me to school I thought it was taking me away from home for good. Little did I know that the Dr. J. P. Lord Parent-Teacher Association had contracted with the city cab companies to transport the children to and from school. I thought the school was going to keep me. This fantasy was strengthened by the boarding home for children who were disabled and who needed medical or educational programs not available in their own home towns. A five-year-old can't tell the difference between himself and the boarding children. So I thought they were going to keep me—just

6   like they were keeping others. I cried because the experience was frightening and made me feel insecure.

I couldn't tell my teachers my fears, so they couldn't help me deal with them. It wasn't the teachers' fault that they couldn't communicate with me, nor was it mine. The teachers had other children to teach—or try to teach. All they could do was set me out in the hall alone until I got over my crying fits. This didn't enhance my attitude toward school or the teachers.

At home I could communicate with my family by looking at the thing I wanted. If I was hungry, I would look at the cupboard until my mom would guess that I wanted some kind of food. Then she would ask me if I wanted this or that. I would shake my head "no" until she named the right food, which was sometimes the last thing in the cupboard. Sometimes Mom would get so frustrated that she would say, "Does Billy want a spanking?"

I would shake my head no very quickly. It was a slow process of guessing and eliminating, but at least I could talk to my family and felt loved and accepted by them, which was more than I could feel at the school.

One day I went into the kindergarten classroom and saw a seven-year-old boy with a crew cut walking back and forth shouting that he wanted to draw big black gorillas instead of cute rabbits. It was the first time I had seen somebody who was behaviorally impaired, so I didn't know what to think of my new school. Since the teacher was ignoring him, I thought he was the norm at the school. Fortunately, I was wrong. In fact, there was no "norm" at this school.

One bright September morning I was watching the train go by the school and feeling homesick. At the age of five I thought I would grow up and work on the railroad just like my dad and Grandpa Rush. When I turned around to rest my eyes from the sun, I saw Joani Madden, a blonde, blue-eyed doll. I ceased being homesick. She looked frail sitting in the oversized school wheelchair. I felt I had to protect her from the crazy guy who liked to draw gorillas. Just like my hero, Popeye, protected Olive Oyl from Brutus. More importantly, however, Joani was my first friend.

While my brother could make friends simply by going around our neighborhood, I couldn't play with kids in our neighborhood because they were afraid of me or didn't understand how to play with me.

Whenever the neighbors did get together I had to stay indoors with the mothers and listen to them exchange recipes and gossip and compare their love lives (sex education), which then bored me into taking my nap.

But Joani was different. She wasn't afraid of me. Unlike me, Joani had understandable speech so she said "Hi" to me. It was the first friendly word spoken to me at this school. We communicated with each other by playing twenty questions, with Joani as the questioner even though her speech was also affected slightly by cerebral palsy. School seemed worthwhile now that I had a friend.

The school staff encouraged the friendship for two reasons: they thought it was cute that two handicapped kindergartners should become infatuated with each other, and the only way the therapist could get me to do my exercises was by telling me, "If you do this, we'll show Joani. She'll be so proud of you."

Since I watched the Popeye cartoons and the Superman show, I believed the macho image would please the girls. So I did the exercises thinking that Joani would be impressed. Who knows? Maybe she was.

We both went to the Cerebral Palsy Day Camp, which was sponsored by a local women's charity organization. We campers had to put on skits for our parents each year, which suited me—the ham that I was. Somebody arranged for Joani and me to be in the same skit each year. Of course, I was always the hero and she was always the heroine. One year we were Popeye and Olive Oyl; the next year we were Yogi Bear and Cindy Bear. At the time, the skits were very serious productions. We practiced for them all week.

We attended each other's birthday parties. I remember my gift to her was a plastic dimestore engagement ring that I bought from my disappointed brother, Jimmy. He and I were on vacation with our parents. We stopped to eat at a restaurant which had a machine that dispensed either rings or whistles for a dime. Jimmy asked for a dime to give to the toy dispenser in exchange for a whistle. But the machine spat a plastic ring at him. Jimmy came back in tears. Mom tried to compliment him on his prize, but it didn't do any good.

While she was comforting Jimmy, I got an idea. My uncle had just gotten engaged and had given his girlfriend a diamond ring. So I reasoned that if Uncle Dennis was grown-up and gave a ring to his girlfriend, then giving a ring to Joani would be the grown-up thing to

8   do. I motioned towards the ring with my eyes. I kept staring at the ring until Mom finally asked me, "Do you want to buy that ring from Jimmy?" I nodded furiously.

"But this is a little girl's ring. You don't want to wear this, do you? Do you want to give it to somebody?" asked my bewildered mom.

I nodded.

"Who? Is it Grandma Rush or Grandma Brown?" asked Mom.

I shook my head "no."

"Is she at school?" asked my Mom.

I nodded my head "yes."

"Does she work there?" Mom asked.

I shook my head "no."

"Is she in your classroom?"

I nodded my head "yes."

"Joani Madden, that pretty blonde your teacher told me about? From what your teacher says I should have guessed her right off the bat. Did you know her dad was a navy officer?" Mom asked.

I nodded my head as fast as I could. Finally I had gotten my message across.

Surprisingly, my parents did let me buy the plastic ring from Jimmy and give it to Joani. Apparently they were hoping Joani's willingness to work would rub off on me. Since Joani came from a family of eight children, she had to learn to do things for herself in spite of her disability. I, in contrast, was pampered. Mom would try to give me therapy, but as soon as I cried she would stop or else my grandma would make her stop by saying, "You're hurting him!"

So Joani and I were engaged on her birthday. And we honestly believed that we were going to get married some day. I even remember Mom trying to pair off Uncle Alan with one of Joani's older sisters saying jokingly, "We might as well have two marriages in one family."

But the Navy spoiled our beautiful plans by transferring Joani's father to West Virginia when we were seven. I didn't cry, but I felt sick inside for a long time. Fortunately, the hurt was eased by our vows to write each other whenever we could, and throughout a decade and a half we still keep in touch.

The last time I heard from her was just two weeks ago. She sent me a postcard from Hawaii and said she was spending Christmas 1982, there. I felt a tad bit envious. I also felt a twinge of guilt for letting two weeks go by without answering it.

When I was finished with my lunch, my aide asked me about the scraps of paper. When I told him, he asked if he could see what my classmates had asked. I nodded my permission. My aide spread the scraps of paper out on the table. They had all kinds of questions. They were questions about my health, cerebral palsy, friends, my likes, my dislikes, my accomplishments, my parents, my siblings, and my grandparents. The questions triggered both good and bad memories. But more importantly they made me realize my parents had given me a surprisingly "normal" and stable childhood.

I remember losing my first tooth. My parents instinctively felt that I should pull it. I guess that they felt since I was five I should have some control over my body. My front baby teeth started to be shoved out by my permanent teeth. Of course, they were encouraged to vacate my mouth by a few forward falls when I was crawling.

One day my mom felt my front teeth and said, "It looks like the tooth fairy will visit you tonight if you're lucky. What do you say if we pull your tooth and give it to the tooth fairy? Maybe you could pull it yourself and take it to school for show and tell. Would you like that?"

I nodded my head slowly. I wasn't too anxious about self-inflicted pain—or any pain, for that matter.

"Daddy, come and look at Billy's tooth. I think it's ready to come out," Mom called to Dad.

"Let me get my pliers," my father joked as he came into the room to inspect my tooth. He wiggled it, which made it loose if it wasn't loose already. "Sure enough, it's loose."

"I wonder if there's any way for Billy to pull it himself," Mom said.

"Well, Grandpa Rush used to tie one end of a string to an open door and the other end to my tooth. Then, he'd slam the door shut. I suppose we could tie a string around Billy's finger and have him yank on it until the tooth comes out. By the look of the tooth, it wouldn't take much to get it out of there," Dad said, still wiggling the tooth. If he didn't stop wiggling it, the tooth would come out before I could pull it.

My dad put me in my oversized highchair which was built for me by my great-uncle Carroll. Mom got a piece of string and brought it to me. She tied one end to the forefinger of my left hand while Dad held the spastic athetoid hand still. The other end went around my tooth.

When Mom had tied everything securely, Dad let go of my hand.

10

My spastic athetoid left hand jerked. My tooth flew from my mouth. I grinned a toothless smile until I saw my blood coming from the newly-made hole. It was a steady stream, which added color to my drool.

I reacted like any five-year-old would. I cried hysterically.

"Oh, it's all right, Billy. Look, you've pulled your tooth by yourself. I'll go get a mirror so you can see how funny you look," Mom said.

She was right. I looked so funny that I stopped crying and laughed.

The tooth went in a matchbox and was positioned at the top of my bed that night. When I woke up the next morning a dollar was in its place. The tooth fairy had always been generous with us Rush children.

I also remember that no matter how hard they tried to give me a "normal," healthy childhood, some absurdities did creep into my upbringing—like the time when I was eight, eating creamed chicken, and one of my teeth became part of the fare.

It was one of those lovely suppers where I was supposed to hold my head in the center of my body, close my mouth on the spoon, chew each bite with my mouth closed, and swallow each bite. Never mind if I tasted—or enjoyed—what I was eating. Never mind if I had a chance to enjoy the family chatter.

The speech therapists had told my mom that if I just could learn how to chew, suck, blow, and swallow, I could talk. Of course, had the dear speech therapists told my parents that hanging me upside down every day for an hour would have made me walk, talk, and use my hands, my parents would have done so faithfully.

What the professionals had failed to realize was that when I had to concentrate on all four functions at once I couldn't concentrate on what I was saying. For most, talking is an acquired reflex, but for me it would always be unachievable.

I wouldn't have minded working as hard as I did, had I perceived some progress. But every year it was the same dull drills of trying to say the vowels, of trying to blow a feather across a mirror, and of trying to suck (and blow bubbles) through a paper straw.

Still they persisted in the belief that I would be able to have "normal" speech someday if I were just properly trained. One of the methods of training me was to give me speech therapy while feeding

me, which made sense. If I didn't eat properly, I would starve. If I
starved, I wouldn't have to worry about talking.

Since I ate most meals at home, my mother was drafted to play speech therapist.

My tooth fell out during such a game. I felt my jaw clamp down on something hard. "Better spit it out," I thought to myself.

I let it slide out onto my bib, but unfortunately the potatoes and gravy and chicken came with it—a common happening which was nauseating to my family. My tongue was never any good at separating things, be they words or particles of food.

Mom didn't see my tooth, so she routinely scraped the food from my bib and fed it to me again. When she tried to feed me the bite again, I grimaced.

"Come on, Billy," Mom said, "This is good for you, so open up before I spank you. And hold your head up, close your mouth like your speech therapist says you can. Let's get this meal over with."

I obeyed but let it slide out again. If I swallowed my tooth, I wouldn't get to spend my dollar from the tooth fairy. I was getting very mercenary when it came to my teeth. Who wouldn't at a dollar a tooth? "Billy, if you spit this bite out one more time, I'll slap you," Mom sternly said as she scraped the twice rejected bite from my bib. She put it in my mouth for the third time. "I don't care if you like it or not. Just eat it!"

A part of her frustration was caused by my speech therapist's insisting that Mom use dinnertime—a family time—to give me speech therapy. Not only was Mom supposed to prepare the meal, set the table, serve the meal, and join the mealtime chatter, but also see that I held my head up straight while I took the bites off the spoon, chewed them with my mouth closed, and swallowed them. She tried, but she wasn't temperamentally equipped for the task.

So, I swallowed the bite. Maybe the hard piece was just gristle.

After the meal Mom wiped off my mouth and saw the new cavity.

"Did you lose a tooth?" She asked nonchalantly.

I nodded.

"Where is it?" Mom asked curiously.

I looked at the plate with the remains of the creamed chicken and potatoes.

12

"No, it's not on the plate," she said bewildered.

I looked at my bib and opened and closed my mouth several times.

"You don't mean it fell out while you were eating?" Mom asked concerned.

I frowned and nodded my head.

"You don't mean I fed it to you in the bite you kept spitting out," she said hysterically.

I nodded my head sadly.

"Oh, Billy, I'm sorry. I feel terrible, not to mention stupid," Mom said apologetically. "Well, at least you're not a shark. Can you imagine what would happen if their moms fed them one of their teeth? After I do the dishes I'll read you a story or two."

After that, whenever I dropped a mouthful of food more than once, Mom checked it very carefully. But the tooth fairy still owes me a dollar.

Therapy. It wasn't normal but my parents thought it was a path to normality. I hated getting vit as much as Mom did giving it. The word therapist should be hyphenated so that it reads the-rapist. Throughout my early life therapists showed me the same courtesy as rapists show their victims.

I remember once when I was eight the school's occupational therapist had me play a game of checkers with her in an attempt to develop my grasp. The set with which we played was fixed so that students had to pick up a checker to move it. The therapist made a rule that if I dropped a checker, then she would get it. I would be able to pick a checker up out of its square, but when I got it into my hand, my arm would fly around excitedly. Then I would drop the checker and she would get it. This happened on almost every move. After awhile I started to drop the checkers deliberately to get the humiliating game over quickly.

Suddenly there weren't any more of my checkers on the board. The therapist had them all. She said, "See why I want you to develop your grasp? You can't even play a game. Why don't you try? Well, I've wasted enough time with you. I'll take you back to your classroom and let your teacher worry about you."

I remember how relieved I was to hear her say that. At least when I dropped something in the classroom, my teacher gave it back to me. A person with athetoid cerebral palsy has enough frustration trying to make his hands do what he wants them to do without having a therapist say she was wasting her time with him.

But I agreed with her. Time spent with her was wasted when compared to time spent with my Uncle Alan. Born twenty years after my mom, he also helped in giving me a normal childhood. Time spent with him was never wasted. My first memories of him are vivid although I was only four years old. He was just fifteen then. His gift of time has lasted and has been treasured. Before I was to enter kindergarten he spent the whole summer with me.

Uncle Alan stayed with me that summer because Mom was going to have another boy, who would be named Donald Jay, and lifting me was impossible for her. Grandma Brown volunteered Alan's services by saying, "Alan can take care of Billy. It would be good for him to learn some responsibility."

Little did Grandma know that she was giving me the best summer of my childhood.

He was responsible for my ambition and imagination. When I was with him, I didn't feel disabled because he didn't give me charity. He gave me friendship. I guess he was a cross between Mr. Rogers and Big Bird. He could even make therapy fun.

That summer was spent in fantasy land. Uncle Alan did almost everything with me. I think we aged both Grandma and Mom with our stunts. Alan had helped my brother Jimmy, then five years old, build a treehouse. I kept pestering Uncle Alan to take me up the tree and inside the treehouse. So one day he did.

Alan perched himself on the bottom branch of the tree and had somebody hand my squirming body to him. Then, with his feet not so firmly planted on the branch, he hoisted me into the treehouse, where somebody who was inside the dilapidated structure pulled me in. I was scared to death partly because I had never been up that high before, and partly because tree climbing for one is hard enough without having to balance on a branch while struggling to hold on to another person. More than once, I heard my grandma shout from the ground, "Alan! You're going to break both your neck and Billy's neck. Now come down here."

Even though the climb was scary, I did get to climb a tree and play in a treehouse just like any other kid. Sure, I did it differently. But I did it.

. Alan also gave me some disguised therapy. Once he dressed me in my Superman costume and pretended I was on a high cliff (which was really my trundle bed). He then put a hunk of Kryptonite (which was really a wooden block) beside me. Then Uncle Alan pretended he was Superman's arch enemy and said, "Ah-ha. Superman, I have you now. You can't get rid of that hunk of Kryptonite. If you could just get your hand to it and toss it over the cliff, you'd be okay. But you're too weak. The Kryptonite has made you too weak. But wait. What is this? Your arm is moving towards the hunk. It's touching it. You're moving it towards the edge . . . and there goes the Kryptonite. Superman does it again!"

Then my uncle gave me a piggyback ride around the house to celebrate my victory over Kryptonite.

Some Superman I turned out to be. Now I was able to leap curbs at a single bound, faster than a speeding paper wad, and more powerful than a wet noodle.

Not all the summertimes were pleasant or normal. When I was six, Mom had me crawling the length of our backyard during the summertime. Each day she had me struggle from our back door to our sandpile for therapeutic purposes. When you have cerebral palsy nothing is ever done for fun, only for therapy. (When I was older, Mom said that frequently my therapists made her feel like she had to choose between loving me and treating my cerebral palsy because if she didn't give me therapy, she was chastized by my therapists.) The sandbox was located at the far end of the yard. If I did the exercise well, I got to go swimming. If I did poorly, I just got aching muscles and battered knees.

To tell me to crawl was like telling an able-bodied man, "Walk this tightrope over Niagra Falls blindfolded." It required the same amount of intense concentration. I fell flat on my face frequently. Mom would have to come out and pick me up and start me off again.

At first I used to fantasize while I was crawling. I was a secret agent going on a special mission. Each blade of grass was an object invented by the enemy to trip me. But these dangerous blades wouldn't stop me from reaching the sandbox and retrieving the buried message for the chief.

The next day I was Buffalo Bill crawling across the Southwest

desert to save his buddies from being slaughtered by unfriendly
Indians. The sandbox was the site of the would-be slaughter.

But you can only pretend for so long. The daily routine became
boring, and my knees began to burn from the rough ground, and I
began to get tired of playing in the sandpile every day.

One day I started to rebel. Mom had to coax me every inch of the
way. It was hot that day. Tempers were short. I couldn't see what
good this was doing me. I would much rather be lying on our living
room floor watching television. My muscles were so uncoordinated
that it was almost impossible to make them do what I wanted them
to do. It was as frustrating for me as it was for Mom. When we got a
foot from the sandbox, I fell again. Out of frustration and anger I
kicked and screamed. Mom quickly got our garden hose and squirted
me with ice cold water.

"Billy, why don't you do what the therapists and I tell you to do?
Can't you see we're doing this for your own damn good? I'm
squirting you to make you wake up and to keep myself from killing
you, you ungrateful little brat. I know that you're smart enough to
figure out some way to re-route the right message from your brain
to your muscles. Or at least that's what the therapists say. So why
don't you do it? Don't you want to walk someday?"

I continued to throw my fit. I didn't want to walk that badly. So we
threw our normal temper fits and they helped us both.

Even when I was sick and in the hospital it was usually for the
normal childhood illnesses. At the age of nine I had the first surgery
that I remember, a double tonsillectomy. (I had my first hernia
operation when I was two months old and the second at seven
months.) Ironically, it was a common operation and had nothing to
do with cerebral palsy. A routine hearing test showed that I had
developed a slight hearing loss. This, combined with a series of
colds and sore throats, convinced my family doctor and parents that
I should have my tonsils and adenoids removed.

The date for the operation was set for April first, a lousy April
Fool's joke as I recall.

My dad was absolutely no help in soothing my nerves. When we
arrived at the hospital, Dad kept saying, "Where's the son of a bitch
with those long pliers? Why, I could yank those goddamn tonsils

16   out if I had those pliers. Why don't you just give me the goddamn pliers and have me yank them out?"

The nurse who was showing us to my semi-private room didn't pay any attention to him, so I knew he was kidding. Or at least I hoped he was kidding. He was so persistent about those pliers that I was beginning to wonder.

I checked in at 7:30 a.m. and the operation was scheduled for 9 a.m. The pre-operation procedures were enough to make me get up and run out of the hospital. The nurse with a big needle pointed to my arm and told me to relax. She just wanted a little blood. First of all, to a nine year old there's no such thing as "a little blood." Second, you don't tell a person with cerebral palsy to relax when you have a long needle pointed at him and expect him to go limp. But the nurse had to get my blood for testing. She tied a rubber band around my upper arm, which was tightened with fear which made the whole process more painful. I made up my mind not to give blood to the Red Cross right then and there.

Soon another needle-happy nurse came to give me a hypo shot. I didn't like that either. I was beginning to feel like a pincushion. But this time my mom tried to get my attention off the shot by having me look at my secret agent doll, Mike Hazard. She perched Mike on the hospital bed's railing and said, "Mike wouldn't let anything happen to you, would he?"

This worked fine until the needle entered my boney rear. Then my arm instantanously flew forward to knock my friendly doll head over heels on the floor. My reflexes were excellent. If I only just knew how to use them!

When I awoke from the operation, I was in my room and heard the principal of J. P. Lord talking. I tried to turn my head, but my neck was sore. I groaned to let him know I was awake. He came around to where I could see him and said, "Don't try to talk. I just stopped to see how you're doing. Get some rest. I have to get back to school."

I dropped off again. Whatever it was that they gave me was powerful. I had never slept all day before.

I woke up later in the day to see my teacher and two of my therapists hovering over me.

"The school had its Easter party, so we brought your share of candy over to you," said my teacher, Mrs. Clanton. "We realize hard candy isn't exactly what you need now, but maybe when you're feeling better, you'll eat some."

I tried to say thank you to please my speech therapist, who had begun a massive program to make me talk.

She said, "Don't try to talk, Bill."

I looked at her; I was puzzled. For a year she had pleaded, begged, and coaxed me to talk. But now she had told me not to talk. I was confused.

"Your throat has been cut. Its muscles need to heal. I don't expect you to talk now. I'll bet you never expected me to say that to you," my speech therapist said and chuckled.

I stayed in the hospital just one day after the operation because the nurses, professionals in health care, were scared to treat me. They asked my mom to stay with me throughout the night because they didn't know how to communicate with me. So after a night of trying to sleep in a chair, Mom asked the doctor if she could take me home since she was the only one taking care of me. The doctor released me and sent me home. I recuperated normally from a routine operation.

In fact, my recovery went better than a verbal child's recovery because I didn't try to use my throat to talk.

I have had two operations on my legs which weren't normal to any other child. They were corrective surgery. The success or failure of these corrective operations depends on how you look at them. No operation will make a child who is severely disabled suddenly jump out of his wheelchair and walk. But corrective surgery will assist therapists, parents, and child control himself a little better. I'm not advocating or condemning corrective surgery. But the surgeon's knife is definitely not a magic wand and certainly no picnic for the child.

I remember my hamstring operation because I was spread-eagled for six weeks. I was put in a body cast with a foot-long bar between my legs. The purpose of the cast was to keep me immobile while cut muscles were healing. The cast did its job remarkably well. For six long weeks I had to lie flat on my back with my legs spread out like the wings of a 707. During the days it wasn't bad, but during the

18 nights it was hell. I usually sleep curled up into a ball, but now I was forced to sleep on my stomach with my feet hanging over the bed. I had a portable color TV which Grandma and Grandpa Brown bought for me, and I watched the late, late movie to make the nights seem shorter. I was doped up so that I could relax during the nights.

To make this situation worse, I developed bronchitis while I was in my body cast. When I cough and sneeze, my whole body shakes. But when I was in the cast, only my head and arms could move. So when I sneezed my head jerked up and my arms flew around.

Once my aunt baked me a coconut cream pie. When she held it close to me so I could see it, I sneezed and my arms flew up and creamed the coconut cream. The pie went on the floor before my aunt could catch it. My understanding aunt scraped the pie from the bedroom floor and put it back in the pie pan and said, "My latest recipe: upside-down coconut cream pie."

Once during the night, I made the mistake of getting Mom out of bed for a minor problem—I couldn't breathe. My nose was clogged up. Now Mom loves me. But I learned a long time ago that I had better not get her up if it wasn't a matter of life or death. I should let her beat up the alarm clock and have her cup of coffee before summoning her. But my plugged up nose combined with the uncomfortable cast made me lose my senses, and I yelled until I woke her up.

"What in the hell do you want?" asked this Angel of Mercy. "If the cast is hurting you, I don't have the cast cutter. And I won't call the doctor at this ungodly hour."

I stared at the nose drops which were on the night stand with my Valium, ear drops, cough medicaton, rubbing lotion, and pain pills. Mom sleepily grabbed the ear drops and put them in my nose.

As soon as I felt the waxy medicine coating my nose I yelled and cried. I was certain that unless I got medical attention, I would die. I stared a hole into the ear drop bottle trying to get Mom to understand.

When I screamed, she slapped me across the face and said, "Just because you can't sleep doesn't mean you have to wake up everybody in the house. Get to sleep. And if you can't get to sleep, be quiet so that somebody else might get some rest. Do you understand me?"

I understood. I might be dying, but I should do it silently.

In the morning Mom asked me, "What was wrong with you last night? You haven't acted like that since you were two years old." 19

I motioned towards the ear dropper and frowned.

"You said that your nose was plugged so I gave you these. That's what they're for. See, the label says . . . Ear drops. God, no." Mom said as she read the label. "You mean I put these drops in your nose instead of the nose drops? I'm really sorry. I'd better call the doctor. I can just hear him now, 'Well, Mrs. Rush, it helps to read the label. That's why the druggist puts them on.' "

So, Mom sheepishly called our doctor, and said, "Hi, Doc. Guess what I did. I put ear drops in Billy's nose. How much damage did I do? I was half asleep so I couldn't see the label. Oh, I see. Then there's no damage done. Thanks, Doc."

After she had hung up she returned to my room and said, "The doctor said no damage has been done because the nose and ears are connected so eventually everything that enters the nose or ears winds up in the same place. Now that's settled, how about me giving you a back rub? I feel I owe it to you after last night."

Although my mom and I did fight, I remember that I never needed to be told that she loved me and would do anything for me, even being a Den Mother so I could be a Cub Scout when I was eight.

Mom was my Den Mother simply because I would freak out any other mother. But my mom and dad insisted that I be given the chance to do everything that other kids did. If there was a requirement that I couldn't do like sit-ups, push-ups, or skipping rope, we improvised. Mom made arrangements with my physical therapist to set up some exercises that I could do, like rolling over ten times and holding my head up straight. (The physical therapist was secretly watching me. If she caught me with my head dropping twenty times, I didn't get the credit.) I remember that I felt sick when the therapist told me that she had caught me nineteen times with my head down. I could have sworn that I did better than that. But a lifetime habit of letting my head droop almost kept me from becoming a Wolf Scout.

A weird thing about me was that I tried to do things that were impossible for me to do, but I didn't care about doing things I could do. I can remember getting a wooden block and being told to whittle an Indian face necktie slide from it. The block had a profile of an

20   Indian on it, and all the scouts were to whittle the block down so
that its shape was like that of its picture. I was determined to whittle
that piece of wood. Dad reluctantly let me try. We fastened the block
down with a C-clamp. I gripped the Boy Scout pocket knife in my
left hand (This was before the headstick entered my life.) and began
to carve on the block. I wasn't making much progress when
Grandma started helping me with the project. And I wanted to do it
myself. So I yanked the knife away from Grandma and accidentally
drove it into my right forefinger, making a deep cut across it. Blood
gushed out and covered the block. Mom rushed me to the bedroom
and bandaged the clean deep wound which my bullheadedness and
bad temper had caused. It was the last time my parents let me touch
a knife and I don't blame them. The scar from that fiasco still shows.
It should remind me to keep my cool and to pick tasks that I can do
instead of picking the impossible to do and stubbornly pursuing
them. It should, but it doesn't. In a way, I'm glad it hasn't.

I even tried to wrestle with another Cub Scout. We squared off on
our knees. I really thought I could pin him. When my uncle (also the
Den Chief) said to go, I lost my balance and fell down because I was
so excited. The other Cub Scout pinned me in three seconds. I don't
think he took advantage of me unjustly because if he had lost his
balance, I would have pinned him. That is, if I could have.

My Cub Scout troop had a softball team and I was its mascot. My
job was to heckle the other teams when they were up to bat. It made
sense to me. Suppose you were an eight-year-old kid and heard this
bullmoose yell behind you. Wouldn't that throw your concentration
off the ball? But unfortunately sometimes my teammates would
lose their concentration as well. At the time I thought I was being
invaluable to the team.

My dad was the coach and he hauled the team in his white pickup
truck. Of course, I had to go to the games with my team. So Dad
lifted the wheelchair and me into the back of our truck and told the
guys to hold onto me.

I was never a sports fan outside of rooting for my Cub Scout team,
which was the only thing that made me abnormal to my family who
were avid sports fans. I never was contented to sit and watch other
guys do things, especially when I had no means of participating.
That's why my parents made me think I was contributing to the

team by heckling our opponents. Who knows? Maybe I did.

For one project, our troop put on a skit for the pack meeting. The plot was a simple one. A dragon was terrorizing a village. A brave knight fought a deadly duel with the dragon and eventually the dragon was stabbed, went up in a puff of smoke, and was replaced by a beautiful princess who presumably married the brave young knight.

I was the evil dragon. My mask was a bucket with the bottom cut out of it. With Uncle Alan's help and imagination, I used green egg cartons for the eyes. We covered the outside of the bucket with black crepe paper and the inside with yellow paper for the fire. We even gave the dragon a red forked tongue. We were that technical.

I even had a speaking part for the skit. When the narrator said, "And the dragon roared," I let out a yell. We practiced that line many times because when a person with cerebral palsy wants to do something, he can't and when he wants not to do something, he involuntarily does it. So getting my vocal cords to cooperate with the cue was as hard as memorizing a Shakespearian play. But after weeks of practice I growled right on cue. More importantly, my costume won first prize in the audience applause for best costume. My prize was an orange with a quarter attached and a handshake from the scout master.

I also remember my grandmas and how each in their own way tried to treat me as they would any other grandchild. Although their approaches differed I never questioned their love for me.

My most recent memories of both were when I visited them in the hospital. In 1975, Grandma Brown contracted Crohn's disease, which changed her lifestyle from an independent one to a dependent one. She neither accepted it nor adjusted to it.

Once, when she was in the hospital undergoing one of her many surgeries she endured while I was in high school, I asked my high school teacher if she would take me to see her. The hospital was across the street from the school. When we entered her room Grandma Brown introduced us to her roommate as her "crippled grandson and his teacher." I guess she wanted to make sure her roommate knew I wasn't taking one of the hospital's wheelchairs for a joy ride.

Grandma Rush died in 1980, two months after we celebrated our

22 mutual birthday. I was 25 and she was 85. She let me know in many ways that she considered me her sixtieth birthday gift. One weekend when I was home from UNL Mom said softly, "Grandma Rush is dying. Do you want to go to see her to say your goodbye to her? I don't know if she knows she's dying."

I nodded and told my mom that I wanted to hug Grandma. Mom said, "I know, but we have to see what happens. If we make too much of hugging her, she'll suspect something's up."

When we entered the hospital room Grandma Rush's eyes lit up and she said in a weak voice, "Nurse, this is my grandson. He's going to college at the university in Lincoln. And I'm so proud of him." Then to me, "I suppose you're too big to be hugged by your grams."

I shook my head no and tried to laugh. Mom pushed me closer. Grandma Rush reached out through her guard railing, I bent forward, she grasped my hand and said, "Thank you for coming. I love you." She knew she was dying and was saying good-bye.

She died the next week.

My grandmas were both from farms. They had immigrant parents and strong work ethics. Both let me know they loved me. But those were their only similarities.

Grandpa and Grandma Rush had four children plus two nieces for whom they had to care during the Great Depression. Grandpa had to scramble to find and get jobs. In contrast, Grandma and Grandpa Brown had only my mother, and Grandpa Brown worked every other week as a first class diamond cutter and jeweler.

This, in turn, affected how my parents viewed the Depression. Mom doesn't remember the Depression and has a carefree attitude about money. But the Depression had a lasting impression on my dad. He has always saved money and has never wasted it and tried to teach his sons to use money wisely.

World War II also affected both my grandmas in different ways. While both their husbands were too old for combat, Grandma Rush had a son serving in a highly active and dangerous area. At the age of seventeen, my dad was a part of the hell which was called the Italian Campaign. As a result, Grandma Rush spent many hours on her knees praying for her son's safe return. Grandma Brown didn't have any such personal stake in the war, nor did my mom who sat in her high school's auditorium, heard the radio broadcast of Roosevelt declaring war on Japan, and wondered why her teachers were crying.

Grandma Brown trusted in her own ability to work her way out of any problem. Grandma Rush trusted in God to lead her.

Grandma Brown spent her time with me in ways that she thought would "cure" me. For example, the therapists said, "Puzzles will help his motor coordination. They would help any child's coordination for that matter."

So the day after Grandma Brown heard this she bought me a cardboard picture puzzle. I did it and did it until my drool warped its pieces. Mom told her, "Billy drooled on his puzzle until it's so warped that I can't make the pieces stay together. He's worn that puzzle out."

The next day Grandma Brown came over with another puzzle. I wore that one out too. Grandma Brown didn't give up. She bought me wooden and magnetic puzzles saying, "The therapists said these puzzles would help him. So it's worth it. Anything to get him to use his hands."

Once when I was three, Mom and Dad went elk hunting in Idaho. Grandma and Grandpa Rush stayed with Jimmy and me. We had an apple tree in our backyard which yielded green apples. She picked its apples and made apple sauce. Then, she would feed me her homemade apple sauce covered with cream. When Mom and Dad came back from elk hunting I was chubby. It was the only time in my life that I had any excess weight.

One summer when I was thirteen both sets of my grandparents went to Minnesota on a vacation with my parents and us four boys. Grandma Brown insisted I bring my big Sherman tank walker with underarm supports because my dear therapists wanted me to maintain my walking skills—what little there were—throughout the summer.

Taking a trip with me became nearly as complicated as moving the space shuttle across country because I needed, or my family thought I needed, my wheelchair, my highchair, my standing table, my special swing, an inner tube, and now my walker. We looked like the Beverly Hillbillies going down the highway with our car and pickup truck loaded to the brim.

24   I voted to keep my Sherman walker home. I didn't like exercising because I couldn't see any use in it. But Grandma, instead of going fishing, was out in the back of our cabin coaxing me to walk like my therapist wanted me to do. I rebelled every step of the way. Sometimes I wouldn't budge. After all, this was my vacation too. So Grandma said, "If you walk ten steps, I'll buy you a new wooden puzzle every day for ten days."

      I slid my feet along the path ten times begrudgingly. When Grandma sat my body down in my wheelchair, I saw sweat running off her forehead and into her hazel eyes. She took her glasses off to wipe the sweat out of her eyes and said, "Whew. We had a workout today, didn't we? I'm glad I'm going walleye fishing tonight. Well, let's get you ready to go swimming and play in the sand."

      But Grandma Rush came out of the cabin and announced, "I just got done with a batch of cinnamon rolls. I don't suppose you'd want one?" Grandma Rush made heavenly cinnamon rolls. It seemed like Grandma Rush wanted to fatten me up with her baking and that Grandma Brown wanted to keep me skinny with plenty of exercise.

      That night in Minnesota when Mom heard about Grandma Brown's bribe, she told her thirteen-year-old son, "You should be ashamed of yourself. Grandma Brown is walking you for your own good. In fact, you should be paying her for helping you. Think about it."

      I did. Mom was right. After Grandma Brown came in from fishing, I tried to tell her to forget the puzzles.

      But she said, "Today we made a deal, and by God I'm sticking to it. Get some sleep. Tomorrow we'll try twenty steps."

CHAPTER 2

CLANTON YEARS

I remember when I stopped taking little steps and began taking long strides. It was in October 1966 when Miss Neff, my occupational therapist, took me into her stale, windowless room. She was a thirty-year-old woman who stood only about five feet one, but she could make every uncooperative student at the Dr. J. P. Lord School for the Physically Handicapped tremble in his wheelchair with fear. As one of them, I was scared to death when she came to get me for an unscheduled visit.

Then, as I recalled, I was a really horrible little boy who wouldn't do what his thearpist told him to do. I was rebellious partly because I was so uncoordinated and partly because, after years of physical, speech, and occupational therapy, I still could not walk, talk or use my hands. Why, I asked myself, should I make the effort?

As Miss Neff told my parents, "We always try to do what we've done in other similar situations, and if that doesn't work, we look for something new." But nothing—old or new—was working for me.

There I was, at any rate, following Miss Neff to her office when it wasn't even time for my therapy. I was petrified! What had I done wrong this time? Had they finally given up on me? Was I getting kicked out of school? I felt like Daniel wheeling into a stuffy lions' den.

Miss Neff parked me in front of her steel teacher's desk; then she sat in her armless chair behind it. Instead of scolding me, as I had anticipated, she showed me some mimeographed diagrams of what looked like a large, but poorly shaped slingshot that was rounded at the fork. It looked ridiculous to me. Then Miss Neff showed me another diagram of a kid typing with this contraption on his head.

During that year's teacher's convention, Miss Neff, along with the

26 school's speech therapist, physical therapist, and Jean Clanton, my new classroom teacher, attended another special school that was in Iowa City. At that school they saw a student using a headstick to type his schoolwork.

"This is a headstick," she said sternly. "It is not a toy or a weapon. We think that you will be able to use it if you want to, but it will be very hard work. And if I ever see you using it to poke somebody, I'll take it away from you and set it on this desk. Understand?"

I nodded stiffly.

"Now," she continued, "at the next PTA meeting I will give your mother some directions for exercises to strengthen your neck. I also suggest that you do them at home every day. I also suggest that you do them in the morning when you are fresh. It will be tiresome work, but you just might be able to do it."

Miss Neff took me back to the classroom after this lecture. Mrs. Clanton, who, unlike all my therapists, had not witnessed my many failures said, "Did Miss Neff tell you about the headstick? I think you can do it. Do you?"

I nodded. So my journey from solitary confinement had begun.

I cannot give you a day-by-day description of my first real taste of success. Every day I did my neck exercises before going to school. As a result, my neck muscles are now the most well-developed in my body—honest! Have you ever seen a skinny person with a huge, thick neck? Well, that's me exactly!

At school, I practiced using the stick to turn the pages of a spiral-bound book and to point to words on an elaborate language board made by my speech therapist. I also did neck exercises there. It was like a dream. Up until now, everything the therapist had tried on me had not worked because I was so uncoordinated that I gave up in frustration. But this was different.

Mrs. Clanton believed in me. If she'd said I could fly, I would have jumped off the Empire State Building without any reservations and flapped my spindly arms until I spattered on the sidewalk. She was a friend as well as a teacher. I still remember how she played baseball with my class as a reward for sitting through an extremely dull recreation hour when we had to watch an inaudible play. So I worked hard to please her, not minding the very few disappointments of this project.

My teacher and therapists thought that I was intelligent because they watched my eyes and facial expressions during my lessons. But as Mrs. Clanton told my parents, "we had no way of testing his knowledge of each of his subjects."

A friend made a headstick and Miss Neff found an old typewriter with a keyguard which I could use.

The climax of this successful adventure came when Miss Neff put me in a straight-backed wooden chair with arms. She tied me in because I couldn't balance on my own. She put the band with a stylus attatched to it on my head. Then she pushed me up to an ancient black electric typewriter. I swear that typewriter was used by Thomas Edison. In fact, I thought then that he had made it himself, and I still do!

Miss Neff told me to turn the old clunker on. To our surprise, I did—quickly! She told me to type my name. I did. She told me to type the alphabet. I did! By this time the speech therapist, the physical therapist, and Mrs. Clanton had been called into the occupational therapy room to share in my victory over silence.

It wasn't long after that until I was writing test answers, doing arithmetic, including long division math problems, on the typewriter. I began using a language board to help me spell various words in my daily conversations. Active and productive art sessions became possible by using a special head wand that held crayons and pencils. I even found a hobby: Art Typing.

For the first time in my life I found out that I could make something of value to others. All my life I had to sit and watch another person make my Mother's Day, Father's Day, and Christmas gifts. Now I could show people I cared by typing a picture for them. It seemed appropiate that I should type a portrait of President John F. Kennedy as a Christmas present for Mrs. Clanton to thank her for having faith in me.

I remember when both Kennedys were killed. I was eight when John collected three bullets from person or persons unknown. Although I was too young to thoroughly grasp the significance of the murder, I lay in front of my family's television for four days and heard about President Kennedy. Some would say that I was brainwashed. Perhaps I was. All I know is I abandonded Popeye and Superman as my heroes that November and started collecting Kennedy memorabilia. It seemed like my collection snowballed. The more stuff I got, the

28   more admiration I had for John Kennedy. The more admiration I had for him the more stuff I got. By the time Bobby Kennedy ran for president, the Kennedy name was a synonym for greatness. I campaigned for him by wearing his buttons and hanging his poster.

When Bobby died, I was mature enough to know what a loss the nation had again suffered. Mrs. Clanton and I mourned him as we mechanically prepared for summer vacation, a traditionally joyful time. I was determined that one day somehow I would be a spokesperson for the underdog like the Kennedy brothers had been.

But before I could do that I had to learn to speak up for myself, which at times seemed like an impossible task. I will always remember the recreation hour when I was sitting on Dr. Lord School's playground and a bee started to buzz around me. I began to yell because I'd heard stories of death by a bee sting. The on-duty therapist walked over and told me to shut up. I tried to tell her that a bee was bothering me, but she walked away.

A minute later I felt the sharp pain of a bee's stinger in the back of my neck. I still couldn't make the therapist understand that a bee had stung me. She mistook my shouts of pain for shouts of rebellion. She told me to settle down when I flinched at the bee sting.

Back in the classroom Sue took off my coat and noticed a swelling lump on the back of my neck. She rubbed it tenderly and curiously.

Sue Shepard, age 11, had been my sisterly friend ever since we were in fourth grade. Sue was deaf, but she could talk a little. Her life was filled with trying to interpret others' gestures. So to her I was just another person who gestured to her instead of talking. We spent many recreation hours at school playing house or Batman and Robin. Sue wasn't taken aback by my absence of speech because she couldn't hear.

"A bee sting you?" she asked. She made a stabbing motion with her forefinger.

I nodded.

"Mrs. Clanton, Mrs. Clanton, come quick. Bill stung by a bee," she called.

Mrs. Clanton inspected the lump and decided the nurse should look at it.

After I finally got treatment for a sweatbee sting, Mrs. Clanton put my headstick (which I had gotten that October) on me and asked what happened.

"A BEE STUNG ME" I spelled out.

Being a teacher, she was delighted that I knew how to spell bee. She jumped for joy over my spelling. I looked at her and thought how easy it was to delight an adult.

However, I remember a time when Mrs. Clanton was not delighted or amused with my antics. Such a time was when the fifth grade class came back to the classroom from an afternoon in the school's gymnasium. We had beaten the sixth grade in volleyball and we were jubilant. We entered the classroom shouting, "We won! We won!"

During the game I slid down in my wheelchair so that my tailbone was on the edge of the seat. I was tilted to my left so that my neck was resting on my armrest. I wished somebody would straighten me up. But nobody noticed my problem. When I yelled for help the others thought I was yelling because we had won.

When my pusher, Sue, and I rushed into the classroom, my chin, which was where my left elbow should have been, hit a desk. The shock and my poor reflexes set me upright in my wheelchair. Sue and my chair stopped but I didn't. I kept going forward, even without my chair.

"Bill, don't fall!" Mrs. Clanton cried.

As I fell face forward onto the concrete floor, I thought "I tried my best not to fall, Mrs. Clanton. Believe me, this will hurt me more than you."

Mrs. Clanton shot up from her desk and lifted me back into the chair. My chin was spurting blood! Mrs. Clanton grabbed a handful of tissues and whisked me to the physical therapy room, which served as a first-aid center.

The bulky physical therapist looked at the cut with caring concern and said, "We'd better get you over to the hospital. That cut needs stitches." Then to Mrs. Clanton, "Have the office call his parents and tell them I took Billy to the hospital."

At the mention of stitches I began to whimper. A few years earlier my brother Jim got hit with a baseball bat above his right eye and needed nine stitches. It looked like a painful ordeal that I could do without.

30

"Hush now," the P.T. commanded. "You ain't hurt that bad. There's nothing to be afraid of. I'll be right beside you. And you knows I won't let them hurt you." The six-foot 250-pound woman was reassuring in both stature and in calmness.

Since the school was a part of a medical center, it had an underground tunnel that led to one of three hospitals. Although the physical therapist used it frequently, this was my first and only trip through the dark passageway. Some students she took through the tunnel had minor accidents like mine; some became ill at school and had to check into the hospital. Still others, such as those who were terminally ill, never returned to school.

So in my mind the tunnel was linked to pain, illness and death. It was an eerie place. It was cold, dark, and forbidding. All I could think of was how many friends had entered this dark place never to return again. Most students just had the principal's office to fear. We had the principal's office and "The Tunnel."

When we arrived at the hospital, we were rushed to an emergency room. A nurse greeted us with, "The doctor will be right with you. Would you put him on the table so the doctor can examine him?"

The P.T. lifted me onto the table. Then she locked my braces in a straightened position. "We might as well stretch your legs and get some therapy out of this," joked the physical therapist. "Besides, this will keep you from kicking around and throwing yourself off this table."

We waited. Thirty minutes had passed. Mom walked into the emergency room with her hair in curlers and said, "I heard you won. What a way to celebrate! I just came from the beauty shop. I was right in the middle of getting a permanent."

I started to whimper again. The P.T. stopped me by saying sternly, "You have been doing fine 'til now. What are you trying to do? Get sympathy from your mother?"

Another thirty minutes later a doctor came in saying, "Sorry, but we had a bigger emergency."

As I lay stretched out on a narrow table, my chin bleeding, my legs growing numb from being stretched for an hour, and my anxiety growing each passing minute, I thought, "A bigger emergency? In whose opinion, Doc?"

The woman doctor covered my face with a cloth.

"Watch his hands," my mom said. "They tend to fly around and he might bump you when you're sewing."

"Don't worry," the heavy physical therapist said calmly, "I have your hands, Billy. Believe me, they won't go anywhere. If they hurt you, squeeze my arms, and keep squeezing hard. Don't worry about hitting the doctor. You know there's no way you can get away from me!"

The doctor used a local anesthetic, which was administered via a long, sharp needle. I let out a low moan when the needle penetrated my chin.

"Hush Billy, just squeeze my arms. We know that hurt, but you're a big boy," the physical therapist kept saying. I didn't make a sound throughout the operation except when the anesthetic was administered. I knew what was expected of me so why did she have to keep reminding me not to cry?

When it was all over, my chin had five stitches and the physical therapist's arms had bruises from being squeezed.

"Now," the lady doctor was telling Mom, "keep those stitches absolutely dry."

"Did you hear that?" asked Mom. "You'll have to swallow your spit for your chin to heal. So concentrate on swallowing all the time!"

It wouldn't be easy. I could swallow my saliva if I thought about only that. But as soon as I thought about something else I would drool. It couldn't be helped.

We exited the hospital the same way we went in—through the tunnel.

When we got back to school, Mrs. Clanton was waiting in the hall with my coat in hand.

"Well," she said, "is he going to be all right? I didn't want to leave until I knew for sure that he was all right. You're my first accident victim. I hope you're my last!"

"He's okay. A little shaken, but he'll survive," the physical therapist said and patted me on the back.

As Mom wheeled me out of the building she laughed and said, "I hope you now know when your dad says that you must learn to take it on the chin, this is not what he meant."

CHAPTER 3

BROTHERHOOD DISCOVERED

I remember that some of our family friends didn't know how to deal with me. Once, when I was in high school, a neighbor lady complimented me on my first published story which appeared in the local newspaper. Then she turned to Mom and asked her, "Does he understand me?"

Fortunately, the majority of Dad and Mom's friends saw how naturally my parents dealt with me and followed suit. I will never forget one such person.

He was from Thatcher Idaho, about ten years younger than my Dad, and a Mormon married to a Catholic. He had blond hair and a twinkle in his blue eyes. He and his family had lived in a lot of places, wherever the Air Force ordered him. He didn't mind. He was an adventurer. In 1956, during his hitch at Offutt Air Force Base in Omaha, Jay Mendenhall pumped gas with my dad.

Pumping gas was one of the many extra jobs that my dad had to pay for my two hernia operations, braces, and wheelchairs. Although Jay was in the Air Force, he too worked an extra job.

Dad and Jay were as opposite as night and day; Jay was boisterous, quick-tempered, and impulsive with money, while Dad was quiet, a slow boil, and thrifty. But there were a couple of things that linked them together: a love of hunting and fishing and a lust for telling tall tales.

The most important thing about him as far as I was concerned was his natural, carefree attitude toward me. To him I was just one of the boys, and I loved him for it. Perhaps since the Air Force had exposed him to so many different people, Jay had learned to accept me as just one of the Rushes more easily than had other family friends.

In 1967, when he was stationed at Davis-Monthan Air Force Base in Tucson, Arizona, Jay somehow talked my dad into visiting him.

After several phone calls, a map from Jay showing us the best route, and everyone coaxing him, Dad finally agreed to make the trip during Easter school break, saying, "I suppose that if I don't make this trip, that Mendenhall and this family won't let me have any rest. Let's go."

So one Saturday our new white station wagon was readied for the journey that would take us south through Kansas, across the Oklahoma and Texas panhandles and west across New Mexico to Arizona. The weather was hot and dry. New Mexico was boring because the scenery never seemed to change; it was flat and sandy for miles. Arizona was the same. The blue mountains bordered the biggest sandbox I'd ever seen. We saw little mud huts speckling the desert. Dad explained these were reservations for Indians. I wondered how the federal government expected anyone to be satisfied with living in a hot, dry sandbox.

The trip took just two days, but we drove twelve hours on the first day and drove until we got to Davis-Monthan Air Force Base late on the second day. I was lucky. I was used to sitting so I fared better than anybody in my family. But I was happy to see Sergeant Jay Mendenhall.

Jay had to meet us outside the base to lead us past the guard at the gate. When we finally arrived at his house, Jay hopped out of his car and flung open my door saying, "I have to get you out of this damn car before it grows to your rear! Man, it's good to see you! Judy has been waiting for you."

Judy was his 14-year-old daughter. She was interested in helping people with disabilities, so I was her favorite. Also, the others talked hunting, a subject that bored us, so Judy entertained me while the others told old hunting stories for the millionth time.

Jay carried me into his house over his shoulder like a sack of Idaho potatoes. He sat me in a chair from the Philippines. Its back was rounded and it had a foot rest built into it. It was made of bamboo. Had I been able to straighten out my legs, it would have been comfortable. But my legs kept bending and dragging me forward and down. Judy kept trying to pull me back up, but to no avail. I kept sliding down.

34   "Daddy, can't you make Bill more comfortable?" Judy said when Jay came in with an armful of luggage.

"Just a minute. We'll unload the wheelchair and put him in it. Is that okay, Bill? Just hold on to him. I don't want his head to dent our floor!" Jay grinned at me as he said it.

When my family and Jay finally unloaded our stuff, they put me in my throne with wheels. The headrest fell off when mom put me in it.

"Damn this headrest," Mom said while fumbling with it. "I wish someone would make one that stayed on. Bill, why don't you learn to hold your head up straight? Then we wouldn't have this problem!"

Jay and Dad saw Mom's problem and helped her. Jay said, "Christ, if we designed airplanes that flimsy, we would be tarred and feathered! How much does one of these things cost?"

"Plenty," Dad said.

"We're going to see Old Tuscon tomorrow," Jay said while he and Dad were fiddling with the headrest, "It's a movie lot. They use it for westerns. I thought the kids, including the Old Man, would like it! There, that should stay on for now."

"Now Jay, you don't have to entertain us all the time we're here!" Dad said.

"Who's entertaining? My kids have been bugging me to take them to these damn places, so we thought you could help us keep them in line," Jay said. "Of course, you can stay home if you want. But Old Tucson is a fabulous place! You folks should get to bed after your long drive. Bet you're tired."

The next morning I woke up with stomach cramps. I groaned for somebody to help me. Jay came staggering into his guest bedroom and asked, "What's wrong, buddy? We'll get you up in a little while. Can't you wait until then?"

I shook my head.

"Do you hurt somewhere?" Jay asked.

I nodded.

"Your head?"

"Your neck?"

"Your shoulders?"

"Your arms?"

"Damnit, Bill, I'm sorry I'm so slow at this."

"Your chest?"

"Your gut?"

"Do you have to shit?"

"That's easy enough to fix. Just a minute, and I'll get my coffee cup and I'll sit in the can with you. It'll give me an excuse not to help Eleanor with breakfast."

Apparently Jay hadn't heard of the Eleventh and Twelfth Commandments. The Eleventh Commandment came from Dr. J. P. Lord's matron and was, "Thou shalt not have a B. M. during school hours;" and the Twelfth Commandment, which came from Mom partly to appease the matron, was, "Thou shalt have your daily B. M. after breakfast and before the taxicab comes to take you to school."

I was surprised that anyone would voluntarily sit and hold me on the toilet, but Jay made it seem natural and relaxing to go to the bathroom before breakfast.

Old Tuscon lived up to Jay's billing. It was the Old West reconstructed down to hitching posts and wooden sidewalks. There was an adobe church, a gold mine with skeletons in it, and a general store that sold souvenirs to the tourists instead of bullets to cowboys. It was a tourist trap, but we kids—our parents included—loved it.

Stuntmen staged a shootout using blanks in its dirt streets. One stuntman was on the roof of the town's hotel trying to get the drop on the hero. But the hero turned and shot. The cowboy dramatically fell off the roof, bounced in and then out of the wagon and into the street.

My seven-year-old brother, Donny, was impressed with the man who fell off the building and lived. Donny asked him, "Where are the bullet holes in you?"

The cowboy stuntman jokingly replied, "They're there. You just have to go around on the other side of me and look towards the sunlight."

So my little brother walked around the stuntman, seriously looking for signs of bullet wounds, but to my brother's disappointment, he couldn't find any.

The next day Jay took us to see statues of real cowboys as they were at the O K Corral. The statues were of Wyatt Earp and the Clanton gang shooting it out. They were severely weathered. The statue of Billy Clanton had lost its nose and right hand to the elements. But Jay said, "Old Wyatt shot the nose right off that guy!" I shook my head fast.

36

"The hell he didn't, Bill. Then why doesn't he have a nose? Wyatt must have shot it off. They are buried close by. Let's go and see. I'll bet his tombstone says his nose was shot off."

So we went to Boot Hill. On the way there Jay said, "This place is the original Boot Hill. Other places have copied it. But this place is the real McCoy," Jay said.

My dad laughed and said, "Bill, you shouldn't believe this guy. He'll tell you that Chief Sitting Bull took a piss right where this highway is and you're dumb enough to believe him even without a plaque."

Jay and I laughed. Jay kept insisting that we were going to see the original Boot Hill, and I kept believing him.

When we got to the "original" Boot Hill, Jay got the wheelchair out of his trunk while dad got me out of the car.

The ground was white gravel. It would be rough going for a wheelchair. Dad put me in my wheelchair and said he would wait for the others. Jay began pushing me up the rocky hill when the headrest fell off. Jay stopped and put it back on and continued touring the graveyard. The headrest fell off again, so Jay stopped and fixed it again. We went a little farther and it fell off again. This angered Jay.

When we got back to the base, Jay said to his wife, "Hey Eleanor, where's my drill and a couple of nuts and bolts? I'm going to bolt this damn headrest to Bill's wheelchair, so he doesn't have to worry about it coming off whenever someone pushes him two steps."

When he was finished he said, "There! That headrest will never fall off again. I should go into designing wheelchairs when I get out of the Air Force!"

Jay didn't let the Rush family rest. He took us to a desert museum, to Mexico, up a mountain for a picnic supper, and around his air force base. He included me in all the activities so naturally that sometimes I would wonder how many other people in wheelchairs he had taken on mountain hikes and across the border. During that week in the Arizona desert I experienced more things than in any other week in my life because an Air Force sergeant and my family regarded me as just one of the boys.

I remember other times when, no matter how hard my family tried, other people wouldn't—or couldn't—regard me as just one of the boys. Surprisingly enough this happened at our neighborhood church.

I don't remember much about early Sunday school except that

Uncle Alan accompanied me to the sessions. He was a combination baby sitter and aide. His presence was helpful and reassuring to the Sunday school teachers. He was a security blanket for them—a buffer between them and me.

Our church was semi-accessible. The sanctuary was accessible but the area for the elementary Sunday school wasn't. So my uncle had to carry me down two flights of steps each Sunday. When I graduated to junior high status in the church, Mom insisted that my older brother, Jim (a six-foot, 2-inch tall 14- year-old), and I take confirmation classes. Whether we joined the Church was our choice. But Mom was determined that we should at least take the classes to learn about our religion and about the Bible and about the Presbyterian faith. She also wanted Jim to replace Uncle Alan. Jim didn't want the duty but he felt an obligation to do what Mom wanted.

In retrospect, having him assume such a responsibility was a mistake. Jim was big for his age and self-conscious about it. He was shy and didn't want to draw attention to himself or to his size. He wanted to fade into the background. But with me at his side he couldn't. We stuck out like a couple of sore thumbs. On the other hand, since Jim was so big, our parents — as did everyone else— expected him to be as mature as he looked.

Our pastor then was Rev. Cruckshank, a gentle, elderly man who believed God shouldn't be taken grimly, so he tried to make the lessons as entertaining as possible. This disturbed Jim but I loved our pastor's approach. Another thing that endeared him to me was that he treated me just like the rest of the students — something that was rare in my church.

Although I took my headstick and letter chart, I didn't use it. Jim wouldn't let me. Each time that I tried to participate in the discussion or answer a question I felt his fingernails on my wrist and heard his voice quietly say, "Forget it, Billy please. There isn't time to let you talk. Let it be."

What Jim didn't understand was that this was the first chance that I had to interact with my mental peers and I wanted to take advantage of it.

I told our mom that Jim wouldn't let me take part in the discussions. "I WANT TO ANSWER THE QUESTIONS BUT JIM WONT LET ME"

38   Jim countered with, "It takes too long for him to spell things out on his letter chart. He should be glad just to get to go."

"All right, you two," Mom said. "Billy, Jimmy is right. It does take too long for you to spell out what you want to say. Accept it. Jimmy, Billy should be able to participate in the group discussions . . ."

"But, Mom!" Jim shouted in exasperation.

"Let me finish! You both have weekly assignments for this class, so why can't Billy write a note and include what he wants to say with his assignments and that could be his class discussion? His class discussion would just be a week late."

"Okay, but I won't stand up and read his notes in class," Jim said quickly.

"No, no, you will just hand them in to Cruckshank. He can read the notes to the class if he wants to. Now, I'll ask Cruckshank if this is all right with him the next time I see him."

At the next confirmation lesson, Rev. Cruckshank came over to me and whispered, "I'm looking forward to your notes."

But he never discussed my notes with the class.

The class lasted from September to April. The most important thing I learned was how to define a miracle.

"A miracle is not magic," Rev. Chuckshank said. "God is not a magician. A miracle is a sign that God is fulfilling His covenant with an individual or with a people. God doesn't make a miracle happen overnight. Sometimes it takes years."

Palm Sunday, 1968, Jim, twenty-seven young people, and I were confirmed as members of the Church. And for three years I attended the worship service faithfully. But no one from our confirmation class spoke to me. With the help of Grandpa and Grandma, Mom took the whole Rush brood, without their dad, to worship service.

I was under strict orders to sit up straight, to swallow my saliva, to keep my hands in my lap, and not to sing.

"Just listen to the sermon and pray silently," Mom ordered.

On several occasions I felt the urge to remind her that the Bible said to "make a joyful noise to the Lord" and to remind her that the Good Book didn't say to make a joyful noise only if it could be understood and appreciated by others.

Mom wanted me to be inconspicuous but that was impossible since

I had to park my wheelchair in the aisle. People noticed me. One elderly lady always greeted me with a sloppy kiss on the forehead instead of a hearty handshake. I had the impression I was the congregation's Tiny Tim and I hated it. I was frustrated because I couldn't interact with the other members to let them see that I wasn't a Tiny Tim or a poster child and to let them understand that I was merely another member of our church. Church began to become for me a meaningless, hollow ritual. So, I stopped going.

While going to church provided me with a solid lifelong faith in a merciful and loving God, I never had the feeling of belonging to it. No one was to blame. I should have been more patient. Mom and Jim should have been more assertive and less self-conscious. The church members should have been more accepting. But as Mom always says, "It's easy to have 20/20 hindsight."

I still believe in God and love Him. But my church now comes from all denominations and is composed of people who accept me just as I am.

PART TWO

JOURNEY INTO

UNCERTAINTY

CHAPTER 4

DEANNE AND DAY CAMP

I met Deanne Kelley two weeks after my eighth grade graduation. It was on Flag Day, 1971. When the day camp director was handing out little flags to commemorate the day, I was more interested in Deanne than in getting a flag. I was coming of age—teenage, that is.

My eighth grade graduation had been a nice goodbye from Dr. J. P. Lord School. I had received a certificate of attendance that verified I had completed eleven years of a special program in the Omaha Public Schools for children who were physically disabled. I didn't know what I would do for high school because in 1971 the State of Nebraska didn't have a high school program for young teenagers with severe disabilities. The eighth grade graduates before me stayed home, but neither my parents nor I were excited about that much togetherness.

So, not knowing why, I went to day camp for the eleventh time. I expected the same horseback riding, the same sloppy joes, the same sing-a-longs, the same parents' day, the same arts and crafts, the same scavenger hunts, and the same counselors. But the camp was the only one of its kind in Nebraska.

It was run by a group of well-meaning volunteers who were as varied as we campers. The one thing they had in common was their grandmotherly love for us. They rented a city park for a week so that the students from Dr. J. P. Lord could have outdoor fun. They also asked local high school students who were experienced baby sitters to be our counselors.

When I was five, I looked forward to camp, but now I was fifteen. I had outgrown camp but didn't realize it.

I arrived at the camp on that Flag Day and was wheeled into the old pavilion with its maze of picnic tables, two brick fireplaces and cement floor.

44   Two counselors were wondering how to talk to me and were talking to each other about me, as though I weren't there.

"I wonder how we are supposed to treat him," one counselor said to the other.

I motioned for my headstick and my language board, and spelled, "WE HAVE FEELINGS TOO JUST LIKE YOU DO SO TREAT US THAT WAY"

While the two counselors were trying to regain their composure, another girl counselor came up and said, "Hi, I'm Deanne, Bill Rush. I'm your day camp counselor. I overheard what you told those two girls." The black-haired girl nodded towards the two counselors that had just left, "Don't worry. I got your message."

I nodded and spelled, "GOOD MOST PEOPLE DONT KNOW HOW TO TAKE ME AT FIRST I FREAK THEM OUT"

"You don't 'freak' me out, I've heard a lot about you but you haven't heard anything about me. So why don't we go outside and sit in the grass and get acquainted," Deanne suggested.

I nodded. I was surprised at how readily she had talked to and with me rather than at and about me. No one had granted me validity so quickly and naturally as she did.

We found a shady spot on the meadow in back of the pavilion. She sat down beside my wheelchair on the grass, but that didn't work because she had to strain to look at my language board. She then perched herself on her haunches, which made her neck level with my language board.

"Now that we are adjusted, you can ask me anything about me or my family—anything at all," Deanne chimed.

I had to think. When somebody makes her life an open book, it's hard to decide where to begin. So, I asked the typical beginning application form questions.

"HOW OLD ARE YOU"

"Fifteen. How old are you?" Deanne shot back.

"1-5," I pointed out.

"One-five? One-five? I don't understand, Bill. Could you explain. You're obviously not six," Deanne puzzled.

"FIFTEEN," I spelled out slowly because I wasn't sure of the spelling, which had been my reason for resorting to numerals.

"Oh, fifteen, not one-five. I'm such a dummy. It must be frustrating to talk to a dummy," Deanne joked. "What month were you born in? I want to see who's older. A-U-G-U-S-T. August? I was born in September. So I'm older. No, wait. You're older. I never was any good with the order of the months. I tell you, Bill, they gave you a real winner for a counselor this year."

Before I could reply, the day camp director's voice boomed.

"Flag raising five minutes. Flag raising five minutes. Counselors, get your campers over by the flag pole. Counselors, get your campers over by the flag pole."

The voice was unaided by a loud speaker but we could hear it loud and clear.

The daily flag raising ceremony was routine. We raised Old Glory, sang the National Anthem, and learned new day camp songs—songs that I had known for years. A lot of oldies but no goodies.

"Today, I want you to get acquainted with your campers. And make sure they do their arts and crafts project for today," the director was saying as she was passing out the flags. "Have a fun day with your campers." She dismissed us—or rather—she dismissed the counselors.

The gathering was dispersing when Deanne suggested, "How about doing your arts and crafts project now, and then after lunch we could go for a walk to get acquainted more?"

I said that her plan sounded good. I didn't particularly like the arts and crafts part. But the camp director had said that we had to do a craft project daily, so I might as well get it over with.

"The project today is to do a picture out of dried beans," the fifty-year-old art director said. "You have your choice among several patterns: a wise owl, a funny clown like the one at the Shrine Circus, and a shining fish. Which would you like to do?"

I chose the owl since I had graduated only two weeks ago and owls are wise.

"You're supposed to fill in the lines with these various dried beans by gluing them onto the picture. The lima beans could be used for the yellow spots, and the sunflower seeds could be used for another shade of yellow and so forth," the craft lady instructed Deanne.

We worked on the owl all morning. I had suggested to Deanne, "YOU PUT THE GLUE ON AND I WILL PUT THE BEANS IN PLACE"

It was an hour later and we had done just the head of the owl. At this rate we could be doing this all day and I definitely didn't want to do that. I had another idea.

46   "WHY DONT WE JUST DUMP THE REST OF THE BEANS" I spelled out with my gluey headstick.

Deanne thought I meant abandon the project and said with minimum conviction, "Bill, that's not nice. C'mon, we can finish it. And besides, if we don't finish this and throw it away, the ladies will feel bad."

"NO I MEAN WE CAN PUT GLUE ON THE BOARD AND DUMP THE BEANS ON IT THAT WAY WE WONT HAVE TO SPEND ALL DAY ON THIS"

Deanne grinned and took the glue and bathed Mr. Owl in it, and then she showered him in dried pinto beans. It was quick, messy, easy, and effective.

"I'll take this masterpiece to the craft lady and then we will go for a walk and talk," Deanne said cheerfully.

Five minutes later she came back out of the craft shop and said, "They said you have to decorate a sack to put your projects in. You have your choice between a lamb or a lion. We have to put the little pictures on the shopping bag and think up a catchy slogan for it. Personally, I think the purple lion is cute."

I went with the lion because I didn't care what my sack said or how it was decorated. I came up with a catchy slogan for the cute purple lion: "Drop me a lion."

Just as we were finishing the project, one of Deanne's girlfriends came up and asked, "Hi, Deanne, who's your friend?"

"Bill Rush. He talks by spelling things out with the stick on his head. See what we made from an ordinary bag? He thought up the slogan. Not bad, huh?" Deanne said enthusiastically.

The girlfriend stared disbelievingly at the shopping bag. "You mean he thought of this by himself? That's really good. Well, Deanne, my camper and I are going bowling. See ya."

After she had left, I poked Deanne with my headstick and spelled, "I THINK I FREAKED YOUR FRIEND OUT"

"Oh no, you didn't freak her out. It just takes her some time to warm up to people, honest."

I was glad that the day camp director had assigned me a counselor who warmed up to people quickly.

The unamplified voice of the director boomed, "Sing-a-long out in back of the pavilion in ten minutes. Sing-a-long out in back of the pavilion in ten minutes. Get out there so we can get the tables ready for lunch."

At the sing-a-long I groaned and moaned along with the others. After eleven years of taking music, I still couldn't sing although I understood and could read music. But when I tried to harmonize, I sounded as if I were in great pain. The irony of this is that in my mind's ear I sounded a-okay. So I sang along.

When forty-five minutes had passed, the day camp director announced, "Lunch's ready. Come and get it."

I dreaded having to eat in front of Deanne because all my life people, except for my grandmas, had complained about feeding me. Even my mom, who loved me, had complained. My brothers, who also loved me, would rather wash the dishes, take out the trash, do the laundry, clean the house, and feed our dogs than feed me. I couldn't blame them. I was a slow eater. I was a messy eater. I was an unappetizing eater. Why did Deanne have to see me eat? We were developing a fast friendship. Why did it have to be spoiled by making her feed me?

She carefully scooped up a spoonful of hamburger and macaroni and gave it to me. It fell during the transfer from her spoon.

"Ock. If your mom complains about how messy your pants are, tell her you had an inexperienced feeder today," Deanne said and nervously giggled. "Shall we try again?"

I nodded uneasily.

The second bite made it into my mouth where my tongue tossed it around and where the bite was gummed. Saliva moistened the mouthful until the throat swallowed it.

Deanne, as well as others, could see the entire process because I couldn't keep my lips closed. Some looked away, but not Deanne.

The camp director saw the trouble that Deanne and I were having. She came over and offered, "I'll feed Bill so you can eat. He isn't very appetizing to feed with his wavy tongue and gaping jaws." The camp director had a knack for calling a spade a spade. I respected her for that.

"We're getting along fantastic, honest. Of course, Bill's mom will hang us both when she sees how messy I am. But I enjoy feeding him," Deanne said, surprising both the camp director and me. "But thanks for the offer anyway."

48   After the day camp director had walked away, I spied Deanne's plate. It was untouched.

"MAYBE SHE SHOULD FEED ME SO YOU CAN EAT I AM SORRY THAT I AM NAUSEATING YOU" I spelled out as hamburger and macaroni fell from my mouth.

Once in an attempt to get me to eat better, my speech therapist had fed me in front of a mirror. The experience had nauseated me so I could imagine what the sight was doing to Deanne's stomach.

"I'm on a diet," Deanne said, "so I can get into a purple bikini that I just bought. Honest. I look like an elephant in it now so you aren't nauseating me. Eat up. I refuse to have you go home messy and starving both."

While I ate, I cast an admiring glance at Deanne—one that encompassed everything from her slender neck to her sandals. Her shape did not need any improvement. But I appreciated her sincere attempt to salvage my self-image more than her shape.

After lunch we went for a walk to get better acquainted. I learned that Deanne had come from a closely knit family and because of that she placed a high value on her family. She promised to introduce me to her parents someday. Unlike me, she was sports-minded—with good reason. Her grandpa was then the commissioner of the Omaha Softball Association. She lived in a park—the same park where my first day camp had been held.

Since it had been three short years since Senator Robert F. Kennedy and Martin Luther King, Jr., had been killed, we talked about prejudice. She said, "I don't believe people should judge a whole group of people by what a few people do. That's unfair."

I agreed with her. Somehow I had sensed she would feel that way.

"Tomorrow I want you to meet somebody. He's a fan of Kennedy like you are. You'll like him, I think," Deanne said, half to herself and half to me.

A familiar voice boomed, "Counselors, it's time for the campers to go home. Please get them to the loading area."

On the way home the volunteer driver asked us how we liked the first day of camp. All her passengers agreed that it was fun. I was amazed and a little confused that I had fun. In the past I had drawn do-gooders for counselors and I had expected to get another one this year.

I had gotten used to do-gooders as I had been plagued by them all my life. I had met them at church, and Dr. J. P. Lord attracted them like a garbage scow attracts flies and other parasites. They are parasites because they feed their consciences with good deeds without really knowing how to care about their benefactors. The telethons are their breeding grounds because they chose to give instant sympathy rather than sincere empathy. For the sake of my sanity, I had learned to weed them out and to ignore them.

But I hadn't met anyone like Deanne. She wasn't a relative, a professional, or a do-gooder. If she were, she would have jumped at the day camp director's offer to feed me and she wouldn't have allowed me to get to know her. I couldn't put her in one of my pigeonholes. On the other hand, she was probably having a harder time putting me in one of her pigeonholes.

The next day of camp when they unloaded me from the car Deanne greeted me with a cheerful, "Howdy, Bill, how are you today?"

She quickly fetched my headstick and my spelling board from the back of the car so I could answer her. It was refreshing to meet somebody who would ask me a question, expect me to reply, and help me to do so.

A brown-haired guy was beside her. Deanne said, "This is Reuben. He's a Kennedy fan like you. I told him a lot about you."

"Hi, Bill," Reuben said, "Of the Kennedys, who's your favorite? John or Bobby, or possibly, Teddy?"

I answered without hesitation, "JOHN IS MY FAVORITE I WAS 8 WHEN HE GOT KILLED AND WATCHED AND LISTENED TO THE LONG COVERAGE OF HIS FUNERAL AND HEARD HOW GREAT HE WAS"

"The same here," Reuben admitted, "but he had something besides good press coverage at his funeral, don't you agree?"

I nodded and said, "SO DID BOBBY"

"Hey, can you play chess, not to change the subject?" Deanne asked.

I nodded. I wasn't about to tell Deanne that I was a bad chess player. She didn't have to know that.

"I play chess too," Reuben said. "How's about playing a game after lunch?"

I accepted his challenge. Deanne would soon find out that I wasn't a good chess player, so why tell her?

50

"I see my camper is being unloaded, so I'll be seeing you two after lunch, if not before," Reuben said and trotted off.

Deanne asked, "Shall we go inside the pavilion and play a game until flag raising?"

She looked less enthusiastic than she had yesterday. I chalked it up to "familiarity breeds boredom."

I picked a basketball game because I could trigger its mechanisms with my headstick and, therefore, be an independent player.

Deanne made a couple of baskets from half court, but it was evident that she wasn't enjoying the game. Deanne seemed listless and soon she suggested that we quit and go outside to get some sun. I agreed.

When we went outside, Deanne sat on a green park bench and pulled my chair along side of the bench, and softly said, "Hey look, the reason why I'm so down is because Reuben and I used to be boyfriend and girlfriend and now we aren't. My bad mood has nothing to do with you or camp. It's just that. . . Well, you know how it is."

I nodded sympathetically although I didn't know how it was. I hadn't gone out with anybody.

"I COULD SKIP THE CHESS GAME WITH REUBEN" I offered.

Deanne looked horrified.

"Not on your life. I want to see you play chess. Reuben and I aren't enemies. It's just that he has a new girlfriend and I'm kinda bummed out about that."

The camp hummed with the director's voice announcing flag raising. Deanne and I joined the thirty wheelchairs assaulting the curb separating the flag pole from the rest of the camp. The sight of wheelchairs scaling the two-foot curb reminded me of films of the Normandy Invasion. Most counselors were inadequately trained to push a wheelchair up a curb, but everybody attacked the curb with as much zeal as the soldiers who had charged onto Omaha Beach.

Flag raising went as it did the day before. Consistency is reassuring, and this camp was very reassuring.

After the daily camp ritual the camp director announced, "Today we are going to have horses for the campers to ride. They will be here around ten o'clock so be here at that time. If for some reason your campers elect not to ride, that's fine. Alternative activities are available."

"Also, I have posted a list of campers' names inside the pavilion.
On the list I have divided the campers into groups. Each group is
supposed to put on a skit for Parents' Day, which is Thursday. I
suggest that your group get together either today or tomorrow to
think up a skit. When you have a skit, tell one of us so we can put a
program together. That's all. See you back here at ten for the horse
rides."

I didn't ride the horses for two reasons. I had ridden the horses for
eleven years, and for the past two years I heard the matron say things
like, "Every time I lift him onto the horse my back gives out," or "He's
the oldest kid here, but still he insists on doing everything that he did
when he was five."

I didn't have to ride horses if they felt that way. I thought horseback
riding and the other activities were mandatory, so I rode the horses to
keep from being a troublemaker.

My second reason was more selfish. I wanted to be around Deanne
as much as possible because when I was with her, I felt like a person.
When I was on the horses, I felt like a sack of potatoes.

So my morning was spent making a box out of tongue depressers
and going on a walk with Deanne. On the walk we met Reuben and
his young friend, whom he promptly introduced.

"Well, I suppose that you have your strategy for this afternoon all
figured out, and I'm a goner." Reuben chimed.

I laughed. He would be surprised. I had never won a game because I
didn't have a strategy. I just moved as the spirit moved me, and
consequently I lost.

"REALLY YOU ARE EXPECTING TOO MUCH FROM ME I
AM ROTTEN AT CHESS" I spelled out.

"We'll see," Reuben said.

After lunch Reuben came with a chess set in hand and said, "The
moment of truth has at last arrived."

As we played, we talked about a lot of things. Deanne joined in on
the conversation. We talked about the Kennedys and prejudice, and
how to rid the world of war. We decided world leaders should sit down
and play chess to resolve conflicts. We talked so much that Reuben
and I didn't finish the game.

"HOW ABOUT COMING OVER TO MY HOUSE SOMETIME
AND WE WILL FINISH OUR GAME OR START A NEW ONE.

52 CAMP HAS TOO MANY DISTRACTIONS," I spelled out. It was
the first time that I had a friend over to my house without my parents
being involved, and it felt good.

When I got home, Mom asked her usual question, "Did anything
exciting happen at day camp or was it the same dull stuff?"

I hated questions with the word "or" in them when only a nod was
expected. If I answered yes, would I be saying that something exciting
happened at camp or would I be saying that camp had been the same
dull stuff?

I solved my dilemma by nodding yes and grinning from ear to ear.

"I take it something exciting did happen at camp. Do you want to
tell me about it?" Mom asked.

I nodded my head, "yes."

Our usual game of twenty questions followed with Mom as the
questioner.

"Is it something about one of the campers?

Is it something about one of the volunteers?

Is it something about one of the counselors?

Your counselor?

Another counselor?

Can you spell what this other counselor is doing or did if I go
through the alphabet?

Visiting?

This other counselor is visiting somebody?

You?

When?

Tonight?

Tomorrow night?

Did you know that we had a baseball game tomorrow night?

Would he walk in if nobody came to the door?

Should I leave him a note on the door so he knows you're home and
he can walk in?

Do you need anything when your friend comes?

Is it food?

A book?

A game?

Monopoly?

Scrabble?

Checkers?

Chess?"

My family used this game of twenty questions instead of my headstick and language board because my parents were familiar and comfortable with it. They also thought it was quicker than my headstick and language board. The system had worked for eleven years. So why abandon it?

I was lucky. This time Mom had gotten the whole message by asking only 23 questions. Sometimes Mom asked a hundred questions and got only a partial message.

Reuben came over as planned and he brought his new girlfriend with him. She looked like Deanne but she didn't seem as outgoing.

Reuben spotted my chess set on the TV where Mom had left it. He began setting up the chessmen.

"This is Sherri. Sherri, Bill. He hates the Kennedys, especially John."

"AND FISH HAVE EARS" I spelled and laughed.

Sherri didn't get the joke, so Reuben filled her in.

We started to play chess, but we started talking and were sidetracked.

The next day at camp, Deanne asked me, "Did you and Reuben's new girlfriend have a good time last night?"

"DO I DETECT A NOTE OF JEALOUSY" I teased.

Deanne blushed. Then, she said, "I wanted to come over last night, but I didn't think it would be right to show up uninvited, especially with her over there."

"THATS STUPID YOU SHOULD KNOW BY NOW THAT YOU ARE WELCOME AT MY HOUSE OK IF YOU NEED A FORMAL INVITATION HERE IT IS HOW ABOUT COMING OVER FRIDAY NIGHT"

"I'd love to. Is 7:30 okay?"

On Friday morning Deanne and Reuben introduced me to a curly-haired fifteen year old as, "Bill, a fantastic chess player."

They introduced him as, "Tom Taxman. He goes to Westside High School with us. He plays chess too. Hey, maybe you two could play a game before we have the sing-along," Deanne suggested.

"Sounds good to me. How's about it?" Tom asked me.

I nodded. I couldn't believe that Deanne and Reuben were impressed with my chess playing. At home I was referred to as an "easy win," a "pushover."

54 Tom and I played chess while Deanne and Reuben watched. During the game my arm had a spasm and bumped the board and dislodged some pieces.

"Ah, I see you're using the same technique that Napoleon Bonaparte used. When he was losing, he too knocked over the board to save face," Tom teased. "But fortunately, I think I can reconstruct the game. Now, let's see, you had your knights here and there, right? And, I had my pawns here and..."

Painstakingly, Tom pieced together our game. When he finished, he said, "It's your move, Napoleon."

We all laughed. It was refreshing to be teased by my peers, although it took some adjustment on my part.

"Are we going to visit Kathy tonight?" Tom asked Deanne and Reuben. "John told me that her leg is still in the cast."

"Sure," Deanne said, "but, Bill has invited us over to his house tonight. Can we do both?"

"Oh sure. We can go over to his house after we visit the sick. But, am I invited?" Tom asked.

"YOU ALL ARE INVITED" I spelled.

I was loaded into a volunteer's car for the last time that Friday afternoon. Deanne poked her head in the car window and said, "I'll see you tonight, Bill."

The driver, a lady in her fifties, said, "Oh, you're the reason he's been so anxious to get to camp all week. I knew it wasn't the food."

Deanne giggled and blushed.

To Mom's dismay an army of teenagers invaded our house at a quarter to ten, an hour after I had given them up and fifteen minutes before my bedtime. There were eight of them.

Tom grabbed a chair and asked, "Where's the chess set? The rest of you can do whatever you want, but I'm playing chess with Bill."

"I guess I could show you his room," Mom said trying to figure out from where all the teenage bodies had come.

"Oh, I'd like that," Deanne said.

They stayed until eleven. Tom had beaten me at chess. Deanne and Reuben had seen my room, which was a shrine to John F. Kennedy.

When the group had gone Mom said, "What a super bunch of kids. They can even spell. It must be exciting to be able to talk to someone your own age for a change. You really lucked out this year."

CHAPTER 5

SQUARE PEG WITH PEERS

The rest of the summer of '71 was long, hot, and boring. I sat in front of the television and watched the game shows in the morning, worked on my stamp collection in the afternoon, and watched more TV with my family in the evening.

I also went on outings with a group of young adults who were in the same boat as I was—disabled, teenage, and graduated from Dr. J. P. Lord. The outings provided a change of scenery, but that was all.

The group was composed of ex-poster children who had outgrown their cuteness. They now went to a day care center which was staffed primarily by volunteers from my neighborhood church.

My family thought that I would go to the day care center and that the summer would be a good time to ease me into the program.

The group was transported on a van with a lift which had been given to the Center by a charity organization. The van was uncomfortable for me. I was too tall for it. I had to tilt my head to the side, which was a pain in the neck.

The wheelchairs on the van were clamped to the sides of it by unreliable fasteners. Everytime the van hit an Omaha pothole, one of the clamps would be jarred lose. Then the unsecured chair would roll in the van and wedge itself in an awkward postion.

I saw a clamp fall off on a wheelchair beside me. I tapped my language board to get the chair's occupant to listen to me.

"I can't spell or read your board, so wait until we stop. You can tell the driver your problem then. Relax and enjoy the scenery, man," the endangered passenger said.

But I persisted. Many times before I had wanted just to chat on the van, but this time was different.

56   "Hey, Kath, can you tell what he wants? I don't understand his lingo." the guy beside me said sarcastically.

The girl behind him said, "I'm back here so I can't see his letter chart or whatever you call it. Can't he wait? We'll be at the park in five minutes, and then the driver can figure out what's wrong with him.

"Oh by the way, Joe, are you going to our potluck dinner Saturday? It should be fun.

"It's too bad about Mrs. Andersen having to quit teaching us. She was a good teacher. I'll miss her. Sure wish she could be at the dinner."

Joe agreed, "It's too bad she had that falling out with the occupational therapist. I'll miss her too. We all will."

I wanted to ask who Mrs. Andersen had been and why she had the falling out with the O.T. But I was the odd-man-out then because there was no way for me to communicate with people who couldn't spell.

At the park the van driver discovered the loose clamp and said to herself, "It's funny that nobody saw this and told me to stop. Oh well, all's well that ends well, I guess."

I gave up. I decided to enjoy the outing at the park. After all, I had to get used to this group because I would join it soon.

The park director had a list of activities scheduled for us: watching another person make potholders for us, drinking lemonade, listening to the radio, and playing a washer-toss game.

The washer-toss took minimum effort and skill. One of the goodhearted helpers would put my wheelchair beside the square target, my left wheel touching its right border. Then another would put a heavy washer in my hand. And when I dropped it, the piece of metal would plunge on the target. Sometimes it would hit the bull's-eye, which was a round shallow hole in the center of the square.

For us, letting go of the washer required as much concentration as it did for an able-bodied person to toss it.

But a part of me wanted more of a challenge, such as playing chess with one of my new found friends from Westside High.

I tried to strike up a conversation with another person in the group. She was making a potholder and humming to herself.

"HOW ARE YOU TODAY" I spelled out.

"Can you repeat that. I didn't quite get all of it. Sorry," she said.

I asked my question again. This time carefully pointing to each letter, moving slowly and precisely.

"Oh, just a moment and I'll get the craft supervisor," the girl exclaimed, "Oh, Miss, oh, Miss, he wants to make a potholder like I'm making, only he wants it red and white. Could you help him?"

I stared in astonishment. How could anybody get that I wanted a red and white potholder from HOW ARE YOU TODAY?

The craft supervisor had headed for the craft supply shed for the necessary supplies. When she came back with the supplies and a gentle grin, I didn't have the heart to tell her it had been a misunderstanding. Besides, Mom could always use another potholder.

So I sat and watched the craft girl make a red and white potholder for me, listened to the radio, and got eaten by the gnats.

The radio blared the usual rock-'n'-roll songs continuously. It, combined with the summer breeze, had a hypnotic effect.

I had been drowsing when it came on the radio, but I snapped to attention after its opening lines. It was a composition by Tommy Clay. The record was a salute to the two slain Kennedys and Martin Luther King, Jr. The song, "What the World Needs Now," played softly in the background while the original news broadcasts of the three men's assassinations were played. It was so popular that the radio station played it four times in one hour. I made a mental note to ask Mom to get the record for me.

I didn't have to ask Mom for it. The next day Tom and Deanne came over. Tom asked, "Did you hear that new song on the radio about the Kennedys?"

I nodded and spelled out. "ITS GOOD I LOVED IT"

Tom nudged Deanne and grinned. Deanne, holding something behind her, said, "Good, because we bought it for you. We thought your Kennedy collection needed it."

"THANK YOU" was all I could say.

"You're entirely welcome, my man," said Tom, "By the way, do you have time for a quick game of chess? Deanne and I can't stay long, just long enough for me to beat you in a game."

While we were playing I drooled on the board. I was afraid my drooling would turn off my new friends because my family and therapists had told me repeatedly that it was socially unacceptable.

58   But, Tom just said, "Get the towels. Bill's dike broke again."

About a week after my sixteenth birthday, Deanne surprised me again. About 8:30 one August night, the doorbell rang. It was Deanne. She was carrying an oblong box and saying, "Hi, I can't stay long. I just stopped to drop off this birthday cake for Bill. My mom is waiting out in the car for me."

I was happy to see Deanne although she looked pale. I was thrilled to see the cake. I would have been happy with an ordinary pan cake from her, but this cake was far from ordinary. Shaped like a guitar, it had lollipops to adjust its strings and was decorated with frosting to look like a guitar. Numerous tooth picks held it together. No other girl my age had baked me a cake before or since.

"You must have spent hours on this," Mom commented. "We ought to have a picture of it to preserve it for posterity. Wait until I get my camera."

"I really must be going," Deanne politely interjected. "I have a concussion. Like a dummy, I fell off a horse while we were on vacation. . ."

I jumped and spelled, "ARE YOU OK"

"Yes, Bill, I just need a lot of rest," Deanne replied.

"WONT YOU HAVE A PIECE OF CAKE WITH US" I urged.

"I really would like to, but my mom is waiting out in the car. Thanks for the invitation anyway," Deanne said.

"THANK YOU VERY MUCH DEANNE" I spelled out.

"You're welcome. This cake didn't exactly turn out the way I had wanted, but I hope it tastes better than it looks," Deanne replied.

I heard a car horn honk. Deanne said, "That's my mom. I have to go now. See, since I have this stupid concussion, the doctors want me to rest in bed. Coming to see Bill used up my out-of-bed time for today. I'm doing a lot of reading these days. Bill, I'll see you soon. Hope you like the cake. Bye-bye." Deanne hurried out the door.

Mom looked at the cake and said, "What a nice surprise!"

I looked towards the door and nodded in agreement.

CHAPTER 6

CORRESPONDENCE AND TUTOR

Fortunately, the Omaha Public Schools granted me a temporary reprieve from going to the day care center, although I continued to go on recreational outings with the group. After seeing the findings of my battery of psychological tests the head of special education agreed with my parents: I was capable of doing high school work. The problem was that there were no high school programs for young people with severe disabilities in Omaha in the fall of '71.

So the school system put me under the jurisdiction of the homebound teacher and bought me independent study correspondence courses from the University of Nebraska at Lincoln's Extension Division. They allowed me to study in a corner of a classroom, which had 9- to 12-year-olds. The program was on a trial basis.

I was allowed to study at Dr. J. P. Lord because I needed the stimulation of others and the discipline of the classroom.

The homebound teacher was a silver-haired, no-nonsense lady, who was neither condescending nor jovial towards me. Her job was to administer tests, to help me when I didn't understand the material, to mail in the completed work to the Extension Division, and to show me the corrected work. She did her job. No more. No less.

It was late September before courses came. The homebound teacher was explaining the process when the principal came down to her office and said, "Since you are in kind of a special high school program and won't be getting much help, I have assigned you a tutor."

I looked at him questioningly. Was he so sure that I would fail?

"The tutor is a high school student herself. I shouldn't tell you this. You might get a swelled head," the principal teased. "But the young lady asked to help you specifically by name."

60   Resentment turned to curiosity.

"Her name is Deanne Kelley. Ring a bell?" the principal asked.

I grinned. Curiosity turned to delight. I couldn't believe Deanne was that interested in me. I was elated and inflated.

"I don't blame you," the principal said. "She's a doll. She will be here this Friday."

That Friday Deanne came to school with a woman, whom she introduced as "my mom." "I told you I was going to introduce you two one of these days," she said.

"Actually," the principal chimed in, "her mother came to check you out to see if you have honorable intentions." We all laughed.

When I laughed my right arm flew out of my lap and now dangled beside me.

"Can we put in a scratch paper so you can talk to us or is this lesson too important?" Deanne asked. She innocently moved to my right side. A danger signal flashed across my brain: "Hand, stay right where you are. Don't move."

"No, honey," her mother said, "leave his lesson in. We won't be here that long and it would be a shame to mess up his work."

I wanted to tell Deanne's mom that the workbook lesson would be corrected by me and would end up in the wastebasket without a teacher seeing it. But all my concentration was directed at making my right hand stay down at my side. I had a vision of my right hand flipping up Deanne's mini-skirt.

"Oh, hand, please for God's sake stay right where you are. You can knock over as many chess games as you want. Just don't move now." My brain flashed to my arm. The muscles would or wouldn't obey. Chance would decide.

"You're right, Mom." Deanne said, "Where's his letter board? Ah, here it is. Talk to us, Bill."

I couldn't because when I tried to spell something out, I could feel my muscles in my arm start to contract, drawing my arm upwards.

"Stay down, hand. I'm warning you," my brain flashed to the contracting muscles.

I thought of the consequences if I flipped Deanne's skirt up. I remembered my mom saying, "People won't understand if you flip up a woman's dress. They'll think you are a dirty old man, or young man, as the case may be."

This thought made me more tense. I couldn't even point to "YES" or "NO." I was—if you would excuse the expression—paralyzed with fear.

"C'mon, Bill, talk to us. I have told my mom a lot about you, and now here's your chance to show off. Have you gone shy on me?" Deanne teased.

I wanted to explain what was wrong to her but couldn't. I didn't know how. What would I say?

"DEANNE MOVE OR ILL FLIP UP YOUR DRESS"

Somehow that didn't sound like the proper thing to say in front of her mom. On the other hand, I didn't have time to spell out, "DEANNE ONE OF THE PROBLEMS WITH CEREBRAL PALSY IS THAT A PERSONS MUSCLES DO THINGS THEY SHOULDNT AND WE HAVE A PROBLEM NOW RESULTING FROM THIS"

So I just sat there, looking like an idiot, as my mom would say.

To my overwhelming relief, Deanne's mom looked at her watch and said, "It's time for us to go. It was good to meet you, Bill."

"I don't know if the principal told you this but you'll have to put up with me twice a week. I'm coming to bug you on Mondays and Fridays, if that's okay with you."

I grinned and nodded.

Deanne continued, "By the way, today is my birthday. I didn't have the honor of seeing you on yours, but you are seeing me on mine. Bye-bye. See you on Monday."

One day before our tutoring sessions, Deanne wheeled me into a room which we used to study in private and said, "Your homebound teacher called me this morning to tell me that you got an A- on your worksheets and a B on your test in World G."

She knelt beside me so that her eyes were level with mine.

"Bill, that's fantastic. I'm impressed. Really, I couldn't do that good. I'm proud of you."

Emotionally and socially, I needed her, not only because she was a girl, but because she was my age. The Dr. Lord students, like those at the day care center, couldn't understand me since they couldn't follow my language board.

So this is why I fell in love with Deanne. She honestly cared when it

62   seemed that nobody else at school did. I tried as never before to get good grades just to impress her. Most teenage boys do something—curse, smoke, hit a homer—to impress their teenage love. Getting good grades was my way of showing off to my love.

CHAPTER 7

THE CUCKOO'S NEST

The next year I was a man without a school. I had had enough of the arrangement at Dr. J. P. Lord. Twelve years would wear out anybody's welcome.

The placement counselor at J. P. Lord tried to suggest I should go to an individualized learning center which was designed for dropouts and drug addicts but my dad abruptly said, "Listen, you son of a bitch, that isn't an option. My son is not a drug addict or a dropout and I won't have him exposed to that type of people. If you can't find a better place for him, then I will by God."

So in an attempt to solve my dilemma, my parents enrolled me in the day care center with whose clients I had been socializing for the past two years, and asked the Omaha Public School System to continue providing the homebound program with its homebound teacher.

Then, my parents and I considered the Center and the correspondence courses the best of all available options. The Center's staff consisted of two certified teachers, one certified physical therapist, an uncertified guidance counselor, a secretary, and the director. The Center's primary function was to provide relief for the parents of teens and young adults who were severely physically and/or mentally disabled. It also provided camaraderie for the young adults, most of whom lived in nursing homes.

When I was talking to the Center's teacher who would help me with my coursework, another client, a woman in her twenties who was twisted and contorted, and institutionalized, wheeled over and asked the teacher, "Can the physical therapist put some hot packs on me? My rheumatism is bothering me. It happens when you get to be my age."

64   I noticed the teacher wince. She and the woman in the wheelchair were about the same age. The teacher, however, didn't have a ninety-year-old roommate.

"I'll talk to the therapist and see what I can do," the teacher said wearily. "Excuse me, Bill. I'll be right back."

I looked around and saw guys listening to records on the stereo, young women knitting, and a couple playing checkers. They were content to live for the present.

I noticed one of the guys putting a rolled up piece of paper into another guy's hand. At first, I thought it was an act of friendship. Then he lit it with a match.

The guy who had it in his hand had no reflexes to drop the firey paper. All he could do was watch it burn in his hand and shout, "Hey, help, help! Get this damn paper out of my hand, somebody!"

His eyes bulged as the fire consumed the paper and came closer to his deformed hand.

The bearded physical therapist came to see what was happening. He saw the flaming paper in the paralyzed hand. He yanked it out, took it to the bathroom, and flushed it. When he came out of the bathroom, he shouted, "Who did it? It's not funny. Who was the guy?"

The guy who almost got a hot hand fingered the culprit with pleasure.

"Yeah, I did it, but only after they called me fat and stinky. I can't help it if I have to wear a damn bag to go in and that sometimes it stinks," said the guy who tried to make a human torch.

"All right, let's go into the director's office," the physical therapist said. "She will have something to say to both of you." He wheeled the two enemies into the office.

I began to wonder if this was my best option. Was this any better than being with dropouts? Perhaps I should have stayed home. I didn't like those prospects. Would I become as self-involved as the others at the Center?

But in the midst of this insanity, I continued to work on my correspondence work without knowing why. My efforts were bolstered when they were recognized by the University of Nebraska Extension Division. I appeared in its newsletter and was named the outstanding High School Supervised Correspondence Student of the year 1972-1973 in the Handicapped Division.

Receiving recognition helped me to make the best out of a nightmare. But I was blessed with something else which the others at the Center didn't have. Tom from Westside had signed up to do his High School Volunteer Civic Work at the Center because he had heard I was there. He was a breath of fresh air.

"Hi there. I'm Tom Taxman. I volunteered to help Bill Rush with his studying," he announced to the director.

As soon as I heard his voice, I let out a scream. Then I heard, "Never mind showing me where he is. I'll follow my ears. I've come to know his yell. I keep saying he should do the voice for Tarzan. He sounds like him a lot."

When Tom came into the room where I was studying, he asked, "What are you studying, Bill? Please say something easy."

I told him I was studying geography and its effects on the first and second world wars.

"Wonderful. Hey, how's about a game of chess, my man? You deserve a break since I don't know anything about how geography affected the world wars. And, as your tutor, I feel obligated to teach you how to goof off. Everybody needs to know that."

One day at the end of October, as he was leaving, Tom said, "Well, next Tuesday when I come, I'll bring a little surprise for you. I think you'll like this surprise."

Tom came that Tuesday, whistling a merry tune. Deanne was following him. As my face beamed, he said, "I brought another volunteer to the Center. And as you can see, Bill knows her slightly. You've probably heard about her from Bill, so I won't waste my breath introducing her."

"Hi, Bill," Deanne said cheerfully. "I finally found a ride over here. It's so good to see you again! Tell me, when do I get a grand tour of your new school?"

In early November, Tom said, "Hey, Bill, Westside is having a play three weeks from Friday. I think you'd like it. If you could get your family to bring you, I can take you home. A lot of people who you know will be in it. So how's about it? We can do like last time. You could get there and I'll bring you home."

66

I smiled because I remembered the first time when Tom had invited me to a play at Westside. It had been in the summer before I had made my move from Dr. J. P. Lord to the Center.

Tom had talked to my mom and they had decided she would bring my body to the play and Tom would take me home.

I remembered how hard it had been for Mom and Dad, as it would have been for any other parents of a teenager who had a disability, to let me go unescorted. But Tom had proven his friendship.

I recalled how we had to use the fire exit to get into the play because the exit had the fewest steps.

I recollected my surprise when Tom had said that he had arranged for me to have some female companionship during the play, and it had turned out to be Deanne.

But I also remembered how nervous I had been at being out in public and how embarrassed Deanne, Tom, and I had been at my uncontrollable laughter. The harder I tried to control it the louder it became.

Deanne, I recalled, had politely commented, "Remind me to teach you to chuckle softly when I tutor you next year."

I remembered when the play had ended, Tom had come out from back stage and said, "I could hear you clear up on stage. We had a hard time not cracking up ourselves.

"At least we know you enjoyed it. Our director is always telling us we should get the audience involved. I guess we'll have to bring you to every play to show our director that the audience is really involved."

Tom brought me out of my contemplation with, "Oh by the way, one of the people in this play is Deanne."

That settled it. I was going.

Deanne was a part of the chorus and had just a few lines of dialogue, but to me she was one of the highlights of the play.

After the play and the drive home, Tom and his friends struggled to get my tall, skinny wheelchair out of his two-door hatchback, joking all the time they were doing it. Tom had a skill for cramming four teenagers plus my chair into a vehicle designed for two persons.

After clowning around with my wheelchair, Tom carefully opened the car door, unbuckled my seat belt, and started to lift me out of the car. But I jerked. The next thing Tom and I knew, I was on the car floor under the dash inspecting his carpet. Fortunately for me, it was soft. My right shoe was in my mom's flowerbed collecting mud samples. I could hear Tom above me apologizing to me and cursing at himself.

Tom carefully threaded me out from under the dash and got me into my wheelchair. Then he quickly rushed me into the house where we were greeted by Mom.

Tom stammered, "Mrs. Rush, we had a little trouble getting Bill out of the car. Or rather, I should say we had a lot of trouble. One minute he was in my arms. And, the next he was under my dash. Oh Lord, he even got his shoes muddy! I'm so sorry, Mrs. Rush."

"Forget it, Tom," Mom said calmly, "For seventeen years he hasn't gotten his shoes muddy. It's about time he did get them muddy."

The Center also provided a nightlife. It wasn't as satisfying as the one that Tom and Deanne provided. The Center's clients went to movies and to dances for teenagers who were disabled. Had I not known anything else, I would have been as contented with its outings as its other clients.

For Christmas the Center went caroling at several local nursing homes, which were home sweet home for a number of its clients.

The first home was run by the County. It was enough to spoil my Christmas spirit. It had old blind men who sang "Jingle Bells" while we were singing "Silent Night," two old women fighting over a Raggedy Ann doll, and another old man who relieved himself in front of the Christmas tree.

It was where the guy who was almost set on fire lived. He was teased by the females on the nursing staff. When the rest of the group was making its way to the elevators, I heard a nurse tell him, "I understand that you have something special for me and that I should come to your room late at night to get it. All I get from you is promises, promises and no action."

So, I shouldn't have been so angry at him when he teased me by saying, "Last night Deanne came to my room. She's real nice, if you know what I mean."

I felt like setting him on fire myself.

But if I would have been honest with myself, I would have been able to check my own daydreams about Deanne.

68   My fantasy was to go out with her and to develop something more than a friendship. My intentions were honorable, even if they were unrealistic.

I heard stories about other men who were disabled to the point of being in iron lungs getting married. So why couldn't I? Deanne obviously cared about me, and I cared about her.

The Center's inexperienced guidance counselor encouraged me by giving me canned clichés like, "A person can do anything he wants if he really tries. We could double date. Nothing is impossible. Don't let your disability get in the way of your sexuality."

The counselor offered to talk Deanne on my behalf. I naively accepted his offer.

My parents tried to discourage me by saying, "You have a fantastic friendship with Deanne. Don't blow it by acting stupid. You can't date her. Be satisfied with what you do have."

They didn't tell me why I couldn't date her.

The guidance counselor came up with another cliché, "Your parents are just being overly protective. Don't you see that?"

My parents were right. Deanne's visits became fewer and less frequent. There wasn't any scene that ended our friendship.

At first she tried to downplay my romantic feelings by saying, "How could a smart guy like you fall in love with a goofy looking person like me? I thought you were smarter than that, Bill Rush."

When that didn't work (because I tried to convince her she was the most beautiful girl in the world), she stopped coming to the Center because she couldn't handle the situation that I had created.

At first I thought she was sick. So I wrote her letters telling her how much I missed her.

I couldn't see that Deanne was a seventeen-year-old girl and was unprepared to handle my feelings for her.

My parents urged me to stop. But I ignored them and continued writing to her. Ironically, Mom had to take the letters out of my typewriter, put envelopes in my typewriter so I could address them, put the letters into their envelopes, seal them without reading them, and mail them. While she did this she said, "You've scared her off. You're making an ass out of yourself by doing this. But I guess you need to make your own mistakes."

I was frustrated because writing letters was my only form of communication with her. It was hard for me to figure out why she wouldn't answer. When I saw her, which was becoming less and less frequently, Deanne had always said, "Write me, Bill. I love hearing from you."

Of course she said this from a distance.

If she "loved" hearing from me, why didn't she answer my letters? For my part I forgot what 1 Corinthians said about love and let my letters to her become impatient and unkind, not to mention arrogant and rude.

I wanted to call her and talk to her directly. That way she could tell me exactly how she felt and I would have the same opportunity. Who knows? Maybe it would do more harm than good, but at least it would clear the air between us. But I couldn't get the answers that I needed. I became aware of how important direct communication was. I resented that I couldn't have it with Deanne. I wanted it so much.

Finally, Tom, my gentle friend, made me see the unpleasant light. He came over to my house during Christmas break. We went into my bedroom where we could have privacy.

It had been almost a year since I'd heard from Deanne. I asked Tom if he knew what was wrong with her. Was she sick? Had she been in an accident?

His usual clowning vanished like the chill of a spring morning. He drew a long deep breath, let it out slowly, closed his eyes, put his hand on my shoulder, and said, "I talked to Deanne and casually asked her why she never visits you anymore. She cried. She couldn't talk about you. It was a bad scene. If I were you, I'd back off. I'm sorry. I know how much you cared for her."

I cried. I felt heartsick that I had been inflicting pain on somebody who had befriended me when I had desperately needed a friend. Why hadn't I heeded the warnings? Why had I let determination turn into blind bullheadedness?

I stopped writing her.

I would learn much later that she hadn't known how to deal with my feelings and that she had sought advice from mutual friends, teachers, her parents, and the Center's guidance counselor. I would also learn that she had gotten tons of it, ranging from "See him often. Show him you're human," to "Let him know that you have boyfriends,

70   love interests," from "See him occasionally like once or twice a month, on a friendship basis," and finally to "Stay away from him. You're too close." I would learn that the Center's counselor had been the one who told her to stay away from me. I would learn that he had told Deanne that she was bad for me. Nothing could have been further from the truth.

PART THREE

JOURNEY INTO
UNDERSTANDING

CHAPTER 8

CAMP CAMELOT

The fall of '73, winter and spring of '74 were the most depressing seasons of my life. I thought I had lost Deanne Kelley's friendship. And it became more evident that the day care didn't meet my needs.

By April, 1973, my parents had taken me out of the Center's program. I did my correspondence courses at home and realized that for the first time in my life there was nowhere for me to go. My future looked bleak. My parents and I were tired and hurt because we had tried so hard and for so long to prevent me from becoming homebound.

But the summer of '74 became a time for healing. I went to Easter Seal Camp Kiwanis, an overnight camp for people with disabilities. The camp was just outside of Milford, Nebraska. Mom was astonished that I wanted to go because for years I had resisted going to the overnight camp.

When I asked her to fill out an application, she replied, "But, you hate this camp. The last two times you went, you complained about old dilapidated cabins that leaked when it rained, bad counselors, and the mosquitoes. Don't get me wrong. Dad and I will send you if you want to go, but it has to be your decision, understand?"

I nodded. A part of my decision was influenced by what I had heard at the day care center—new cabins, better counselors, longer and wider sidewalks, better shower stalls, and more activities. I also was tired of being homebound. I needed a vacation from my family, and my family needed one from me.

So with a certain amount of apprehension, I went to camp. Unlike the Cerebral Palsy day camp, which had a camper-counselor ratio of one to one, Camp Kiwanis had a ratio of five campers to two

74 counselors. The campers and counselors were assigned by cabins. One counselor was in charge. Usually each cabin had two campers who used wheelchairs.

My cabin leader, Ed Henry, a blond Kansas farmboy, reminded me of a chunky bulldog with glasses and a mustache.

Our first meeting wasn't too pleasant. It was during lunch. Another counselor was trying to hold my head while feeding me. It wasn't working because, as one of my speech therapists had explained to me, holding my head causes an overflow of athetoid motion. In other words, I was jumping around, spraying food everywhere, and making an unbecoming mess out of myself although I had been covered by a plastic garbage bag which was supposed to serve as a bib.

"Feeding him will be fun," Ed remarked wearily. "But, we'll manage somehow."

Between bites I motioned for my headstick and tried to explain the problem. My feeder got the message but didn't heed it because his training had told him to support the head. Bad habits are hard to break.

After the meal I told Ed, "I AM EASIER TO FEED IF YOU DONT HOLD MY HEAD LIKE HE DID"

"Okay, next meal I'll feed you, and we'll try it your way. That guy who fed you works for the State Hospital in Beatrice. He has to do volunteer work for a day," Ed said. "Anyway, the next activity is swimming. So how's about going back to the cabin to change into your swimming trunks. Is there anything special I should know about to assist you better?"

I considered. I was so used to others telling me how they were going to do things. Ed was the first person to let me have some degree of control over my body.

"MY FEET SHOULD BE TIED TO MY FOOTRESTS AND MY KNEES SHOULD BE TIED APART TO GIVE ME MORE BALANCE AND STABILITY MY BOOTS SHOULD BE ON WHEN I AM IN MY WHEELCHAIR I CAN LIFT MY WEIGHT IF I HAVE MY BOOTS ON BUT I CANT BALANCE AND DONT PUT ANYTHING ON MY TRAY WHERE I CAN REACH IT OR MY ARMS WILL KNOCK IT OFF"

"Okay. Anything else?" Ed asked sincerely.

"I CANT SHUT MY EYES IN THE SHOWER SO BE CAREFUL

OF GETTING SOAP IN THEM AND SINCE I CANT BALANCE I
NEED A STURDY SHOWER CHAIR WITH A BACK AND
ARMS"

"Like a folding lawn chair?" Ed suggested. "I know where we can
get one. Will that do you?"

I nodded.

"Okay. Let's go for a swim," Ed said. "Do you use a life jacket, inner
tube, or both?"

"BOTH" I spelled out.

Ed took me to our cabin. There he wrestled me until he had
threaded my spindly legs through narrow trunks. After he put his
swimming trunks on, he pushed me to the camp's swimming pool
with my brother's size twelve tennis boots still on me. (I was a size
nine.) I had viewed myself in the cabin's mirror. I looked like I had just
stepped out of a "before" picture in an advertisement for a body
building course and had someone install pontoons on my feet.

When we got to the pool, he introduced me to the lifeguard. The
lifeguard, Karen, smiled at me, and asked Ed if I needed a life jacket or
an inner tube.

"He told me that he uses both."

"Good. Ed, hand me a life jacket from over there, and put a tire in
the water. I have to make sure the jacket is secure."

I knew the lifeguard was doing her job, but she could have at least
spoken to me instead of about me. It also made me feel a little leery
that she seemed to expect me to drown. In a way, with all her
precautions, she had taken all the fun out of swimming for me because
she had eliminated all the risk.

Before we submerged, Ed asked, "Do you have any last words?"

"YES IF I DROWN HAVE HER GIVE ME MOUTH TO
MOUTH" I joked.

"Smart-ass," Ed retorted.

That night my appreciation of the farmboy grew. At supper he fed
me without using a garbage bag bib as well as without holding my
head. We were spilling a lot of food on him and me. But when I
suggested that he use a garbage bag for a bib, he replied, "Those bags
are too bulky."

"BUT MY CLOTHES WILL GET DIRTY" I spelled.

"So, if they get too messy, I'll wash them. I don't like those damn

76 bags. They don't look dignified. I wouldn't put one on myself so why should I put one on you? Besides," Ed added jokingly, "a garbage bag wouldn't let these gals around here see you in a T-shirt, and I don't want to deny them that."

I laughed and out came a mouthful of corn. But I was delighted Ed was that concerned about my appearance.

After the meal the camp had a mock Olympiad on a grassy meadow. During a relay race the bottom of my foot pedal caught on a bump and almost flung another counselor and me head over heels.

Fortunately, my pusher and I regained our balance before we hit the ground. Unfortunately, my footrest was bent and had a broken pin.

My pusher and I panicked. He said, "Oh my God, why does this always have to happen to me? We'll have to call your parents and have them bring out your other wheelchair. I'll get Ed! Stay here!"

Where did he expect me to go? I wanted to tell him that I didn't have an extra wheelchair but he was gone before I could point to a letter on my board.

In five minutes he came back with Ed, who calmly inspected the damage.

"Yep, the pedal's broken and slightly bent," Ed said. Then to me, "Do you have an extra wheelchair at home that your folks can bring out?"

"NO" I spelled out.

"Figured that. You don't look like a two chair person," Ed joked. "I can rig something up to hold this one together tomorrow. C'mon, Let's get some shut-eye. It's getting late. Can we cross your legs and tie your foot to the other pedal until I get this one fixed?"

I nodded.

The next day at breakfast the other counselor commented to Ed, "I have been noticing Bill's oblong face. It seems to me that all C.P.'s have that same gross facial distortion. What do you think, Ed? Haven't you noticed it?"

Ed, who was feeding me and putting salt on his oatmeal, sensed my neck hairs begin to rise. He quietly gave me a look that told me he was just as exasperated at the other counselor's insensitivity as I was. Ed ignored the question.

After lunch Ed borrowed a hammer from the camp tool shed and

pounded the bent and twisted bracketing of my footrest back into
shape.

"This is how I take out my frustrations," Ed joked as he pounded. "Now, if we can find something to replace the little pin that used to hold this in place, we're in business. Any ideas?"

"HOW ABOUT USING A WIRE CLOTHES HANGER WE COULD TIE THE PEDAL TO THE CHAIR USING A PIECE OF A THAT" I suggested.

"Damn, you're a smart bastard, or else I'm a dumb one! That won't require a comment from you!" Ed then asked more seriously, "Do you have any other problems?"

"YES THE OTHER COUNSELOR IS BEGINNING TO RUB ME THE WRONG WAY I WISH I COULD STRAIGHTEN HIM OUT WITH A HAMMER" I spelled.

"I kinda figured that after this morning. He's young. I've been talking with him, trying to get him to see the total camper but he's studying pre-med. So he's wrapped up in the medical aspect. Bear with him, and I'll have a talk with him again," Ed assured me. "Now, how's about going to the main lodge for a snack before the next activity?"

I reflected on Ed Henry's attitude. After eighteen months of being engulfed by panic over my dismal future, I needed someone like Ed to help me calmly put life back into perspective. I knew I needed him to help me put my life back in order. However, I didn't know the process had already begun.

As we went to the main lodge I noticed how the campground was arranged. The camp wasn't so different from others. It had a rifle range, a cement swimming pool, a wooden bathhouse, a small infirmary, a big main lodge, and two groups of newly-constructed western style cabins. But the camp had the signs of being for people with disabilities: ramps on the infirmary, on the main lodge, and on some of the cabins; shower chairs, urinals, and bed pans in the bathhouses; floating lawn chairs, an abundance of life jackets, and inner tubes in in the pool area; and a long sidewalk from one end of camp to the other. The sidewalk reminded me of a river with tributaries that fed into the different cabins, the main lodge, and the swimming pool's bathhouse. These modifications didn't invalidate the beauty of the sky that served as the camp's blue dome, or the trees that served as pillars, or the lush green grass that served as a carpet.

When we arrived at the main lodge, Ed said, "I'm getting a Diet Pepsi. What do you want? Your parents gave the camp's general store a couple of bucks for you to spend on snack food like pop and candy and to buy a camp T-shirt if you want one."

"ILL HAVE JUST A COKE" I spelled.

"Okay, I'll be right back."

While Ed was getting my Coke, I viewed the old dilapidated main lodge. It was the most prominent place at camp since it was two stories high and one city block long. The top floor was a combination dining hall, general store, and town hall. The bottom floor was a combination bathroom, tool shed, storage room, tornado shelter, and laundry room. The decrepit old building had screen windows and a leaky unshingled triangular roof. The building's antiquated wiring, wooden frame structure, and a single wheelchair ramp made it a potential firetrap. The ramp, which reminded me of a cattle chute, came from a rickety pale blue porch.

But the lodge was kept spotless. It also had a big brick fireplace which made it comfortable and friendly on chilly nights.

I engaged in girl watching. Two had caught my eye. Both were counselors, both were slender, and both had dark blonde hair. One had short hair and wore a red Iowa State T-shirt as well as blue cutoffs. She took a girl camper out of the lodge. The other had extremely long hair and wore bib overalls as well as a camp T-shirt. She came over to me and said, "Can I get you anything?"

"NO MY COUNSELOR IS GETTING A COKE FOR ME" I spelled.

"Okay, catch you later," she said and went to help another camper.

"Rush," I thought to myself, "you like them skinny and able-bodied. Shame on you."

Soon Ed came back with my Coke and said that he had forgotten to have me sign up for my daily activities and that we had to take care of it right away.

"OK WHO IS THAT GIRL WITH THE LONG HAIR TAKING ORDERS FOR THE GENERAL STORE" I asked.

"She's Judy—Judy Jennings. She's a helluva gal. She is the camp's Spanish instructor," Ed said as he gave me a swallow of Coke. Then he took out a sheet of paper and a pencil from his pants pocket and said,

"For the first activity you have a choice of swimming, nature, or Spanish. Which one do you want?"

"SPANISH" I spelled with hesitation, expecting to be rebuked.

My mom's response would have been, "Bill, you can't even speak English, so why in the hell do you want to learn Spanish?"

But the Kansas farmboy's remark was merely, "Figured that. I had Spanish marked already. Now for the second activity you have a choice of music, swimming, riflery, or nature. Which one?"

"MUSIC"

"Good," Ed said. The third activity period has swimming, canoeing, Spanish, or music. You can't sign up for one activity twice so your choices really are swimming or canoeing." Ed gave me another swallow of Coke while I was making my decision.

"SWIMMING"

"Okay, let me run this sign-up sheet up to the office. Then, we'll go swimming. Here, have the rest of your drink. Keep an eye on the gals for me until I get back."

After swimming, we heard the dinner bell signaling time for supper. Ed pushed me up to the main lodge where some of the other campers and counselors were having a "rap session." It was being held in a small corner of the main lodge.

Ed suggested that I join the session while he went back to our cabin to help the other counselor with the rest of the group.

I nodded my agreement. I found the session interesting, not so much for what was being discussed—the Watergate scandal—but rather for how it was being discussed. The counselors let us campers disagree with them and among ourselves. It was the first time I was allowed to express a contrary opinion and have the authority figures—the counselors—respect it. That was a good feeling.

Until then, I wasn't supposed to argue. If I dared to disagree with my dad, I was being stupid. If I dared to disagree with my mom, I was being snotty. If I dared to disagree with my teachers and therapists, I was being lazy and uncooperative. If I dared to disagree with my brothers, I was always wrong.

The approaching clatter of plates made the group facilitator say, "I see it's time for us to quit for now, but we'll continue this tomorrow, same time, same place, same station. Now let's eat!"

The group vanished, leaving me alone. I couldn't ask for help

80   because no one had the time to watch me spell. I started to count the nails in the lodge wall, figuring that I would have to wait for Ed to get seated at a table.

Fortunately, I had to stop counting when I reached my fiftieth nail. The red Iowa State T-shirt counselor saw me sitting in the middle of nowhere and came to me and offered to escort me to a table. I nodded my acceptance.

She took me to a table and put my plate and glass on my wheelchair tray so they covered up my letter tray and were within reach of my spastic athetoid arms. A danger signal went off in my head and I wondered if the plate and glass were breakable. If Ed didn't come quickly, we would soon know.

I resented my arms. They were always getting in the way. They got in the way when I met Deanne's mother and they were getting in the way now when I wanted to strike up a conversation with the female counselor. Amputation was fine with me but I doubted that my parents would allow it.

The female counselor interrupted my thoughts of self-mutilation with, "Do you want me to dish your plate for you?"

I shook my head since my letter board was covered with the endangered plate. I noticed a slight lisp in her speech. The lisp was attractive in a way. It gave her speech an unique flavor. I also noticed that there was something subtly attractive about her, although I couldn't put my finger on exactly what it was. In a way, she was plain looking with wire-rimmed glasses and an average figure. Still, she had something. I didn't know quite what.

"Okay, see you later then," she said and went to help another camper. Just as she was leaving, Ed came with the rest of our cabin group.

Ed saw the plate and glass setting in the danger zone and quickly took it off my tray before I knocked it off.

"WHO WAS THAT" I asked.

"Sally Stone," Ed replied while he was dishing my plate. "She's a real nice gal. She embarrasses easily, so we counselors play little practical jokes on her. Fortunately, she's also a good sport about it. She's in our sister cabin. I'll be happy to introduce you two after supper."

"I WOULD LIKE THAT"

"Guess who has a crush on who," the other counselor chimed in.
"I DONT HAVE A DAMN CRUSH ON HER" I spelled out angrily "I WOULD JUST LIKE TO MEET HER."

I resented that when I expressed a natural and healthy interest in a woman, people like the counselor automatically invalidated it by labeling it as just a crush. That way they aren't forced to deal with it.

"Okay, Bill," Ed calmly said. "You don't have a crush on Sally. He misunderstood. That's all. Sometimes you're too damned sensitive."

Ed was right. But, he didn't know why I was so sensitive about women. The memory of what happened with Deanne was fresh, and the wounds hadn't healed. I guess I had developed a conditioned reflex to the word "crush." I was still trying to sort out what had happened and why it had happened.

"Open up. Here comes some food," Ed said cheerily.

After supper Ed wheeled me to the bathroom. After we took care of business Ed asked his usual, "Do you have any other problems?"

I hesitated, then told him about Deanne. Confession is good for the soul. When I had finished, Ed took a deep breath, let it out slowly, and said, "Once when I was in college, I had a rotten day. I mean not a damn single thing had gone right. I got a bad grade on a paper, flunked a test, and I don't know what else. Anyway, I was walking back from the dorm's cafeteria, bitching to a friend. The friend stopped me and said, 'Ed, be glad that you can feel. So many people are strung out on dope and can't feel anything.' So Bill, be glad that you can at least feel.

"And, besides, from what you have told me, it sounds like your guidance counselor at that day care center made a bad mistake. A counselor never tells anyone what to do. His job is to help the person who he is counseling to reach his own decision, not to tell him what to do.

"Anyway, now I understand your reaction to the word 'crush,' but you can't stop reaching out to gals just because of one bad experience, dammit!

"C'mon, let's find Sally, so I can introduce you to her properly. And, thanks for trusting me enough to confide in me."

Eventually Sally and I did meet. It wasn't under the best of circumstances for her. The camp had a talent night and some of the campers in our cabin wanted to dress up as female strippers. They

82 were discussing where to borrow—steal, actually—bras for their skit.
I suggested using one of Sally's. After all, her cabin was by ours so
taking it would be easy. Ed loved my idea, saying that Sally could take
that kind of a joke. I then suggested that I be the one to give back her
bra after the show. It would make her notice me and remember me.

The plan worked. Sally accepted the bra with a mixture of
embarrassment and humor.

"Oh, I'm embarrassed!" she said with a giggle. "You guys always do
this to me! I wondered where this had gone."

"THANK YOU FOR THE USE OF IT BUT I AM AFRAID
THAT IT DIDNT FIT ONE OF THE GUYS QUITE AS GOOD AS
IT FITS YOU" I spelled.

"You're a flirt, Bill Rush, but thank you for the compliment. It's
late, so see you tomorrow."

Ed leaned over and said, "Good job. You're really a lady's man at
heart, aren't you? There's a fifties sock hop tomorrow night. Maybe
you can invite Sally to that. Sleep on it."

I did and decided to do it. But the next morning I had the Spanish
class with Judy Jennings. The class was more of a time for socializing
than for learning Spanish.

Judy let us campers decide what we wanted to learn, then taught it
to us. Most of the time the conversation drifted away from Spanish to
other things because Judy was natural, friendly, and light-hearted. She
made us campers feel accepted and welcome in her class.

"Well, Bill, don't worry about how to pronounce the words. Just
worry about how to spell them," Judy told me. "I'll spell the words for
your benefit, okay? Actually, you have a tougher job than the others
do. But, you can handle it, can't you?"

I nodded and laughed.

During the class I asked Judy what her plans were after camp was
over.

"Well," she said, "This past May I graduated from the University of
Nebraska at Lincoln with a degree in Special Education, and this
coming fall I'm starting to teach at Dr. J. P. Lord School. I'm really
excited. I'll teach first grade."

I felt a twinge of regret for having been born thirteen years too
soon, and I also felt a strong anger for having to leave Dr. J. P. Lord
before my high school education had been completed. But deciding

not to burden the young idealistic teacher with my contempt for the
Omaha Public School System, I spelled, "I HOPE YOU LIKE IT AT
DR LORD"

"Thank you. I hope I do too. Do you go to Dr. Lord?" Judy asked.

"I USED TO BUT NOT ANY MORE I GOT TOO OLD FOR IT"
I mechanically spelled out.

"Oh, that's too bad. I was looking forward to seeing you at the
school. Perhaps we could still get together if you live in Omaha," Judy
offered.

I nodded my head.

"Okay, it's a date! Oh, I see it's time for lunch," Judy said as she
glanced at her watch. "C'mon, I'll push you up to the main lodge."

The day was ungodly hot so at lunch the camp nurse gave me and
Ed a salt tablet each. Then she asked Ed, "When are you going to find
time to come to get your injection? It has been a day and a half since
your last shot."

Slowly, I began thinking—the salt on his oat meal, the Diet Pepsi,
and now the shot.

When the camp nurse had gone, I asked Ed, "DO YOU HAVE
DIABETES"

"Yep, sure do. My mom has it too. Are you ready to eat, Sherlock?
By the way, did you ask Sally to the fifties dance?"

I shook my head and spelled, "I DIDNT HAVE TIME"

"She'll be at the general store. You can ask her then, okay?" Ed
suggested.

I took his suggestion. When I saw Sally roaming around during the
general store period, I motioned to her to come over.

"What do you want?" she asked. "Sorry, we are all out of bras
today."

I laughed and started to spell, "DO YOU KNOW ABOUT THE
DANCE TONIGHT"

"Yes. Will you be there?" she asked.

"YES I WAS THINKING SINCE WE ARE COMING FROM
THE SAME GENERAL DIRECTION WE . . ." I started to spell.

"Are you asking me for a date to the sock hop?" she asked.

I nodded stiffly.

"Okay, I'll pick you up around seven, okay with you?"

I nodded a little less stiffly and smiled.

84   "Thanks for asking me to the dance. See ya at seven," she said as she walked away.

That night our cabin was buzzing with primping activity. For many of us this was our first chance to go to a dance although many of us were either old teenagers or young adults. Professionals didn't see the need to allow us to participate in mixed gatherings, and most parents didn't have the resources or desire to let us date.

Ed dressed me in my brother's tennis shoes, dark pants, and a white shirt. He lent me a pair of bobby socks to give me that fifties look. Ed used good old H_2O to plaster down my jet black hair.

While grooming me Ed said, "Brylcream is a pain to get out, so I thought water would be better since shampoo and you don't get along too good."

I looked at him and nodded my approval.

At seven, Sally showed up at my cabin door wearing a light brown pullover sweater, a dark brown skirt, and, of course, bobby socks. She had her dark blonde hair pulled back into a ponytail. When we started towards the main lodge, Ed stuck his head out and jokingly yelled, "Have him back at 10!"

Sally leaned over and whispered, "Parents and counselors are such a drag."

As we strolled down the sidewalk, I realized that this was my first dating experience and I prayed that I didn't blow it. At the sock hop Sally took off my and her shoes and checked them in.

Next we boogied with waving arms and rocking wheels. Sally had to lock my brakes so that I didn't roll over her stocking feet. Sally took my hand and twirled herself under my arm. For the more tender dances she unlocked my brakes, put my arm around her waist, and swayed back and forth. However, Sally instinctively knew when and how to keep it friendly. After a couple of dances she said, "I have to circulate and make sure the others have someone to dance with, understand?"

I quickly nodded.

"Hey, don't be so anxious to dump me and get another girl. I'm saving the last dance for you, and if you don't walk me home, I'll be hurt," Sally reassured me.

I looked around and saw Ed dancing with a girl camper. Soon Judy came over to me and asked me to dance with her. Slowly I realized that no camper was being left alone for more than a dance. The counselors made sure of that. It was their responsibility to see that we campers had a good time. I wasn't sure how I felt about that. On one hand, I could understand why the counselors felt an obligation to see that we campers were having fun. But on the other, I resented the contrivance. I wanted and needed to know that Sally and Judy were dancing with me because they really wanted to, not because they were obligated to do so.

When the sock hop was over, Sally escorted me back to my cabin.

"I had fun tonight," Sally said. Then she gave me a peck on the cheek and a hug. "I have to get back to my cabin but I will see you tomorrow. And thanks again for inviting me."

That night when I was in bed, I reflected. Camp was a Camelot. It was isolated from outside norms that dictated how people with disabilities were supposed to be treated. At camp I was allowed to be and act like a valid person. But in the larger society I was denied the right to normal sexuality, the right to flirt, and the right to reach out. For the first time in my life I had been able to ask a woman for a date without worrying what others would think and a woman was able to kiss me out of friendship without worrying if others would think she was leading me on. I didn't understand why I couldn't date. What was so damn wrong with it? Why couldn't Camp Camelot be extended to the outside world?

Suddenly, I realized that camp consisted of an empathetic staff who had at least a basic understanding of how to treat and what to expect from people with disabilities. I also realized at camp we were the majority, and in the outside world we were the minority. This explained the injustice, but didn't excuse it.

I decided to raise this isssue at the next rap session to see how the other campers and the counselors felt about it.

I opened a can of worms. One camper said, "I want to have children, but the people at the hospital won't let me."

A counselor said, "If you had a kid, who would support it, you or the taxpayers?"

"Good point," I thought to myself. I hadn't considered that aspect.

"I would," the camper defiantly shouted to the counselor.

"Hey, I'm on your side. I'm just pointing out arguments that you should be aware of," the counselor said. "If you want to have kids,

86 that's fine with me. But, you must logically convince the hospital administrators that you can be responsible for a child. That's all I'm saying."

"Okay, I'm sorry that I flew off the handle, but I'm sick and tired of people telling me that I can't have kids because I'm handicapped," the camper angrily said.

"I HAVE A QUESTION" I spelled. "COULD AN ABLE BODIED GIRL FALL IN LOVE AND MARRY A DISABLED GUY"

"Of course. That's possible," the group facilitator said.

"BUT IS IT PROBABLE" I spelled out quickly. I was tired of clichés. I had enough of those from the day care center's guidance counselor.

"Well," Sally said hesitantly, "I, personally, wouldn't be able to handle it. I'm a basically insecure person and I don't think I could take the daily hassles. But I'm not saying that it's totally impossible."

The dinner bell rang and the plates began to clatter.

Again the approaching clatter of plates made the group facilitator say, "I see it's time for us to quit for now, but we'll continue this tomorrow, same time, same place, same station. I think this has been one of our more interesting discussions. Now, let's eat!"

I just stared blankly into space, letting the activity around me become a dull din. In one way, I was relieved that the other campers were as concerned as I was about sexuality. But in another way, I felt so helpless because the problem didn't seem to have a solution—only more and bigger problems.

Fortunately, camp kept me too busy to ponder too many more deep philosophical problems. The days were filled with picnics, swimming, games, music, and Spanish. The evenings were filled with hayrack rides, cookouts and campouts, a kangaroo court (where I was convicted of being a hopeless flirt and was sentenced to wear blinders for a morning), a coffee house, and a good-bye banquet-dance. My friendships with Ed and Sally continued to grow as fast as my admiration of the camp's Spanish instructor.

Judy was always willing to help out wherever she could, and she had a knack of making the camper feel like he was doing her a favor by allowing her to help him.

Once, her camper was taking a long time to eat breakfast. The dining lodge began to empty and the other counselors began to clear off tables. When they came to Judy's table she, pretending to be indignant, said, "Hey don't rush us, guys. Food is supposed to be enjoyed, not gobbled down like you do it. We have read that you should chew your food 32 times, and we are doing that! So leave us be! I can clean off this table."

Most counselors would have stopped their camper saying, "Next meal you'll get your fill. We have a schedule to follow. I'm sure next meal will be longer."

I think all the males at camp admired Judy because once I heard a male counselor jokingly tell her, "When you die, will that beautiful long hair to me, please."

Blushing, Judy shouted back, "Okay! Hey, I'll bet your grandpa scalped mine at Little Big Horn!"

During the camp's coffee house night Judy was giving me a swallow of spiced tea when another counselor ran into the lodge and announced excitedly, "I just heard. . . on the radio. . . Nixon has decided to resign. No shit!"

I let out a scream that made Judy say, "Oh, you like that? But, Bill, Nixon was such a honest, law abiding president! You don't buy that, huh? Well, I won't even try to sell you my great beach property on the Antarctica! How about finishing this drink?"

I was glad that both the country and I had finally started the slow healing process.

The next night was the last night of camp. To commemorate the end of a session as well as the camping season, the camp had a banquet and a dance. This dance was more serious than the fifties dance because it was a good-bye dance for the counselors as well as for the campers.

Since it was so special, I asked Sally if she would escort me to it.

"No, I don't want to," was her reply.

I nodded my head and didn't ask for a further explanation.

But Sally felt compelled to give one. "I like you. Don't get me wrong. But we aren't going steady, understand? I hope we can continue our friendship after camp. And besides, at this dance I'll have to circulate even more than at the fifties dance, so it wouldn't be fair to you or to me for us to go as a couple. I'm sorry if this hurts you. Still friends?"

I nodded. I now knew what had attracted me to Sally. She respected

88   me. When we first met, she respected me enough to push me to a table. Now, when we were friends, she respected me enough to be honest with me. How could I be mad at her for that?

The night started with a bigger than usual dinner. Then we had speeches by the camp director and a representative from Nebraska Chapter of the Easter Seal Society. He ended his speech with, "Each year since 1972, we have had the counselors vote for a member of the counseling staff who, in their estimation, has exemplified the spirit of what a counselor should be. This year is the first year that the award goes to a female counselor. Her name is Judy Jennings. . ."

The campers clapped, stomped, banged their lap trays, screamed, cheered, and anything else to show approval for the choice. I was afraid that our ruckus would either have the Milford police department rushing to camp to check on our well-being or reduce the old dilapidated lodge to a pile of rubble. The rejoicing lasted for at least five minutes.

"I can tell by your reaction that you campers approve of the counselors' selection," the speaker shouted above the din.

When the presentation was over, Ed escorted me to Judy's table so we could congratulate her. She hugged me as well as Ed and said a tearful, "Thank you, you guys." I had the impression that at that moment Judy would have hugged anyone, even my family dog.

The dance went as did the fifties dance. Everyone danced with everyone else but it seemed a little bit less contrived and a little bit more sincere.

Sally came over to where I was sitting, extended her hands, and asked, "Wanna dance or are you mad at me for not coming with you?"

"LETS DANCE" I spelled and smiled. At least now I knew that she was dancing with me because she really wanted to, not because she felt obligated.

"Will you write to me if I write to you? I'll write you if you'll write me back. I don't write people who don't write me back, understand? Good. I'll be sure to give you my address before you leave tomorrow, okay?"

Damn, Camp Camelot would be over in less than twenty-four hours! I knew camp had to end, but I didn't want the spirit of camp to end.

The next morning Ed gave me his address and said, "I really want to keep in touch with you, so write, dammit!"

My mom and Grandpa and Grandma Brown came to pick me up from camp. My grandma was pleasantly surpised to see that I wasn't malnourished like the other two times that I had come back from camp.

Ed loaded me into my grandparents' car and said, "Remember to write."

Sally kissed and hugged me and said, "You're still a flirt, but write anyway. Love ya."

When we were on the interstate back to Omaha, Mom said, "I have good news, I think. J. P. Lord School is starting a high school program this fall and you're eligible. The Nebraska State legislature passed a law saying that the State has to provide the handicapped with a high school education. Can you believe it?"

I shook my head in disbelief while thinking, "It's about time. It's about time."

"Do you want to go back and give dear old Lord School another shot?"

I considered. Why not? It beat staying home. Besides, Judy would be there.

I nodded my head.

CHAPTER 9

DAVID

I first met Mrs. George, the teacher for Dr. J. P. Lord's new high school, in a small room that was designed for one teacher and one student—the same room in which Deanne had once tutored me.

The room had been converted into a classroom for four teenage boys. Three of us were in wheelchairs and one walked with a cane. Those of us in the class had a variety of medical problems. The student with the cane was legally blind. As for the three in wheelchairs, one was victim of a gunshot wound in the head, one had Muscular Dystrophy, and one had Cerebral Palsy. I was the one with Cerebral Palsy. When I tried to vocalize, Mrs. George kidded me by saying that it sounded like the mating call of a bull moose.

Each of us had different academic and emotional needs, ranging from preparing for college to preparing for death. Mrs. George did everything she could to help the first class of Dr. J. P. Lord High.

Mrs. George was about five feet tall, in her fifties, had graying black hair (which would be a lot grayer at the end of the school year), had olive skin, and a high pitched voice. She had a habit of talking too fast and she ended her explanations with, "Do you see that?"

She greeted us the first day of school with a cheery, "Good morning, you guys. This room was thrown together at the last minute but I think we'll do okay. This high school is the first in Nebraska so we are pioneers. Pioneers have to put up with a few troubles. I understand all of you know one another except Bill and David. David, this is Bill. He has Cerebral Palsy. He left school about the time you came because this school didn't offer high school then. Bill, David is a Hawaiian transplant, and he has Muscular Dystrophy. He'll be nineteen May 6th. We'll have a birthday party with dancing girls."

I wondered if she knew what Muscular Dystrophy was. I knew that David wouldn't last until his birthday. He already had more birthdays than most suffering from this disability. Already his lungs were affected, which meant his breathing would require effort all year.

"Now I'll get you started on what I want you to do. I have expectations for all of you, do you see that?" the new idealistic teacher stated.

When she came to me, I was classifying rocks to fulfill a requirement in earth science. Sitting down beside me she said, "I hear you have been taking correspondence courses from the University of Nebraska at Lincoln and haven't gotten very far for the past three years. I know these courses are bearcats and take a lot of time. But I will help you with them, and we will shoot for graduation next spring. Also, I'll feed you lunch if that's okay with you. I know you would rather have one of those young chicks that are just out of college, but you're stuck with the old hen for your feeder. Do you have any questions?"

"I DONT THINK DAVID WILL MAKE IT TO HIS BIRTHDAY HIS LUNGS ARE TOO WEAK AND THESE WINTERS ARE HARD ON ANYBODY" I spelled out slowly.

"You and I know that, but he doesn't know that. Just as you want that diploma, David wants his nineteenth birthday cake."

Mrs. George was true to her word. I completed courses and started new ones at amazing speed. However, David worsened during the holiday season. He was afraid to go to sleep at night for fear that he wouldn't wake up. So Mrs. George let him sleep in class saying, "We have hospitals across the street, and if we have to visit them, we can be there in five minutes. So David, you are safer here than anywhere else."

Once when David was having trouble breathing, she had to massage his chest all afternoon. While she was doing it she said to the aide standing by with oxygen, "David is helping me build up my tennis arm, so if you see a five foot woman with bulging biceps on the tennis court, it will be me. This is fantastic exercise! Do you see that?"

One day we were discussing some dull subject for my world history course and she said, "When I'm working with the other two guys, I can't keep an eye on David's breathing so I'll leave it up to you, Bill,

92   because I can't watch him all the time, okay? If he slumps over, make one of your bull moose noises to get my attention. He doesn't look good, does he? But we'll keep him in school as long as possible. At least his mother doesn't have to watch over him when he is here. Now we should be able to finish this damn history course in March if we are lucky. This is a dry course, and I'm sure you're fed up with it because I am!"

Frequently, when he was gasping for air, David would look at me and say, "I'm all right, Bill. I'm all right. Thanks for watching over me."

Fortunately, my bull moose yell was never needed. The vigil, however, matured me greatly. I watched him and in doing so, I became aware of David's desire to live. Seeing him fight for every breath he took, I suddenly knew the value of living. So when I had to do some boring research, I didn't mind because at least I could do it without worrying about breathing. I think this was the lesson that Mrs. George was teaching me by having me keep an eye on David.

April tenth was David's last day at school. That night he took a turn for the worse. He was rushed to the hospital where life-supporting machines could maintain his breathing.

On April 15, 1975, I had planned to visit him after school. But that morning I found a hand written note beside my typewriter saying, "Don't go to the hospital tonight, David died in his sleep. I didn't want to tell the other guys because today the school is going to the circus, and there's no reason to spoil that. We will mourn him together. J. George."

CHAPTER 10

DAVID'S NINETEENTH BIRTHDAY

Mrs. George seemed distant all day, so just before I went home I asked her, "IS THERE ANYTHING WRONG"

"No, Bill, nothing is wrong," Mrs. George replied. "I'm just in a bad mood. Today is David's nineteenth birthday. He almost made it, didn't he?

"Plus, I don't like the way the clouds are beginning to take shape."

The air was calm—almost too calm. But I welcomed the May sun after a hellish winter. Little did Mrs. George or I know on this day, May 6, 1975, Nature would make David's nineteenth birthday unforgettable.

On the way home in the school wheelchair van, I heard a disc jockey broadcast a typical tornado watch. Omahans get used to tornado watches in the spring. One tornado might develop out of a hundred watches, so I was unconcerned at first. Then golf ball hail began to beat on the van while the trees did the twist. This would be one hell of a ride home.

"Don't worry, kids. This storm won't amount to much," said the van driver. "Bill, do you remember when we were out in that blizzard? Wasn't it worse than this little storm?"

I nodded. But I noticed her wiping her sweaty palms on her faded blue jeans three times in five minutes. Sure, the blizzard had been bad. But I had been the only one in the van that time, and I could take anything she could. But now in this hail and wind storm the driver was responsible for a boy with muscular dystrophy and for a girl with brittle bones. If the van were to be blown over, they would certainly die. The boy's muscles weren't much stronger than those of a rag doll, and the girl's bones, including her rib cage, were as brittle as

94 toothpicks. If the van overturned the boy would flip flop around, possibly injuring something vital. And since a minor fall breaks the girl's bones, it would be a disastrous if the van were to tip over. But silent prayers were answered and nothing happened to the brown van with its fragile cargo.

Upon arriving home, I watched a poor Rock Hudson comedy with Mom while she fed me supper. The movie was interrupted by numerous weather advisories. Apparently the storm was worse than I had first thought. As the reports grew in number, they became more ominous.

Then the tornado watch turned into a tornado warning. A twister had touched down in Omaha. The television was now giving constant up-to-the-minute information on the destructive trek of the funnel. The tornado was coming from the southwestern part of the city where Deanne and her family lived. And it was coming fast.

I was controlling my anxiety until the weatherman said that the tornado was less than five blocks away from our house and headed straight towards us. My brain and body have never co-operated. So while my brain told my body to remain calm, my body wasn't listening to the message. My poor wheelchair rocked under my jerking, stiff body. I looked like I was directing a hundred piece orchestra playing the *Flight of the Bumblebee*. Most people, even panic struck, can run somewhere or do something. But all I could do was to jump up and down in my wheelchair and yell. The poor wheelchair. If the tornado didn't blow it away, I would stomp the hell out of it.

I panicked because I couldn't help myself get to our basement. Mom could no longer carry me. My dad was at work. My 6'5" blacksmith brother, Jim, wasn't home from work yet. My two younger brothers, Don and Bob, were carrying papers. Don, the elder of the two, had called and had said that he was in a customer's basement. Bob, in contrast, had run home when he had heard the civil defense sirens sound.

The television announcer, who was tracking the destructive path of the storm, said that the twister had demolished the area where Deanne and her family were living. The announcer didn't say whether there had been any casualties. I said a quick prayer that there weren't.

Suddenly Bob, soaked to the skin, came in and said, "Damn, there are things floating around in the air and it's heading our way! I've never seen anything like it!"

"Do you think that you and I could get Bill downstairs?" Mom asked Bob. "Jimmy hasn't come home yet, and I think we should head for the basement right now!"

If given a choice, I would have taken my chances with the tornado. Our basement steps were steep as well as splintery, and I could just see Bob and Mom dragging me down the steps while my bony rear collected bruises and splinters. Besides, even if I did get downstairs in one piece (which I doubted), my wheelchair, which was my legs, would be blown away, leaving me immobile. So why couldn't I be a good captain and stay with my four-wheel ship?

Bob replied quickly, "Jim is home. I saw him across the street watching the storm. Should I get him and tell him he gots to take Bill downstairs?" Mom was so nervous that she didn't bother to correct Bob's use of "gots."

"Yes! yes! I don't know what's wrong with him! Here we are, in a tornado, and he's watching it like a dummy! Tell him that he has to take Billy downstairs for me. And hurry!" Mom shouted in a frantic voice.

Moments later Jim came in followed by Bob. Putting his lunchbox and Thermos on the television and taking off his grimy blacksmith boots, he said as he was carrying me to the stairway, "I could see the storm. It veered towards the west. I think it might miss us if we're lucky!"

If you ever had to carry a six foot pole down a three foot wide stairway, you can empathize with Jim. I was beyond being calmed down with words. If the tornado hadn't veered, our house and I would be flying—without an airplane. All I could hear was Jim saying in a tense low voice, "If you jerk or leap, I'll kill you. These steps are dangerous so if you move, we'll fall! So relax, stupid, relax!"

Telling a person like me to relax while you're carrying him down steep, wooden, backless, uncarpeted steps when you are not too calm yourself and threatening him with murder is like telling a hundred-year-old redwood to uproot itself and move to a different spot.

I saw the bare wooden stairs. My arms scraped the rough plaster on

96 the walls. Several times Jim almost lost his footing. I was certain we would fall to the bottom of the steps at any moment. But we didn't. When Jim's foot hit the basement's floor, I felt we deserved a fanfare.

Jim carried me to Don's room in the southwest corner of the basement.

"Put the skinny body under the bed, Jimmy!" Mom shouted.

"He won't go under it. The bed is too low and I can't straighten his damn legs and arms out so he'll go. C'mon, Bill, straighten your legs out!" Jim said angrily.

"I'll pull the mattress over him then. You shut off the gas and electricity and open the windows. Bob, get under the desk, and stay there. Oh Jimmy, bring your portable radio down here too." Mom ordered. As the confusion and panic mounted, I thought to myself, "Straighten my legs? How? Hadn't my dear family realized that after twenty years of wearing super strong braces, getting intensive therapy, and having two operations on my legs, I couldn't straighten my legs at will?"

When Mom pulled the mattress over me, she had to lie down beside me and hold the mattress off my face to keep it from smothering me. Soon Jim, having completed the necessary precautions, came back down with his radio and waited for whatever would happen next. Under the mattress I could hear nothing except the damn radio.

The radio was maddening to me because the D-J kept saying that the tornado had completely devastated the area where Deanne and her family lived. Irrationally, I wanted the disc jockey to say, "Those who have survived the tornado include the Kelley family."

Silently we waited, then a tired sounding disc jockey announced the tornado was over. We climbed out of our hole, expecting to find our house in shambles, but instead we could hear our phone ringing. Jim was the first upstairs (even carrying me), answering it he handed it to Mom saying "It's Dad; he wants to talk to you."

She reassured Dad that we were okay and that the house was still on the same street. She hung up the phone and said, "I don't believe it! In all our years of marriage that's the first time that your father has ever called me from the railroad to see how we were. It must be bad.

"Bill, are you all right? You have a weird expression on your face. Did you get hurt?"

I shook my head.

"Are you okay?"

I nodded my head, but I was far from okay. I was worried about what had happened to Deanne and her family. But when I brought up the subject of Deanne my parents said, "Leave that girl alone, dammit! Haven't you done enough damage to her, Stupid?"

I didn't need to be reminded of how immature I had been so I decided not to bring the subject up. But nonetheless, I was concerned about her. She had been my friend. I just wanted to find out if she and her loved ones had survived the tornado.

Jim and a neighbor were already going around on foot to see how bad the neighborhood had been hit. A cousin stopped by on his way home from the local race track. He told us that the streets were closed due to fallen trees and that he was having a hard time getting home. He tried calling his wife to tell her that he was okay, but the phone lines were overloaded and he couldn't get through. He didn't want to wait around until the lines cleared so he left to try to get home.

The National Guard had been called in. I could see them establishing a base across the street from our house. Mom took me for a stroll up and down our block so that I could see the aftermath of the storm. Our front yard was filled with debris from the tornado.

In times of disasters, people inventory what they value. Dad and my cousin did this and showed their concern for what they valued by phoning, or trying to phone, home. While I was grateful to God for sparing my immediate family, I was frustrated that I didn't know about a certain family in the southwestern part of the city. I was frustrated that I couldn't pick up a phone and ask the Red Cross about the family or couldn't ask someone to call for me. I felt invalid that I couldn't check on them personally and offer them goodwill when they needed all the help they could get. After all, Deanne had been around when I had needed her friendship and support. I felt so damn helpless and useless.

The next morning Dad and Jim laid off work to help a friend who had lost his home to the storm with his task of cleanup and salvage. They took chain saws and the pickup with them. With chain saws in their hands, they worked out their feelings of frustration, of helplessness, and of devastation. I, on the other hand, didn't have any choice. I had to go to school. Business as usual.

98   I wished I could take a pickup and a chain saw over to my friends.

On my way to school I heard my schoolmates discuss the Great Tornado and viewed more of the rubble of Omaha.

One said to the other, "Man, am I glad that we were too far west of the storm for it to do our house any damage! We could see the funnel. It sure was scary! How about your house? Was it damaged?"

"No, we were just north of its path," was the other's response.

When I arrived at school, I overheard a teacher from the southwestern part of the city saying, "It completely demolished parts of where I come from. I wanted to cry when I saw the destruction!"

"If it's that bad in the Kelley neighborhood," I thought to myself. "I have to do something to let Deanne know I care about her and her family. It's the least I can do."

However, it took me several days to muster enough courage to talk about my feelings with Mrs. George.

"THE RADIO AND OTHER PEOPLE ARE SAYING DEANNES NEIGHBORHOOD WAS DESTROYED AND I WANT TO DO SOMETHING TO. . . " I spelled out slowly.

"To let her know you are concerned and care about her and her family, right?" Mrs. George asked.

I nodded.

"So write her a note," Mrs. George flatly said. "Send it to her grandparents'. I'm sure that Deanne and her family could use all the support they can get. Don't make it long. In fact, you can do it here and mail it from here."

I wrote the note and felt better for having done something besides sitting and worrying.

I guess using chain saws, calling home, and writing notes say the same thing: "I care."

1. June/July, 1958
   Mom, Dad, Bill and Jimmy

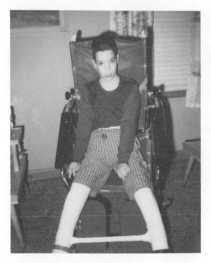

3. April, 1964

2. Bill, 1967

4. Bill with an early model headstick, 1967

5. L to R Bob, Jim, Bill and Don
   Christmas, 1966

6. 1969

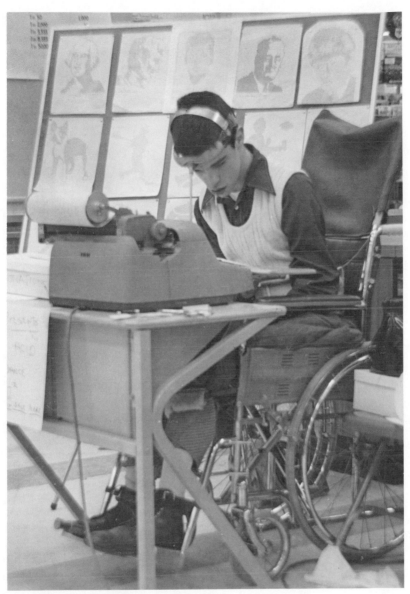

7. Fund Raising for the "Echo," 1973
   Photo, courtesy, Jerry Richardson

8. The Rush family, 1980

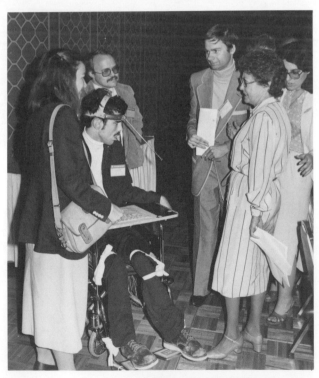

9. College graduation, 1983
   L to R Anne Fadiman, Bill, Ed Henry,
   Tom Rieter

10. Bill, Grandma Brown and the college diploma, 1983

11. Anne Fadiman and Mark Dahmke at the University of Nebraska
    Photo taken by Bill Rush, October 1979.

12. The computer and phone arrangement at Bill's apartment.
    Lincoln, Nebraska, 1986
    Photo by John Butler

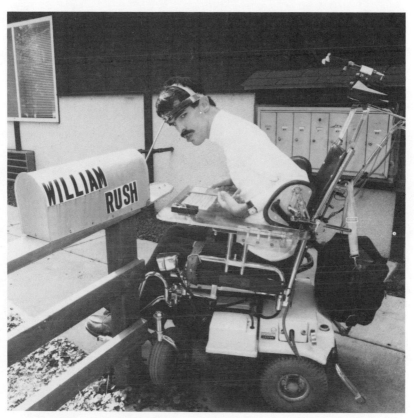

13. In front of Bill's apartment.
    Lincoln, Nebraska, 1986
    Photo by John Butler

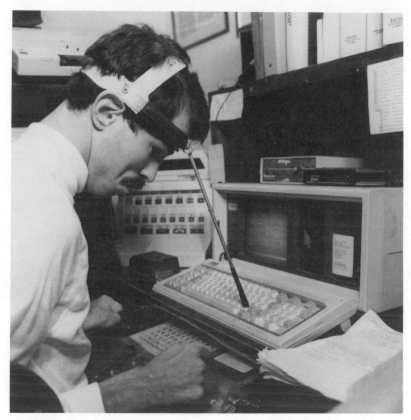

14. At home, Lincoln, Nebraska, 1986
    Photo by John Butler

CHAPTER 11

LET IT BE NOT FORGOT

"Got a cigarette?" somebody asked in a deep guttural voice that set my teeth on edge. I looked up to see Carl in his wheelchair in the doorway of our classroom. He was handsome in a peculiar way. He had large brown eyes laced with long thick eyelashes. He looked rather muscular crumpled down in his wheelchair. His yawn revealed nicotine-stained teeth that were in poor repair. Since he had come to school a few days ago, he vomited and urinated at will, threw books and chairs at whomever he pleased, and flipped his chocolate milk at the principal. For these reasons Mrs. George, the high school teacher, promptly denied his request for a cigarette with, "This school doesn't even let teachers smoke during school hours." Then she firmly said, "Now I want you to get started on your workbook."

Suddenly, Carl boomed, "What are you doin' tonight, Cute Baby!" when a young, pretty aide entered the room, "Wanna go to dinner at Mister Steak and later to my room at the hospital?" He had the same anticipatory gleam in his eyes that the fabled frog must have had when it was waiting for the beautiful princess to kiss him. Mrs. George calmly explained, "Carl, this aide is a married lady, and the hospital won't let you have females in your room after visiting hours. It's impossible for you to date this married lady."

Carl persisted, "I love her. I can make her so happy that she'll forget her damn husband by smuggling her into my room and then. . ."

From the corner of my eye I saw Mrs. George take a long deep breath and say, "Carl that's enough of that! Now get your head in your workbook and out of those soap operas that you watched in the hospital! I have to help Bill now, but when I get back to you, you had better be prepared to answer the questions over what you have read."

100   When she came to me, I was mechanically finishing a rough draft of an English essay while thinking about another frog that wanted to be kissed by a princess.

As Mrs. George sat down beside me I spelled out on my language board, "YOU KNOW SEEING CARL PROPOSITION THAT AIDE WAS KIND OF LIKE LOOKING AT MYSELF"

"You've never been quite as bad as Carl. You just have a way of professing undying love to the object of your affections but Carl wanted that aide to be his 'lady of the evening.' There's a difference. I think you have learned your lesson. I wouldn't worry about it if I were you," Mrs. George said before reading my English paper.

In a way, I felt sorry for the obnoxious cigarette smoker across the room. Experience had taught me a lesson that he had yet to learn. Wanting and wishing does not make it so. Friendship cannot become a romance unless the feeling is mutual.

Suddenly through the fog I heard Mrs. George saying, "Your spelling stinks, Bill, as usual. But otherwise this is good. Clean up your spelling and I'll send it in to the Extension Division." My reverie broken, I looked at Mrs. George.

Taking off her glasses, Mrs. George said, "Welcome back. You looked like Carl had hypnotized you. What were you thinking about? Your lost love? It hurts, I know. But be glad you can understand that hurt."

After circling my numerous misspelled words on the rough draft, she felt she had to tell me about Carl. She began, "Carl has been in and out of institutions since he was five. You see, when he was five, he was diagnosed as having a terminal disease. But his strange disease didn't follow its projected course and he still lives. I feel sorry for his parents. Upon hearing the fatal diagnosis, they asked for advice on raising a terminally ill boy. They were told to indulge him because his every day was precious. So they did, thinking it was the best thing for him.

"But to everybody's surprise he grew up! Now he has the sexual desires of a teenager and the self-control of a two year old. Understandably, his parents can't cope with him, so they regretfully hospitalized him.

"Now since public schools have to provide high school for the physically handicapped, the hospital has asked us to help him. I thought I'd tell you this to show you that there's a difference between you and Carl. Carl gets carried away with every girl he lays eyes on while you are a little bit more selective!"

I laughed and spelled, "YOU MEAN CARL IS A GLUTTON WHILE I AM A GOURMET I SEE YOUR POINT"

"Right," Mrs. George replied. "Oh, speaking of food, I can't feed you lunch today because I have a conference with Carl's parents during lunch hour. So Miss Jennings said she'll be glad to feed you. She told me that you and she met this summer at Camp Easter Seal and became good friends. I can see why you like her. She is honest and sincere. I like her too. Lunch will be appetizing today with her feeding, right? Oh, it's that time already. C'mon guys, it's feeding time."

When Mrs. George wheeled me into the bustling plate-clattering cafeteria of the school, I saw Miss Jennings helping a little girl get into a chair and I smiled. I was glad I had met the blonde primary teacher before she had begun her teaching career. Of course, the whole school staff thought I had a crush on her because I smiled everytime I saw her, and this upset me. I rather wished I could get to know Judy better, but I didn't have a crush on her. Again, my desire to develop a relationship with a woman was being invalidated with that damn word "crush."

Fortunately, Judy ignored the rumors saying, "People around here don't understand that people of opposite sexes can be friendly without romantic involvement and that we are just good friends."

About five minutes after Mrs. George had seated me at my table, I saw Judy coming towards me with my plate in hand saying, "This school is over populated, so they asked me to kill off some students. Since you're the oldest, you're the first to go. Sorry about that. We'll miss you."

Looking at the dish with typical cafeteria fare, I spelled, "THIS FOOD CAN KILL ME WITHOUT YOU HELPING IT"

"I guess you're right. Look at this pizza. It's cardboard! I'll get you a honey sandwich. Don't go away!"

I smiled. How different Judy and Mrs. George were from the other teachers who made no secret of their hatred for feeding the students. Judy and Mrs. George, in contrast, made lunch seem like a joy, not a job.

Judy came back with the honey sandwich and said, "I'm sorry I took so long but Carl asked me to go to Mister Steak with him. I tried to tell

102 him teachers weren't allowed to date students but I don't think he understood me. Oh well, I'll bet he keeps things hopping in your room."

Suddenly she remembered something and said, "Hey, did you know there's a camp reunion tonight. I'll be there. Will you?"

I nodded. I wanted to ask her if she would dance with me at the reunion. She had danced with me at camp. Did her being a teacher change our friendship? I would ask Mrs. George for her opinion.

Back in my classroom I told Mrs. George, "I need to talk with you." Since my face had a troubled expression, Mrs. George pulled up a chair and listened.

"IS IT ACCEPTABLE FOR A STUDENT TO ASK A TEACHER TO DANCE WITH HIM AT A CAMP REUNION" I typed out slowly, "TONIGHT IS THE CAMP REUNION DANCE AND I WANT TO ASK JUDY I MEAN MISS JENNINGS TO DANCE BUT AFTER HEARING HOW CARLS REQUEST FOR A DATE SOUNDED I DONT KNOW IF I SHOULD ITS NOT FAIR"

"Well, I think if the young man really cared for the teacher, he wouldn't put her in that position. If Miss Jennings asks you to dance, that would be different. Play it cool at the dance. Maybe Miss Jennings will surprise you.

"What in the world do you see in camp counselors? Men are supposed to fall for airline stewardesses and their secretaries. I know, you don't fly and you don't have a secretary. It was just a suggestion," Mrs. George joked.

When she had finished counseling me, Mrs. George tried to help Carl with his work. But Carl said in his booming guttural voice, "I'm going to throw up unless you get me a goddamn date with the girl that fed Bill today. If I can't date that aide I saw this morning, I'll take her. She's sexier anyway!"

I wanted to laugh and cry. After all, hadn't I felt like Carl at lunch today? What made his desires to date Judy any less valid than mine?

Aware that I was listening, Mrs. George closed her eyes and said carefully, "Miss Jennings is a teacher. She can't date students. Even if she could, she wouldn't date you. She's picky about her friends. Now you may vomit, but you'll clean it up afterwards. The same thing goes for urinating."

A second later Carl had slapped her across the face, knocking off her glasses. With controlled anger Mrs. George wheeled Carl to the principal's office. After five minutes she came back and announced, "Carl has been expelled temporarily. It may be permanently. We tried to help him, but we couldn't."

She came over to me, turned my head towards her, and said in a hushed voice, "David is gone, and Carl is still here. Is that fair, Bill? I think it's pretty damn unfair."

I worked in silence. I had never seen my teacher angry. It surprised me. And I began to wonder if she had accepted David's death.

At three o'clock the school van driver appeared in the doorway of the classroom and asked, "Is Bill ready to go home? What books does he want to take?"

"I'm giving him the night off. He's going to a dance, which is good because as the old saying goes, 'All work and no play makes Jack a dull boy.' So, Bill, go chase skirts but remember what I said about a certain one." Mrs. George dismissed me with a smile and a pat on the shoulder.

At the dance Judy greeted me with "Hi stranger. Long time no see," and pinned a name tag on my navy blue suit. We both laughed at her greeting. "Hey, I'll see you later and we'll talk. Right now I'm in charge of pinning name tags. Knowing me, I'll probably have them on the wrong persons. But what the heck?"

I nodded and chuckled. She looked pretty, dressed in a blue print dress with a low white collar. Anybody would ask her to dance. But I didn't. Mrs. George was right. Judy was a teacher. I had no intention of acting like Carl. I watched the others dance and visited with some at the reunion.

Unfortunately, Ed Henry and Sally Stone couldn't be at the reunion. But I had heard from Ed and Sally several times since camp and they had become an item. During the past six months they had been seeing each other. At first they tried to tell me as well as themselves it was only as friends. But friends don't travel across Kansas every weekend just to see each other. I enjoyed sharing this piece of news with the others.

"Hey, Wallflower, wanna dance?" Judy asked as she walked over to me.

"YES BUT YOURE A TEACHER AND I AM A STUDENT DOESNT THAT MAKE A DIFFERENCE" I spelled.

104 "This isn't a school. I'm Judy, the counselor. I fed a friend today, not a student. Now do you want to dance with me or not? If you don't, I'll put poison in your food next time," Judy said in mock anger.

"LETS DANCE" I spelled out, "I AM SORRY FOR BEING SUCH A STICK IN THE MUD BUT TODAY HAS BEEN A DILLY"

As we moved onto the dance floor she said, "Mrs. George told me about Carl after school. I guess I should be flattered. I think we all have some of Carl in us. It's too bad that people have to let sex and love be the basis for male-female relationships. You and I enjoy each other because we get along together, not because we have a thing for each other. That's what the staff doesn't understand, agreed?"

I nodded. Suddenly I realized what had made camp a Camelot. The counselors loved and cared about us campers. The Camelot could be extended beyond the campgrounds only if the love and caring could be extended into the outside world. Judy was trying to do this, but the outside world wasn't ready to let the Camelot be extended beyond camp and camp reunions.

Judy couldn't keep the spirit of Camp Camelot alive between us, which is tragic because if the spirit is not allowed to exist everywhere and all times, all people with disabilities will end up as sick as Carl.

PART FOUR

JOURNEY WITH
TECHNOLOGY

CHAPTER 12

THE IMPOSSIBLE DREAM?

With Mrs. George's guidance I was moving quickly towards my high school diploma and enjoying some social life. The nagging question was still: "Where do I go from here?" Would I go back to some cuckoo center where I would play checkers all day? Was that my fate?

I was thinking about this unsavory future when my mom opened a letter from my childhood sweetheart, Joani Madden, and put it on my tray. The letter began, "Dear Bill, I'm going to college, and I'm living in a dorm with other able-bodied students. . ."

I reared up in my wheelchair, waved my arms, let out a Tarzan yell, and pointed to the letter with my headstick until Mom read it. Her first reaction was "but Joani has speech and some hand-use. I don't know if you can do what she is doing. I always thought you could go to college via correspondence. I think you should take the letter to school and see what Mrs. George says."

The next day the van driver asked Mrs. George, "Is there a party at school today? Bill acted so excited that I thought Charlie's Angels were teaching the high school today."

I looked at my headstick until Mrs. George put it on me and asked, "What's up? You look like you're ready to burst."

I pointed to the letter and spelled, "I WANT TO DO WHAT JOANI IS DOING WHAT DO YOU THINK"

"I know you're college material," she said when she read the letter, "I hope you realize you do have a few extra things to consider, kiddo. But you're graduating from high school next spring, and I don't have any better suggestions. We can go for it and see how far we can get. It won't be easy."

It wasn't easy. I wrote Joani to get more information about how she

108   was doing it. She wrote back and said she was living on campus and had students as her aides. She also had the college send me an information packet. The program looked good, but was too expensive. Plus, she suggested I contact my state's Division of Vocational Rehabilitation.

With the principal's cooperation, a meeting with the Nebraska's Division of Vocational Rehabilitation, Voc Rehab, for short, was set up in the spring of 1975. Mrs. George, Mom, myself, and two men from Voc Rehab, Counselor Bob Gellner and Client Advocate John McGill, met in the library of Dr. J. P. Lord School. I would discover that Bob and John made an outstanding team, which was what I needed.

Mrs. George spoke first, "Bill is going to graduate next year and we're wondering what lies ahead for him."

Bob Gellner too quickly replied, "Voc Rehab has worked closely with ENCOR [Eastern Nebraska Commission on Retardation] many times. We have placed many clients like Bill —"

I didn't let him finish. I let out a fierce bullmoose yell and started flailing my arms.

Mom ordered, "Calm down!"

Bob and John chimed in unison, "What's wrong?"

Mrs. George said, "Bill shows no signs of being mentally retarded. He is, we hope, college-bound, and anything like ENCOR is out of the question." She also pointed out that going to college was the best way for me to get a job.

John quipped, "You mean ditch digging is out of the question?"

I nodded and laughed. The tension was broken, and a friendship had been started.

"Well," Bob said, "As long as a person is in high school, our agency can't help. But it's good that you had us out early because our fiscal year starts in July. So since I know about you, Bill, I can put in a request to fund you. So I would suggest that you contact us next January. We'll go from there. I look forward to working with you. This should prove to be interesting."

When Miss Neff found out about the meeting and the possibility of college, she mentioned a new operation that was designed to control drooling that she learned of while at a conference in California. She explained it worked by rerouting the salivary ducts towards the back of my throat and removing the secondary saliva glands. She said the operation was relatively simple (She lied—they cut my throat from ear to ear) and gave me the address of the doctor who was familiar with the operation. She pointed out if I go to college, I would be using library books—those books couldn't be drooled on.

"I'm finally convinced that you can't swallow your spit and concentrate on something else," Miss Neff said almost sympathetically. "So, this operation is an option."

The doctor in California was very helpful. He described the operation to me the best he could in a letter. I was leaning towards having it. I asked Mom and Dad what to do.

To my astonishment they said, "You decide. You want to go to college and be independent. This is your first major decision."

So I asked them what they thought.

"Well," Mom said hesitating, "it would make you more socially acceptable. When people see anyone drooling, it turns them off. They don't understand." Mrs. George added her two cents: "When I come over to help you, I feel like wearing skates so I can glide over your pool of drool."

When I looked at the school's tile floor I could see where my saliva had eaten away at its shine. That wasn't all that my saliva could do. It glued pages of books together, it glued magazines to my tray, it gave off an unpleasant odor, and, as Mom said, it repulsed people. It was a thorn in my side. When I was about nine, we tried to control it with a drug known as belladonna for a brief time. The drug was supposed to dry up my saliva glands. When it dried up my sweat glands too, Mom and my family doctor stopped the drug immediately.

I decided to have the operation because it seemed like the perfect solution. I had the surgery that summer on the day before my 20th birthday. It was my birthday present to myself.

I haven't decided whether it was a success or whether I would recommend it to anyone else. It did cut down on my drooling. But I sacrificed the natural moisture of my mouth which diluted mucus drainage. This thick mucus causes an annoying cough, more trouble eating, and dries on my lips, leaving a white crust. I guess in my haste to make my first major decision I forgot that the surgeon's knife is definitely not a magic wand.

Also, during the summer of '75, Mrs. George participated in a workshop where she met a professor from Southern Illinois University. He told her that anybody with a physical disability could go to college and that the university can make accommodations for the physical limitations so long as the students could do the mental work. I also applied to the University of Missouri because I heard that it had an accommodating attitude towards students with disabilities. Mrs. George, Mom, and I were probably making Robert Frost turn in his grave because we were taking all the "roads less traveled by." We went on the premise that taking the wrong road was better than taking no road.

I wrote letters to any and all colleges that were rumored to be accessible, letters to agencies and institutions asking for financial help, letters asking where I could get an electric wheelchair, and letters to follow up on those letters.

In the fall, Mrs. George had me taking four correspondence courses plus an adult night school class. "If you're going to college you must learn to juggle classes. Plus the night school course will give you a taste of a regular classroom," she said.

I nodded, but the night class was an eye-opener. I wasn't prepared. My brother, Jim, would take me to class, leave me, and pick me up afterwards. When I was in the classroom, I was ignored to the point of feeling invisible.

When I told Mrs. George about this, she said, "Welcome to the real world, Bill. I know, you thought Westside was the real world. I hate to tell you this but you got the cream of the crop at Westside. What you're getting at night school is the norm."

I grimaced.

"But that's why I'm having you go to night school," Mrs. George explained. "I want to expose you to this element while I am still around to support you. Do you see that?"

I thought about the Westside gang. They had graduated the year before. Tom was now studying pre-med in Missouri. Reuben was in Dartmouth studying international banking and was a candidate for a Rhodes Scholarship. We still kept in touch. They supported me in my try for college. However, nobody encouraged me more than my family.

Mom developed the habit of clipping stuff from the newspaper that was remotely connected to college and taking it to Mrs. George and asking, "Is this something that would help Bill go to college? If it would be helpful, I'll send away for it."

Mrs. George always said, "Yes, go ahead. Let's give it a shot." It was by this modus operandi that we discovered a modified version of the Scholastic Aptitude Test. The ad said this version of the college entrance exam was just like the regular one except this one didn't have any time limits. Since I had to type my answers letter by letter, the time restrictions would have been like blindfolding someone else who was taking the test. On the other hand, I wanted to take the college entrance exam to prove to myself that I was college material. I thought I could go to college, but I wanted to remove any shadow of doubt. Besides, the exam was required of all prospective college students.

The test arrived in December of 1975 and was administered by Mrs. George. It took me two days. Mrs. George put the test book beside my typewriter, and I would type my answers. The test was entirely multiple choice, or in some cases, multiple guess, so after the test I asked myself: "My brain has been turned into: (A) oatmeal, (B) cream of wheat, (C) jelly, (D) the school's peach cobbler and will be served later this week, (E) None of the above. It has disintegrated."

The results indicated that I was, indeed, college material. They didn't say that I was a genius.

When Mrs. George saw the results, she said, "You're weak in math, but your verbal skills are good. Bet nobody told you that before. I think it's time to call Bob and John back in."

This time John and Bob were ready to talk college with us. Bob began, "Since we all are in agreement that a trade school is out of the question, as is ENCOR (See, Bill, I'm learning), we need to decide on a college. The trouble is voc rehab won't send you out of state if there's a college in your home state because the out of state tuition is too high. So, that leaves us with the University of Nebraska at Omaha or the University of Nebraska at Lincoln. Now —"

"Excuse me." Mrs. George said. "I have a daughter who graduated from UNL last year, and I hate to tell you this, but its campus isn't accessible."

John said, "I've done some checking into this, and UNL is trying to get its campus accessible to comply with Section 504 of the Rehabilitation Act of '73."

"What's that?" Mrs. George asked.

John explained that Section 504 mandated that any college or university receiving federal money must become accessible within five years or provide reasonable accommodations within five years. John admitted that UNL had a long way to go. He also suggested that UNO was more accessible.

Mom spoke up "If he goes to UNO, he could stay at home, but I don't know how long his dad and I could take care of him. We aren't getting any younger."

I grimaced and shook my head.

Bob saw my signs of protest and said, "You're like me, Bill. I didn't want to live with my folks when I went to college either. Don't get me wrong. I loved them, but I had to get away to be my own boss. That's what you need, right?

I nodded enthusiastically. Bob had hit the proverbial nail on the proverbial head. I wanted to see if I could make a life for myself away from my parents.

Mom asked teasingly, "You mean you don't want to be a 60-year-old man living with your 90-year-old mother and 92-year-old father? Neither would I. So I guess UNO is out because if Bill were in Omaha, his dad and I wouldn't be able to keep our noses out of his business."

"Okay," Bob Gellner said. "John, remind me to check with UNL to see if they're accessible.

"Bill, I need a psychological evaluation and a physical examination done because I need to give VR justification for our decision to send you to college. In the past Voc Rehab has funded 'bad risks' and has gotten in hot water for it. For example, the Agency put another client through college and bought special equipment, and then the client died."

"So you need to be reassured that Bill won't keel over on you," Mom said jokingly. "We can have our family doctor do the physical."

"And the psychologist for the Omaha Public Schools can do the psychological testing," Mrs. George said.

"Good. VR will pay for both exams. Should we set up another meeting for a month from now?" Bob asked. "I think we should meet at least monthly for now. Then, when things get moving, maybe we should meet once every two weeks."

In January, 1976, when I was taking the psychological test for college, Mrs. George came in saying, "You have a female visitor." With that, Deanne entered the room and shyly said, "Hi, I thought you would like to know that I'm going into special education at college. And I'm engaged."

I nodded and typed (ignoring capitalization and punctuation), "im planning to go to college theyre finally getting rid of me—if this test certifies me as normal im beginning to detest tests though congratulations on being engaged thats far out"

"Thank you. And that's great about you going to college. I have a class, so I have to go." Her conversation was different from the time she enthusiastically told me what my grades in world geography were. It was dry and stilted. My childish stupidity had hurt her like it had hurt me. In her way, she was trying to tell me she was no longer available, and I was trying to tell her that I understood.

I thought how ironic it was that Deanne was preparing for a career in special education, which had been my world, and I was preparing to enter the world of the able-bodied, her world.

Dad thought Mrs. George, Mom, and I were crazy. He thought that I was trying to do the impossible. He didn't want any of us boys (who were slowly becoming young men) to leave his house where he could protect us. To add insult to insecurity, I was the first to journey outside his nest. He did encourage me when he said: "We'll help financially as much as we can, but if college doesn't work, we'll try something else. Don't let these silly women get you all mixed up. You know how women are."

I think a part of my dad's problem was he was still seeing me as his little boy, a child, he would always take care of. He hadn't been conditioned for my leaving home.

For those who knew me as an adult, college wasn't that hard to imagine. When I wrote and told my Camp Camelot friends, Ed Henry and Sally Stone, of my plans and of my fears, their reply was that they didn't have any doubt that I could do it. They offered to help in any way. They also invited me to their wedding.

In March, 1976, Bob and John came to school and told me that I had been accepted as a client by VR. John said, "One guy down at the office read your file and told us we were crazy to try this. He said that there was no way a person like you could go to college. I told him that he hadn't met you. Bob pulled out five dollars and offered to make a

114   friendly wager that you would make it. The guy wouldn't take the bet."

"John pulled out ten dollars to go with my five," Bob said and laughed. "Seriously, you are now officially our client, so we need to discuss things like your major. Do you have any thoughts on this?"

"ALL I CAN DO IS WRITE" I spelled out. "SO I GUESS ENGLISH WOULD BE A GOOD MAJOR"

"I don't know about that," Bob said. "The problem I have with a degree in English is that the job possibilities are slim for non-speaking majors. Most people with degrees in English teach it. Let's see, the results of your psychological evaluation say that you could do writing, research, or a combination of both. So how about journalism? It involves writing and researching."

I thought about it. "HOW WOULD I INTERVIEW PEOPLE" I spelled.

"Good question," Bob said. "Wait a second. Why couldn't you type out your questions, tape record your answers, and transcribe your answers at your typewriter?"

I nodded enthusiastically. "I CAN DO THAT" I spelled out. I HAVE EVEN BEEN PUBLISHED IN THE PAPER"

"Good. The next thing that we need to talk about is another evaluation by the Vocational Service Project." Bob said and grinned. "Voc Rehab loves to have people evaluated, don't we?"

"HOW MANY TIMES MUST I BE EVALUATED" I spelled out impatiently.

"As many times as VR feels necessary," Mrs. George cut in sharply. "They're paying the bills, so cool it, kiddo."

"No, no," Bob said. "If I were Bill, I'd be asking the same thing. Let me explain this evaluation to you, Bill.

"This evaluation isn't to see how smart you are or if you're college material. You have already proven that to us. This evaluation is to see how we can help you function better. Your psychological evaluation mentioned something about an electronic wheelchair and a feeding machine. This evaluation will take that a step further. It will determine exactly what you'll need to live on campus. It has a grant from the State Council on Developmental Disabilities to make people with disabilities, such as cerebral palsy, as independent as possible."

"THAT SOUNDS GOOD TO ME WHEN DO I START THIS EVALUATION" I spelled out.

"Well, we have a slight problem which John can explain. You can yell at him. John, be my guest."

"Basically," John said, "you're caught in a power struggle between UNL and a rehabilitation institution. Both want to evaluate you. UNL feels that since you're coming to Lincoln, you should be evaluated by them. On the other hand, the rehabilitation institution points out that you are under age 21, and, therefore, under their jurisdiction. They won't let UNL infringe on their territory. Normally, we would just wait until you turn 21 to have you evaluated, but, as you know you turn 21 eight days before school starts. It wouldn't be enough time. We're caught between a rock and a hard place.

"SURELY WE CAN DO SOMETHING" I spelled out.

"If you would write me a letter telling me how you feel about this mess," John said thoughtfully, "I then could rattle enough cages to shake things loose somewhere."

I did write John a letter. I said that going to college was my dream, a dream not unlike that of Martin Luther King's dream of equality. I pointed out that it would be only through higher education that I could achieve equality in a society of people who were able-bodied.

In April the evaluation was still up in the air. But two things happened to distract me from the stalled evaluation.

First, a man and his wife came to school selling tickets to wheelchair basketball. He was with a woman, and he had limited hand dexterity and was operating a motorized wheelchair.

When Mrs. George saw him, she ran after him crying, "Where did you get that wheelchair? One of my students would die for an electric wheelchair. Would you come in and talk to him for a second?"

He and the woman were a delight. The man told me that he got his wheelchair from a place in Denver, Colorado. According to him, this dealership could put anyone in the driver's seat of an electric wheelchair. He asked the woman to give me the address of the dealer and urged me to write. I thanked him and said he had a nice sister.

"Thanks, but she's my wife," he said.

How naive could I be? Very, very, very, very.

I wrote the dealership a long letter detailing what I needed in a wheelchair. I explained that I needed a control that I could operate with the back of my head. When I told the dealers in and around Nebraska my ideas, they wouldn't touch me with a ten-foot joystick.

116   But Colorado had Craig Institute, the most complete rehabilitation center for people with spinal cord injuries in the nation. It followed that Colorado would know about the latest technology.

Secondly, Dr. J. P. Lord High School was publishing its first year book, and I was its co-editor. For that I earned the final credit that I needed to graduate from high school. The year book was called "1976 Wheeler." It had the symbol of access on its cover. It was dedicated to the Memory of David. I jotted down my thoughts about David, and Mrs. George liked them and they became a part of the dedication page. "He didn't shout, but everybody listened to him. He never complained, though he had pain. He struggled to live, though he knew he was dying. We remember him, though he is away from us."

On the morning of May 27, 1976, my graduation day, as Mrs. George and I were going over last minute graduation details, John McGill came into the room saying, "What are you doing June 4th? Cancel whatever it is because you are going to UNL for the evaluation. We rattled enough cages."

"THANKS FOR THE GRADUATION GIFT" I spelled.

"Just doing my job and I'll see you tonight," he said as he left.

Graduation night was wild. Getting everyone in my family out of blue jeans and into their monkey suits was a trick that would have made Houdini pale. The complaining could be heard for blocks. Dad complained the least but hated it the most. We had to be there early as I had to get in my cap and gown. The gown was easy. The cap was another matter. Mom tried bobby pins, safety pins, scotch tape, and masking tape. Thank God she didn't take Mrs. George's suggestion of a spike seriously. I had a corsage for Mrs. George. She gave me a medallion commemorating the nation's bi-centennial. Mrs. George said that it was symbolic of my quest to be independent.

As I was the only high school graduate that night, I pretty much had control of the program. I chose "The Impossible Dream," "You'll Never Walk Alone," and "Climb Every Mountain" as the music. A nervous Bob Gellner was the guest speaker, which was Mrs. George's idea. As we were going onto the stage, Bob said, "How did I let Mrs. George talk me into this? She can talk faster than anyone I have seen. Just learn to have her gift of gab, and you'll have it made at UNL."

As I sat on the stage under the class motto (which was also chosen by me), "They can because they think they can." I saw a large crowd, a good portion of which was my family and my friends, filling the school auditorium. Two very important people in my life were missing: Grandma Brown, who was in the hospital, and Deanne whom I hadn't invited—not because I didn't want her there but because I was afraid any overture by me would be misinterpreted.

The eighth graders received their certificates of attendance first. Then the assistant superintendent in charge of special education stepped up to the podium and said, "Excuse me. This wasn't planned, but I have to say it anyway. . ."

"Oh-oh, Rush," I heard a little voice in the back of my mind saying, "they counted up your credits and you're short."

". . . .There's no other student in the Omaha Public School System who has worked longer or harder than Bill Rush for this diploma."

He walked over to me and handed me my diploma. The crowd gave me a standing ovation. I guess they were so relieved to be finally rid of me that they had to stand up and clap.

After all the festivities were over at school my folks gave me the okay to go out and raise cane with my friends. Tom Taxman, who was in Omaha on break and whom I had nicknamed Doc, threaded me into his car one last time. We met John McGill at a quiet bar and grill where we talked about how the first verse of my "Impossible Dream" was over and how the second verse was about to begin.

On June 4th Dad dropped my mom and myself off at UNL's East Campus. The evaluation was about to begin. It took three days. The UNL staff took very good care of us. We were assigned a driver who drove us to several places at the university where a team of professionals checked me from stem to stern.

We went to the independent living specialist first. She determined that I was a typical bachelor because I couldn't cook, wash clothes, clean house, or dress myself without help.

A speech pathologist was next. She determined that I was the strong silent type who could not chew, blow, suck or swallow.

Then a physical therapist. She determined that I would definitely not qualify for an athletic scholarship. She was impressed with my straight spine but I thought how many dates will a straight spine get me.

The last stop, the one that did the most for my self-esteem, was at

118   UNL's College of Engineering. They determined that I could hit a button with my headstick and control my head and neck well enough to operate an electric wheelchair.

In the cloistered world of special education that I had just left I was led to feel that the problem was always me. These engineers were saying the problem was not me, rather the surroundings. They suggested adaptations that they could and would make in my environment to help me, not surgery. No pain, a lot of gain.

The evaluation basically reinforced what Bob, John, Mrs. George, Mom and I felt. I needed a lot of help. I was college material and my hope for the future lay in getting the best education possible. In other words, using my head in more ways than one was my key to success.

In July I flew to Denver with Bob, John, and an engineering professor from UNL. We needed to find an electric wheelchair that I could operate with the back of my head.

On the way to Denver, as the engineering professor watched John give me a Coke, he said, "You guys simply amaze me with what you are doing for him."

"We aren't doing anything for him," John shot back. "He's doing it. We're just along for the ride."

When we got to the dealership that I had written to three months before, we were greeted with, "I'm sorry that we didn't get back to you, Bill. Is this the kind of control you need?"

The dealer showed us a picture of a hand control that had been modified so it could be used with the back of the head.

I nodded enthusiastically.

John turned to the engineering professor and said, "See what I mean? We are just along for the ride."

Also, in July John, a worker from United Cerebral Palsy, and I went back to UNL for New Student Orientation. I registered for nine hours, reserved a room at Selleck Hall, and familiarized myself with the campus.

August was approaching and I was going to camp, desperately hoping that I could find an attendant there. Everyone had been looking but no luck. Without an aide college would remain a dream.

My counselor, Roger Bacon, was tall, blond, handsome, 18 years old, and from Westside. He was an actor between jobs. So in response to my persistent query that I asked anyone who would listen, "WOULD YOU LIKE TO BE MY AIDE IN SEPTEMBER AT UNL?" Roger said, "Let me think about it." Three days later Roger said, "We make a good team. Let me try."

That night John McGill visited camp and said, "I hate to tell you this but we have exhausted all our resources regarding attendant care."

Roger said, "I'm going to take the job."

John said, "Rush, how do you do it? Roger, when camp is over, come to my office, and we'll discuss how you'll get paid.

"I have another piece of bad news for you. Your new wheelchair won't be here until late October. I guess it's coming by dog sled." When I got back home everything was set for UNL—everything but the big three: Mommy, Daddy and me. We were all scared to death. But the countdown had started, school was about to start.

Two days before I was to move to Lincoln when Mom and I were packing, the doorbell rang. It was John. "I got a job offer in Lincoln and I'm moving there next week." he said. "Personal reasons. I'll explain another time. I will help you all I can."

I could tell John was not happy and I felt guilty because I was so glad he was going to be in Lincoln. My mother, always quick to speak what she felt, said. "Thank you, Lord."

The big day finally arrived, car packed with my college survival kit. My mother must have thought they didn't have stores in Lincoln. Roger was to meet me at my dorm and take over from my folks. We were early so my mother fussed around putting a few things away but total unpacking was not possible because Roger needed to know what was where. We waited. John McGill stopped; he showed me the bathroom. We waited. Dad hung my lamp over my typewriter. We waited. John called Bob Gellner. We waited. Dad said, "Let's go back to Omaha and wait. Hard telling where this kid is."

We got back to Omaha about three o'clock in the afternoon, Mom called Roger's house and his mother told us he had missed his ride. We made arrangements to pick Roger and his things up (now that we had room) after supper.

While Roger and Dad loaded the car, Roger's mother told Mom and me, "Roger is irresponsible and aiding Bill is too much of a

120   responsibility for a 19-year-old kid. Bill, when you spelled out on
your board the day I visited camp that Roger would be your aide I
thought it was a joke."

Mom just said, "I'm sure that they can do it, they can grow up
together. Besides Roger is the only prayer we have. No Roger, no
school for Bill. Bill trusts Roger and I trust Bill and I've just put this
whole school thing in God's hands. It's the only way I can deal with
it."

Before the semester started I got together with Roger. I showed
him my class schedule and from there we planned my morning
routine. There were some definite aspects of care that had to be
done, such as toileting, dressing, and transferring me into my
wheelchair, and some that could be done if there was time such as
brushing my teeth, combing my hair, and shaving. If Roger decided
to be a student and to take morning classes, we would have to decide
on our priorities all throughout the semester.

My morning routine started when Roger entered my room.
(Roger had a key to my room.) I asked Roger to greet me when he
arrived, as it was a nice way to start out the morning.

My room was usually dark—due to the time of morning and/or
the pulled draperies. The light over the medicine cabinet was
usually the light used. The fluorescent overhead light was quite
shocking and startling, especially early in the morning. Not many
people wake up by turning on a spotlight.

I set my alarm so that the radio had me awake before Roger
arrived. Usually I would be wide awake when Roger entered. If the
radio wasn't on, Roger played a cassette tape. Deciding on what
type of music we would hear was a struggle. Roger liked Frank
Zappa whom I detested. I liked country/western music which
Roger abhorred. So, we compromised. One day we listened to ol'
Frank. The next day we listened to Mac Davis.

There was always a blanket or quilt padding the side rail on my
bed. This helped prevent bruising when I had muscle spasms, which
caused me to kick or hit the rail. Removing the quilt and placing it
on the top shelf of the closet was part of the routine. The side rail
was taken down via two small buttons; one at the head of the side
rail, the other at the foot. Pulling out or pushing down on the rail

required some experimentation to master. If I was lying on my stomach, I needed to be turned over. My left arm needed to be straightened out so that it extended above my head. Roger then placed one hand on my shoulder and one hand on my hip and rolled me away from him. This motion sometimes caused me some leg spasms. They usually didn't last long but waiting for them to finish was a necessity. Then it was possible to uncross and straighten out my legs.

To quote Roger, "He is able to pee in any position." During the morning routine, I was on my back. The plastic urinal was kept on the top shelf of the closet. I told Roger to be gentle because that was one part of me that was not bionic. I was glad Roger understood gravity when he took care of this part of my routine. I occasionally moved my legs or hips around in bed and the urinal would fall out of place. I let Roger know with an urgent low pitched moan. He simply readjusted the urinal when this happened. Roger always asked me if I was finished with the urinal. That way, he didn't take a chance on poor timing and wet sheets. When an accident with the urinal did happen and the sheet got wet Roger avoided the wet spot while dressing me and then changed the sheet after I was in the wheelchair.

Roger attended to my bladder needs again in early afternoon (after lunch), early evening (after supper), and again at bedtime.

Roger always listened to the weather report before he dressed me in the morning. I did not have a lot of fat on my body for insulation. It was nice in the summer, not so hot in the winter. I got cold faster so I always had the layered look.

Sometimes if we had time Roger even asked me what I wanted to wear. Example: "Bill, it's going to be 99 today, do you want to go naked?"

If I needed something special that I wanted to wear I let Roger know at least two days ahead of time. I didn't want him dragging it out of the dirty clothes bag.

I always slept in my underwear as it saved putting on and taking off of pajamas. In the morning then I always got a fresh set of underwear. I did the twist every morning getting in and out of my boxer shorts. Only Roger had to roll my hips from side to side as he

122   threaded me into my clothes. My boots had to be put on while I was still in bed. In order for me to stand for bed to wheelchair transfer I needed the ankle support.

The upper half of my body remained naked because it was easier putting deodorant, undershirt, shirt on while I was sitting up in my wheelchair. Dressing my upper half was not any easier than dressing my lower half; only different. Head first was best because then I could continue breathing while my arms were pushed, pulled, jammed through the sleeves.

Hair combing was not one of Roger's long suits and was sort of an exercise in futility anyway because my headstick was as important or more important than anything else I wore and kept my hair in a constant state of motion and disarray.

Roger and strong male members of my family transferred me from bed to chair by picking me up and putting me down. My mother and others allowed and needed me to support my weight during the transfer process. Every person had his own method. Once the transfer was completed my feet and knees had to be tied to my chair to help stabilize my body. I could not use a safety belt as this interfered with my ability to use my headstick and head control. My feet and knees were tied with a soft knitted material that gave some flexibility and allowed circulation. Feet were tied first and then I adjusted my bony bottom, and my thighs were tied to the wheelchair sides.

After I was tied in my chair the tray with my letter chart was secured to my chair, and with my headstick in place I was ready for the morning.

Roger always checked the bag at the back of my chair to be sure it contained my headrest for eating, a clean bib and/or paper napkins for meals and cleaning my lips, school books, and my assignment for class. The bag was zipped shut when it was possible to keep me from littering the campus. It was sometimes necessary for me to play Evil Knievil when going over curbs.

I needed the same kinds of basic personal hygiene that anyone else used. I used a deodorant daily and after showers, and it was always a part of the dressing routine. Roger and I both felt the same way about my hair or almost. Roger saw no point in bothering and I always told my other aides "Why mess with a masterpiece?" Still and all it was good to have a comb or brush used even though the headstick held down a multitude of "masterpieces."

Roger always used shaving cream and a double edged safety razor. My jaw line and Adam's apple were a real trick to shave but Roger was much better at it than my mother. Bleeding was kept to the minimum. He once asked me if my mother used a chain saw when she shaved me. She did indeed like for me to be clean shaven. It took me over a year to grow a mustache as she would always shave it off on my trips home. After much argument and soul searching she finally left my upper lip alone.

On busy mornings tooth brushing tended to get left out of my routine but I did not like to go to class with swamp mouth. I cannot spit and swallowing toothpaste all my life has left my stomach with absolutely no cavities. I always used a water chaser with my toothpaste.

So-called zits (especially under the headstick) were always a problem and from time to time pressure sores caused problems. Roger dealt with these as he did everything else.

I ate all my meals in the Selleck Cafeteria. I had a Validine meal ticket I carried in my billfold. Roger went ahead of me to get in line and asked me what I wanted to eat. The menu was posted outside of the food line doors. I preferred meat, potatoes, dairy products, pastries. Spicy food, fresh fruit or vegetables were not possible for me to eat. After I had selected my food Roger continued in the line and I found a place in the cafeteria. Before Roger could feed me he had to make a few alterations to my wheelchair. He unplugged the cords by my head control. Then he pulled the head control out of the back of the chair and rotated it around to face the opposite direction. The headrest that I carried in my bag was then inserted into the back in place of the head control. I was then ready to be fed.

Liquids had to be poured into my mouth. Roger always cautioned me that I couldn't breathe and swallow at the same time, so small swallows worked best. Choking, always a concern, was prevented best by making sure bites—especially meats—were cut in small pieces. Chewing was never a skill that I could master. Cracking jokes while feeding me was a no-no as laughing on my part always led to coughing and sometimes choking.

Roger always used a modified Heimlich maneuver when I choked

124   making a fist with one of his hands and punching me in the abdomen above my navel. The amount of power behind the punch depended on how far down the piece of food was lodged.

Roger once comforted my mother with the fact that he did not allow anyone to feed me that did not know this Heimlich maneuver. My mother told him then she would not feed me on weekends anymore as she did not know the maneuver and merely pounded me on the back.

Sometimes my jaw locked when my mouth was open, food gummed up in the roof of my mouth. All these little things made meal time interesting.

Spacing the fluids during the meal prevented food gumming but jaw locking and coughing seemed to be the will of the gods.

Fluid intake was different every day. Hot days and in the middle of the winter I needed more fluids to prevent dehydration. I always kept in my mind how long and how far I would be from help to empty my bladder before quenching my thirst.

I usually went home on weekends and holidays. My Dad or brother Jim picked me up at my dorm Friday nights and returned me Sundays before bedtime. I always took my dirty clothes home with me in a green duffel bag and returned with the clean clothes Sunday. Roger would put the folded clothes away before leaving my dorm on Sundays. My dorm room was small although it was called a double. With a bed, a desk, two wheelchairs, an electric typewriter and other electronic marvels it was very important to keep things picked up and put away.

Bed pan duty or as I lovingly referred to it "The Big Event" was also worked into my and Roger's schedule. I used a bedpan in my wheelchair and was tied as usual. Roger left me alone usually for 30 or 45 minutes. Sometimes mother nature wrecked havoc with this routine and then so much for the best laid plans of mice and men.

I took a shower once a week in the Selleck dorm. One of the bathrooms had a shower seat and I was strapped in this with a safety belt. A hand-held shower attachment helped. I always got a shampoo and soap in my eyes but clean hair. Weekends I got a tub bath and soaking at home. My brother or Dad put me in the bath tub and my mother did the scrubbing.

Before I went to bed at night I always received my two Valiums, a multi-vitamin, and a vitamin "C" along with a full glass of water.

Getting ready for bed was a reversal of my morning routine. Roger always placed me on my stomach and I got myself in a sort of three-quarter side lying position.

In this position I did not rub ankles and knees. Roger then covered me up with sheet, blankets, pulled up the side rail, put the padding on the side rail to prevent bruising and keep my legs from slipping through the railing. He then inserted a country-western tape I had picked out earlier. Roger then shut the lights out, locked the door and left.

CHAPTER 13

AFFIRMATIVE ACTION?

" 'I think you should meet the affirmative action officer here. He might be able to help you find a steady source of aides," John suggested. He was now the Client Ombudsman for the State Rehabilitation Services. "It's not the responsibility of Vocational Rehab to locate aides, so maybe we could get the university to help. I could set up a meeting—if you want."

I nodded my permission. The constant search for attendants was getting desperate and was beginning to drain both Roger and me, not to mention wearing on our friendship. Roger had been my only aide for two years and was getting tired of it. He smiled when I told him of John's plan to involve the affirmative action officer with our search for attendants.

"Do you think it would be helpful if I went to that meeting with you? I could tell him exactly what is involved, not that I'm trying to get rid of you."

"GOOD IDEA," I spelled out.

John had set up the meeting for the following Thursday afternoon in the Affirmative Action Office in the Administration Building. When John told me that I was to go to the Administration Building, I spelled, "IT DOESNT HAVE A RAMP HOW DO I GET IN"

"Oh yes it does. In back, behind the building. Teachers' College kinda hides it," John informed me.

So, on a beautiful March afternoon Roger and I climbed the gently sloping ramp leading to the Administration Building.

I was impressed and a little surprised that it was so easy to climb. I was getting used to ridiculously steep gradients. Even Roger commented, "Gee, compared to the ramp over at the art building, this one is a piece of cake. Hey look, this door even has a sign saying this is a 'handicapped' entrance. How about that? I was getting used to going through store rooms with you though."

The door's blue and white sign said, "HANDICAPPED EN-TRANCE. DO NOT BLOCK."

I made a mental note to congratulate the affirmative action officer on his access door and ramp. When Roger opened the door, I changed my mind. Squarely in the middle of the doorway stood a two-foot thick pillar.

"Jesus Christ. No wonder the sign says not to block this doorway. This pole blocks it nicely all by itself," Roger joked. "Stop before you run into it."

Too late. I had hit it already. Roger then decided that he had better guide the electric wheelchair around the post. When the door shut, the receiving room became dark.

"Now all we need is for the room to fill up with water. If I feel my feet getting wet, I'm leaving," Roger muttered.

We found an elevator and rode it to the third floor to the Affirmative Action Office.

The office was located in a hexagon with other offices, such as the those of the Chancellor and the Vice-chancellor. The room was nicely furnished.

Once we were seated and introduced to the affirmative action officer, John spoke. "The reason Mr. Rush, Mr. Bacon, and I are here is to see if you could help us in establishing some constant source of attendants. For two years Roger has been Bill's friend-aide simply because we haven't been able to find anybody else. Bill, have I left out anything? I'm sure you have several things to add."

"THE JOB IS IDEAL FOR REHABILITATION STUDENTS BECAUSE IT GIVES THEM ON THE JOB TRAINING THAT THEY COULDNT FIND ANY PLACE ELSE " I added.

"How did this attendant get employed?" the university administrator asked.

"I was a counselor at Camp Easter Seals where Bill went. He needed an aide and I needed a job. So here I am," Roger said nonchalantly.

"Well, seeing that students have aides isn't my responsibility. It's the student's. My job is to make sure classes are accessible to wheelchairs. I'm reminded of a disabled girl who had a class in Teacher's College. She couldn't get into the building, so I hired two

128 great big guys to carry the electric wheelchair and her into the building. Or if a deaf student needs an interpreter for a class I can arrange that," the administrator said proudly.

"We're not asking you to be responsible for Bill's aides," John explained patiently. "We're asking for somewhere that a person who is disabled could go to get matched with a prospective attendant. The hiring, training, and firing of the attendant would still be the responsibility of the person with the disability."

Roger added, "The problem is that there's no communication or coordination among the people who are looking for aides. Each person does his own thing, and this causes a lot of frustration. A central office that we could go to would help a lot."

"This is the office that handicapped students should come to if they have any problem. I'll look into this and see what can be figured out. Now are there any other problems? Are all your classes accessible?" the affirmative action officer asked.

I looked at Roger and grinned. It took him a split second to read my mind. He said, "Oh yes. Our Tuesday and Thursday morning encounters of the worst kind. Go on, Bill, tell him about it. Or should I?"

"THE WOODS ART BUILD. . ." I started to spell to the administrator, but he couldn't follow along and apologized. Roger said, "Perhaps I should tell him about the art building to speed things up."

I nodded and Roger told the executive, "The Woods Art Building is very inaccessible. We have to use the freight elevator to get to Bill's art history class. We don't mind using freight elevators, but to get to the elevator we have to go up a 45-degree ramp that has no handrails. In fact, it's so dangerous that I won't let Bill go up it by himself. The ramp's platform doesn't have a guardrail either. To add to the problem, the storeroom's door is frequently locked, and I have to leave Bill alone on a little ledge while I go around and unlock it from inside. We're handling it, but when you remodel, you should keep that building in mind."

"I'll check into it immediately. I'm glad you brought it up."

"Tell you what," the affirmative action officer continued, "Can Bill's aide type up a job description, bring it to this office, and we'll go from there?"

"Bill could do that," Roger interjected.

"All right, have him do it, and you bring it to my office. Now, gentlemen, if that's all, I'll be heading for home."

"LETS SHOW HIM THE ACCESS ENTRANCE TO THIS BUILDING" I spelled to Roger and John, hoping the administrator could improve that entrance too.

John had to relay my idea to the affirmative action officer because he hadn't gotten used to my method of communicating.

"You mean he's having trouble with the ramp to this building? Let's check it out. I'm glad you brought it to my attention. I don't know these things unless someone points them out to me."

When we were leaving the executive suite, the administrator rushed to open the suite's double doors and said, "I'll bet you haven't seen a doorway as wide as this one throughout the entire university system. Have you?"

We rode down on the elevator. When the executive saw the pillar in front of the heavy door, he agreed that it might be a problem for me. But he added, "The only problem is that Bill is the only one who can't open this door. Other wheelchairs can open this door, so the university can't justify spending money for an electric door if only one person will benefit from it. But I'll see what I can do. Thank you, Mr. McGill, for introducing Bill to me."

*****

In 1981, the Administration Building did get an automatic door and other students besides me use it.

The affirmative action officer has helped me locate attendants, but no office has been developed at the university solely for that purpose. However, there is an organization, separate from the university, that has assisted with finding aides since 1981.

The Woods Art Building remains inaccessible. Following is a series of letters between the affirmative action officer and myself regarding the building.

UNIVERSITY OF NEBRASKA
STANDARD MEMO FORM

Date: 5/31/78
Dept. of: Affirmative Action Officer   Attn: Brad Munn
From: Harley Schrader   Dept.: Physical Plant
Subject: Ramp at Woods Art Building

Message:

This is in response to your memo of May 25, 1978. Bill Rush is correct when he says the ramp on the east side of the Woods Art Building is not safe for people in wheelchairs. He should be made aware it is not intended to be used by persons in wheelchairs. This is a service ramp and was never intended to be used as a wheelchair ramp. In fact, the door at the head of the ramp enters into a receiving room consequently it is generally locked and the door from the receiving room to the corridor may likewise be locked. In addition to that, the receiving room may be so cluttered it would be impossible for a wheelchair to move through the room.

Handicapped persons should enter the building through the north entrance, which is at grade. There are adequate walks, curb cuts, etc., on the campus to allow people to travel to the north entrance with ease. It is our opinion there is no need to take any further action.

os   *Harley Schrader*

Brad Munn
Affirmative Action Officer
308 Administration Building
University of Nebraska--Lincoln
Lincoln, Nebraska 68588

June 23, 1978

Dear Mr. Munn:

Thank you for the copy of Mr. Scrader's memo. It upset me, and here's why.

I'm aware that a disabled person can enter the Woods Art Building by the north entrance. However, after the person gets into the building via that north entrance he/she only has access to the first floor. The first floor only has a couple of classrooms and is basically a showplace. Apparently, Mr. Schrader is not aware of this.

I'm painfully aware that the ramp which I have used is, in Mr. Schrader's words, ". . . a service ramp for deliveries and was never intended to be used as a wheelchair ramp." I also agree with him when he says: "In addition to that, the receiving room may be so cluttered it would be impossible for a wheelchair to move through the room."

But a wheelchair must use this service ramp because it leads to a freight elevator which is the only means by which a person can get to the basement, second floor, or third floor--three-fourths of the building! My class was in the basement.

Now, I may never take another class in Woods Art Building, but other disabled people will. It seems to me rather than rearranging classes every time a person in a wheelchair took a class in that building, you could lessen the grade of the service ramp, unclutter the storeroom, and make the freight elevator more accessable to wheelchairs.

It is true that Woods Art Building does comply with the 1974 Rehabilitation Act. I was hoping you would want to do more than just comply with the law. I was hoping you would want to make Nebraska Number One in accessability!

Thank you for your time.

Sincerely,
William L. Rush
2020 North 66 Street
Omaha, Nebraska 68104

cc: Robert Madden
     Dept. of Health, Education and Welfare

     John McGill
     Client Ombudsman
     Neb. Div. of Rehab Services

     Harley Schrader
     Physical Plant

     Harry Jackson
     Lincoln Star

     Don Crouch
     Div. of Rehab Services

132

THE UNIVERSITY OF NEBRASKA—LINCOLN
OFFICE OF THE CHANCELLOR
LINCOLN, NEBRSKA 68588
(402) 472-2116

June 29, 1978

Mr. William L. Rush
2020 N. 66th Street
Omaha, NE 68104

Dear Mr. Rush:

You are to be commended for being on our backs as it relates to programs and facilities for the handicapped. I appreciate your recent letter and would like to add some comments relative to same. Deep within your communication is a statement to which I feel exception should be taken. You said, "I was hoping you would want to do more than just comply with the law." Although I am positive you are referring only to the Woods Art Building, I believe that UN-L has and will continue to do more than the Rehabilitation Act mandates. For example, the new door device that we are purchasing for your dormitory room is not, in my opinion, required by Federal law.

I am a compliance officer for the University, not the designer nor chief authorizer for altering current structures on campus. I have to take the advice and suggestions of professionals when it comes to determining what modifications are necessary for a building. Thus, I had to assume that Mr. Schrader's reply was not only accurate but proper.

In view of your comments, I will ask Mr. Schrader and members of his staff to reconsider your request and mine. I will remain in touch with you.

Sincerely,
M. Bradley Munn
Affirmative Action Officer

clw
xc: Harley Schrader

UNIVERSITY OF NEBRASKA

133

STANDARD MEMO FORM

Date: 7/14/78
To Dept. of: Affirmative Action   Attn: Bradley Munn
From: Harley Schrader   Dept.: Physical Plant
Subject: Woods Building—William L. Rush Letter

Message:

We have reviewed the situation referred to in Mr. Rush's letter, and we are still of the opinion that the primary handicapped entrance to this building should be thru the north doors. Our long-term intent to provide handicapped access throughout the building was to modify the elevator and access to same so it could be properly used by the handicapped. To do this, we anticipated moving the interior entrance doors to the receiving room east far enough so that a door could be provided to gain entrance to the elevator at the 1st floor level on the north side of same. We feel that the development of a handicapped entrance to the building thru a receiving or storage area would be a gross mistake. The elevator itself does need some modifications, all of which were anticipated to be done when funds became available.

It appears to us that Mr. Rush has singled out one isolated situation. We realize there are handicapped needs in many of the buidlings on campus and, as you know, funds have been requested to eliminate all handicapped barriers. We have moved forward to eliminate these barriers on a priority order based on what we considered to be the most important needs to accommodate the greatest number of people. Generally speaking, we have considered the public buildings as the highest priority. Buildings such as Morrill Hall which are frequented by many people was placed high on our list.

We feel we have made definite strides toward the elimination of the handicapped barriers and will continue to work to eliminate all barriers in a priority order as funds are made available.

os   *Harley Schrader*

Bill Rush:
Here's a copy of Harley Schrader's reply for your information.

Brad Munn

CHAPTER 14

FRIENDS

It was mid-September, 1978, my third September at UNL. I was attending a computer fair and was trying to get some information from a computer expert on a home computer system. But the expert had been sidetracked by another questioner.

Why hadn't God given me speech? Life would be so much simpler if I could just talk.

I spied another expert who wasn't busy, so I decided to ask him. I wanted to know if the demonstrated system had a shift-lock since I couldn't hold a shift key down without one.

I expected to be ignored, but this person answered me, "I don't know, but if it hasn't, one can be installed very easily for you.

"I'm glad we finally met, Bill, I'm Mark Dahmke and live in the same dorm as you do. I've been talking to several people here at the university, and we want to develop a computerized speech synthesizer for you."

I looked at him. Mark Dahmke fitted my idea of what a computer programmer-analyst should look like. He had short brown hair that was neatly combed and wire-rimmed glasses. He was slender and conservatively dressed. He knew how to get my undivided attention.

Mark continued, "About six years ago a company in Michigan began selling a speech synthesizer subsystem for use with computers. It was expensive and inflexible. When I was a sophomore in high school, I became interested in building a voice synthesizer for a science fair project. But the project never got off the ground because it cost too much. It would have been just too expensive and impractical. But building a voice synthesizer has always been my dream. Until now it was impractical. But I think we can help each other."

Mark glanced at his watch.

"Well, I'll see you around and who knows? Maybe we can help each other, if that's okay with you," the computer analyst offered.

"YES ITS OKAY YOU NEED A GUINEA PIG AND I CANT TALK" I spelled out. "BUT WHOS GOING TO PAY FOR IT"

"Vocational Rehabilitation, maybe." Mark suggested, "There's a lot of organizations around that can pay for it."

I was skeptical. I was doing badly in my computer course, so Vocational Rehabilitation wouldn't buy me a computer. They would be justified for refusing. But a voice synthesizer would be nice. I could talk on the phone for myself. Now I needed somebody to read what I was saying over the phone. This ruled out private conversations. It also meant finding a time when a third party was available. It sure would be nice if I could dial a push-button speaker phone and be able to say, "Hi, this is Bill. I was wondering how you were doing." Or to be able to ask a professor a question directly instead of asking it through another person and having the professor answering the other student. Or being able to shout "Hi" to a friend who was walking down the street.

All these things would be nice, but I decided not to get my hopes up.

I was a second semester sophomore at UNL with a near perfect grade point average. I was proving that I could succeed in the "normal" academic world. I was enjoying success as a free lance writer with a few nationally published stories. And now Mark Dahmke was talking about building a computerized voice synthesizer for me. I was becoming more independent than anyone could have imagined, thanks to God, family, friends, and high technology.

But something was missing in my life. I didn't know what. Then on a cool October night as I struggled with the outside doors to my dorm, I found out. She grinned when the guys standing by the doors teased me about having such an attractive woman open the door for me.

"How do you do it, Rush? I wish I could get girls to open doors for me."

I nodded my thanks to her and went to the adjoining building. I was too tired to think of a comeback for the smart-alecks.

"My name's Wendy. How are you tonight?" she asked, still holding the doors.

"OK WILL YOU PLEASE GET THE OTHER DOOR IM GOING INTO THE NEXT BUILDING"

"Sure, she said grinning cheerfully. As she followed along, she said

136   boldly, "I want to get to know you. Can I work with you?" She opened the door to the other building and let me enter. "I noticed you have people feeding you, and I thought I might be able to help you with that, if you need any help."

"WHY DO YOU HAVE TO WORK WITH ME WHY CANT WE JUST BE FRIENDS"

"Okay, sure. In fact, I like your idea better," she said. Then another guy walked into the building and she said, "Hi, I'm ready to study." Then, to me, "Would you excuse me? I have a big test tomorrow. See ya around."

I nodded. The young woman turned to climb the stairs that led to the second and third floors. The second floor housed men, and the third housed women.

I let out a bullmoose yell, and she turned to watch me spell, "DO YOU LIVE ON 3RD FLOOR"

"Sure do. Why?"

"JUST MY LUCK YOURE SAFE UNLESS I CAN INVENT A WHEELCHAIR THAT CAN CLIMB STEPS"

Blushing, she said, "Oh, I don't know about you."

As I watched her climb the architectural barrier with the handsome able-bodied guy beside her I felt burnt-out. I was tired of people thinking the only way to get to know me was to "work" with me. And I was tired of being a curiosity, especially to young attractive women like the one who was climbing the stairs. I sadly realized that the flights of steps were the least of my obstacles. I hoped my joke about her safety would start her thinking of me as any other guy, but at the same time knew it wouldn't.

The next night a guy who worked in the dormitory office stopped me to ask, "Hey, did a girl, kinda cute, talk to you? I was in the snack bar getting a Coke when she came up and asked me how to talk with you. And I told her that you talked just like anybody else, except you spelled your half of the conversation. She seemed interested in you and acted like she really wanted to get to know you."

"SHE DID STOP AND TALK WITH ME BUT I WAS TRYING TO GET THROUGH THOSE DAMN DOORS I WAS IN A BAD MOOD AND WE DIDNT GET MUCH OF A CHANCE TO TALK BECAUSE SHE HAD TO STUDY AND I HAD TO GET SOMETHING AT THE OFFICE I WONDER HOW I COULD SET UP A LONGER VISIT"

"I'll call her for you," he offered.

The next evening the young woman knocked on my door and poked her head in the open doorway. "Busy?"

As we chatted and got to know each other, the evening slipped away. It was evident that I wouldn't get as much studying done as I wanted. But I didn't care.

Soon all the guys on my floor gathered in my room. I had a pretty good idea who had drawn the crowd and it wasn't my tape of Jim Croce. I couldn't blame them. My new friend was good looking. She was just over five feet tall and had brown eyes that matched the color of her shoulder length hair. Her skin showed a summer tan and she had a dynamite smile.

"Did he show ya all his electronic stuff?" one of my dormmates asked her. "Go on, Bill, show her."

So I demonstrated the controls for my lights and clock radio. I showed off my door opener, which I could control via a radio transmitter attatched to the plexiglass tray on my wheelchair. She was impressed with the space-age technology.

"Hey, show her your wheelchair and how it works. I'll never understand how it works. It baffles me," another dormmate said.

So, wondering if I should sell tickets, I wheeled about the room. I demonstrated how I went straight, reverse, and turned left and right. I was angry at my dormmates because I was a man, not a side show freak. My wheelchair was a tool for my mobility, not a novelty. Why couldn't they see that? And why couldn't they see that I was trying to get to know Wendy. Why didn't they understand I had a right to my privacy just as they did?

As I was wheeling around the room, I noticed that Wendy was typing something. I was disappointed in her. I thought she knew that I could hear and that she didn't have to write things to me. Apparently I was wrong.

When I was done showing my electric marvels to her and the guys, I rolled back to my typewriter to read, "I wish they would go, so we could talk by ourselves."

They finally left and we finally got to talk. Our friendship had started.

On another night in the same October Mark Dahmke, the computer analyst, came to my room and gave me a long impressive

138   paper on a synthesizer system. He said, "We had a meeting out at the independent living lab on East Campus and copies of these were passed out. I thought you would like to see a copy. It explains the synthesizer that I want to build. Goodnight."

I started to read it, not noticing the byline. As I read I thought the company had put together a thorough public release. And I wondered what company put this system together. When I read the byline I was shocked. Mark had written it. He was serious. He really wanted to make me a voice synthesizer. I felt guilty for my negative attitude. I went to the stairway in our dorm and waited for somebody to come down the stairs. When somebody did, I asked him to get Mark Dahmke.

Shortly Mark appeared and said, "Yes? Do you have a question about the voice synthesizer? I see you have the paper. Comments?"

I told him it had impressed me. I didn't put this much effort into a term paper. It had diagrams and the diagrams looked professional. I couldn't believe how thorough he had been.

He thanked me and said, "During my senior year in high school, I took an English course from a really neat teacher. Part of the requirement for the course was to write a research paper. I wrote mine on bionics and used it as part of a science fair project. I also used it as a requirement in the science course I was also taking. It worked out quite nicely. I learned a lot from it. Enough about me.

"Back to your voice. We have worked it out so that Vocational Rehabilitation and United Cerebral Palsy will buy the actual synthesizer, and the University of Nebraska will pay me for building it. So it looks like we are in business. Oh by the way, I plan eventually to put your voice, so to speak, on your wheelchair so you'll have it wherever you go. It wouldn't be practical to just have it desktop, that would be self-defeating. I will make sure that it's mobile."

I flipped back to the estimated cost. It would cost $2500. He was saying, in effect, I would eventually have a computer that cost $2500 on my tray. I wondered if he knew my arms flew around and knocked things off my tray. I spelled out. "IF YOU DO THAT PLEASE MAKE IT VERY STRONG BECAUSE IM VERY HARD ON EQUIPMENT ASK THE ENGINEERS WHO FIX MY CHAIR"

Mark smiled and said, "Well, mechanical engineering is a little out of my field. Wait a minute. Now that you mention it, when I was a senior in high school, I did some mechanical engineering for the science fair. I made a mechanical arm for my project. It took second place."

I would learn later that the artificial arm project was inspired by Mark's uncle who lost his natural arm in a farming accident.

"IM SORRY I HAVE BEEN SO FLIPPANT ABOUT YOUR PROJECT BUT IM TAKING A COURSE IN FORTRAN AND ITS SHOWING ME HOW MUCH I DONT KNOW ABOUT COMPUTERS AND SO HAVING A COMPUTER WHICH WILL TALK FOR ME IS UNREAL" I spelled.

"I understand," Mark said. "Well, if you don't have any more questions, I'll get back to my school work."

I did have one more. "TELL ME SOMETHING HOW DID THIS PROJECT START YOU NEVER DID EXPLAIN HOW YOU GOT INVOLVED WITH ME" I said.

"Well," Mark said, "One day in September, I happened to be walking past my manager's office at the Computer Network and heard him say something about 'microcomputers.' I stopped to see what was going on and learned that he was sending another employee out to talk to someone in the department of Human Development. I said that I would be glad to go along since their project involved a Radio Shack microcomputer.

"We took a university car and drove out to East Campus. Dr. Lois Schwab met us. After some discussion, I mentioned that I had done some work with artificial arms and was interested in speech synthesis. Immediately, her eyes lit up. We ended up setting a time for another meeting to discuss a 'pilot project.' Since I lived in Selleck Hall and knew of you, I suggested that we consider giving you a voice. Dr. Schwab called in your rehab counselor and I explained what the project would involve. He finally offered to pay for just the speech synthesizer so we could evaluate it and let you use it. If that worked, we would get the rest of the money."

Mark and I were the odd couple of UNL in more ways than one. When it came to prioritizing our appearance and our effort and passion to achieve neatness and order, he was Felix, I was Oscar. But we were alike in several ways. We both were studious. Neither of us was good at mixing with our dormmates. We both hated football in a state that was fanatic about its team. Neither of us was a ladies' man.

140   But I was beginning to feel like a lady's man, thanks to my flourishing friendship with Wendy. Her natural attitude towards me and her total acceptance of my disability refreshed me.

One evening when I was eating dinner in the Selleck cafeteria, Wendy came over and asked if she could sit with me. My male aide, who used his body to experiment with mixing booze with drugs and who thought he could pick up every female within a 10-mile radius, said:

"Sure. There's always room for one more. Pull up a chair. Bill's in a rush. Clever, huh? Anyway, he can't talk to you. What's your name? That's a lovely name. What's your major? Oh, undeclared. Ain't we all? What area are you interested in? I imagine that you'll be good at working with the handicapped. Do you know sign language? I used to be a interpreter for the deaf, and I used to live with a deaf girl for awhile. So I know a lot of it. I could teach you some if you like. It's really simple."

As I was motioning towards my headstick (I wanted at least a chance to tell Wendy "hello"), milk dribbled down my chin. My aide said, "You can't talk now. You have to eat. Your brother is coming to take you home for the weekend. You aren't even packed yet."

Wendy instinctively reached across the table, picked up my napkin without squeamishness, wiped my chin and said, "You'd better eat. I'll come by your room Monday night after my Bible class. We can talk then, okay? I should be getting ready for a date anyway. How's nine o'clock for Monday? Great. See you then. Bye." She left the table.

My aide looked astonished.

"Did you notice how naturally she took your napkin and wiped your chin off? I never saw any thing like it. Interesting girl."

I scowled at him for not letting me talk with her. It was unfair of him to monopolize the conversation, especially when Wendy was my friend. I resented his control over whether I could do something as simple as greet a friend and I resented his ability to chat away, not worrying about the time.

We had different lifestyles. He was a free spirit and I wasn't. He tried to get me to "lighten up a little," but I didn't want to. Education was too important to me. When I didn't go along with him, he became antagonistic. But I was stuck with him because attendants were almost impossible to find and train. The only thing we had in common was that we were both bullheaded. But he had total control over me, and I didn't have any control over him. That wasn't the way it was supposed to work. He was supposed to work for me although he was paid minimum wage by social services. He was supposed to feed, dress, bathe, and toilet me and to assist me when I needed help.

"Did I monopolize the conversation?" he asked sarcastically.

I nodded angrily and silently said, "When I get my new voice, you won't have that chance again, you son of a bitch."

"I did, didn't I? I always do that. I'll try to watch myself in the future. Here, have some more corn, and please accept it with my humblest apologies."

I couldn't tell if he was sincere.

That Monday night Wendy stopped by to talk. Her conversation began, "Last month I read a story by you for an English assignment. It was about your high school teacher. I liked it and wanted to get to know you."

I remembered some of the freshmen had shown me a handout from their English class and how astounded and proud I had been to see my story in it.

"I WISH THERE WERE MORE STUDENTS LIKE YOU ASK AWAY"

"Okay, what would you like most in the whole world? If you had one wish, what would it be?"

I considered whether I should tell her what I really wanted. Why not? After all, wasn't she going to help others who were disabled? She should know what makes us tick.

"TO GET MARRIED BUT IM AFRAID THAT IS THE 1 THING THAT I CANT QUITE DO"

"Why?" She asked with all the idealism of an eighteen-year-old. Her warm, brown eyes were so sincere and so optimistic. "I have heard about a lot of disabled people getting married. I saw a movie on TV just a few weeks ago about a woman who was a quadriplegic and she had a fiance."

"I SAW IT TOO BUT SHE COULD TALK AND I CANT" I pointed out, both literally and figuratively.

"What do you call what we're doing right now?"

"BUT I CANT WEAR THIS HEADSTICK ALL THE TIME

142 AND BESIDES NO GIRL HAS EVER GONE STEADY WITH
ME SO THINKING ABOUT MARRIAGE IS SILLY"

"Bill, 'going steady' doesn't mean anything nowadays. When I
meet a guy I like, I don't think just because I'm spending time with
him I'm 'going steady.' Besides, you're going to college. How many
people thought you could do that?" she persisted.

We argued in a friendly, but irrational manner. I wanted to make
it clear to this girl that I didn't expect any romantic involvement
from her. I should have listened to myself.

"Bill," she said in an exasperated voice, "when you're in love, it
doesn't matter if you can't walk."

"MY POINT IS THAT I HAVE GOTTEN TO KNOW SEVERAL
FEMALES AND THEY HEAD FOR THE HILLS AS SOON AS I
GET EMOTIONAL"

"I won't," she said softly.

"GOOD IM GLAD TO HEAR THAT"

We talked at length of her desire to help people who are disabled,
and I decided that Dr. Schwab and her group on East Campus could
give her helpful guidance. After all, Dr. Schwab hadn't steered me
wrong. Schwab was even making it possible for me to have a voice,
something that all my speech therapists had failed to do.

And thanks to Mark Dahmke, Schwab's dream was beginning to
crystalize. Mark tried to explain what he was doing, but his
explanations just left me with a blank expression. Then he would
say, "Excuse me. I'm being too technical. I have a tendency to forget
others aren't programmers. I'm sorry. But unlike other synthe-
sizers, this will not have a set vocabulary. You can make it say
anything. That's the beauty of it. By typing in a string of phonemes
you can make it say almost anything you want to say. Here, I have
something to show you. He went up to his room and brought down
a paperback book from a company known as Computalker Consul-
tants. "You should have a copy of this material to study. I will run a
copy off for you. This is the way it works: suppose you want to say
'hello,'you type in 'HHEH3LOW1.' Then, it says, 'hello.' You can
store any number of phrases."

He had lost me. But that wasn't anything. My computer science
professor always lost me in class so I asked Mark, "ARE YOU
SURE I CAN OPERATE THIS THING MY COMPUTER SCIENCE

PROFESSOR CAN TELL YOU IM STUPID WHEN IT COMES   143
TO COMPUTERS BUT HERE YOU ARE BUILDING ME A
COMPUTER THAT TALKS I DONT UNDERSTAND IT"

Mark sat on my bed and said, "First, you are working on a big computer system that was written to be generalized for many tasks. It is a very poor system because it was designed by several people who didn't know what each other was doing. If the designers don't communicate, the product will have flaws. Since I'm writing this program especially for you, it will work in a way that's convenient for you. Second, you're taking a course in computer science which even gives me trouble. Finally, if I, as a programmer, do my job right, the system will be so simple that anybody can operate it."

"IM SO UPSET OVER THIS DAMN COMPUTER COURSE I DONT KNOW WHAT IM DOING IM GETTING ERRORS ON TOP OF ERRORS I FEEL SO STUPID MY ERRORS ARE SO UNCOMMON THAT THE TEACHING ASSISTANTS CANT EVEN FIGURE THEM OUT" I said.

"If I can help you with any problem, don't hesitate to ask as long as it doesn't interfere too much with my school work," Mark offered.

"THANK YOU I NEED ALL THE HELP THAT I CAN GET"

I didn't need any help studying Wendy. That beat computer programming any day.

On Halloween night studying was impossible. Along with the ghosts and hob-goblins, rowdy freshmen roamed the halls of Selleck. Some thought it was the Fourth of July and set off firecrackers in the toilet. After the third explosion I gave up trying to study and called Wendy. With my headstick I dialed her number on my push-button speaker phone. Since push-button phones make an audible beep that could be heard on her end of the line, we had worked out a system where she could ask me yes or no questions and I would beep once for "yes," and twice for "no."

Wendy answered the phone with "Hello?"

"BEEP" I responded by pushing one of the numbers on my phone once.

"Hi, Bill. Do you want me to come to your room?"

"BEEP"

"Is it an emergency?"

144   "BEEP BEEP" I responded "no" by pushing one of the numbers on my phone twice.

"Okay, do you just want to talk and listen to tapes for awhile?"
"BEEP"

"How's about I come down in about an hour and a half?"
"BEEP"

"Okay. Goodbye, Bill. See you in a little while." She hung up. As I shut off my phone, I thought how different things would be when Mark finished my voice synthesizer. No more playing twenty questions over the phone. But I thought how good it felt to be able to call and ask Wendy to come over without involving a third party. More important, I thought how good it felt to have a friend who would take the time to play twenty questions over the phone.

Two hours later she came down and sat on my bed in her familiar Indian style. Another firecracker exploded in the toilet. She pushed the remote door control button on my tray. "There, that's much better," she said after the door had swung shut.

"Can I read some more of your writing?"

"OK," I spelled out.

She got my assembled stories from the desk and returned to her seat on the bed. She had a difficult time getting comfortable supporting the big scrapbook. She finally lay on her stomach and propped her head in her hands. The book lay face up on the bed.

"Hey, why don't you come over by the bed so I can see your board and you can see which article I'm reading. I don't like talking to people across the room."

I wheeled near her. It was a different experience for me to be this close to anybody, not to mention an attractive girl.

Once, a specialist in the field of orthopedics described putting a kid in a wheelchair as putting him in a cardboard box. His point had been that both a wheelchair and a cardboard box deform the kid's spine. But what he forgot to mention was as the child grows into young adulthood, his wheelchair continues to act like a box. It serves as a barrier to him touching and being touched.

When Wendy read a newspaper article about me that I didn't like, she curled her brow and said, "I don't like this one because it emphasizes your disability too much and doesn't focus on the real you."

When she said that, I reached out of my electric cardboard box and awkwardly massaged her back. It was soft to the touch. I was tired of mechanically spelling things to her with my headstick and wanted some other means of thanking her for looking beyond my cardboard box. I wanted to show her I cared. She didn't seem to object to the erratic massage. As I was giving her the massage, I realized that I was becoming sexually attracted to her, and I was afraid. Did I have the right to a sex life after all? Since Wendy was letting me rub her back, I began to think that maybe she was interested in me as a lover. After all, hadn't she said, "Bill, when you're in love, it doesn't matter if you can't walk"?

Could Wendy and I become more than just friends? Had the frog who used a headstick finally found his princess?

After she left, I began to worry. If I kept acting like this, I would scare her off for sure. The next time I saw her I would apologize for my behavior.

"HEY LOOK" I started to spell out the next time I saw her, "ABOUT ME RUBBING YOUR BACK THE OTHER NIGHT IM SORRY I DONT KNOW HOW I GOT STARTED"

"What do you mean you're sorry? I enjoyed it. To me, it was a sign of affection between two friends. That was what it was, wasn't it?"

I breathed a sigh of relief and nodded "yes." I was lying to myself as well as her. I resented the fact that I couldn't be honest about my sexual feelings for her. But I sensed that she wasn't ready for the truth so I kept it from her, a bad policy for a journalism major.

I didn't see much of Mark during November and December except for brief encounters in the hall. We were waiting for components for the synthesizer. But I saw a lot of Wendy. And, our friendship seemed to be developing nicely.

Her birthday was in November and I wanted to get her something special because our relationship was evolving into something special. But I didn't know what was appropriate.

I asked a female acquaintance living in the same dorm, "WHAT DOES A GUY GET A GIRL FOR HER BIRTHDAY WHEN THEY ARE JUST FRIENDS" I was getting good at lying to myself.

"Are they good friends?"

"YES THEY ARE DEVELOPING A GOOD FRIENDSHIP."

"Then, how about a yellow rose. It's the symbol of friendship between a man and a woman. Besides, she likes plants."

"HOW DID YOU KNOW" I asked.

146   "Let's just say I'm not blind. You spend all your spare time around her, so it's evident that you two have a good friendship going. And I'm happy for you. Let me know how she likes the gift."

For her birthday I gave my young 19-year-old friend a yellow rose surrounded by baby breath in an ivory vase. It was simple, yet beautiful, much like our friendship. But, it wouldn't last long, and that bothered me. I wished the rose and our relationship could last a lifetime. But something told me that our friendship would be as short-lived as the rose. Neither could survive the elements.

When I bought it, the florist said, "This rose should bloom tomorrow morning, so I suggest that you give it to your lady friend tonight if you want her to see it bloom."

When I saw the birthday girl at dinner, I spelled out, "CAN YOU COME TO MY ROOM TONIGHT ITS AN EMERGENCY" So I lied. I was getting good at it, and that worried me.

That night she came to my room.

"What's wrong Bill?" She asked, "What's the emergency?"

I motioned toward the little rose.

"Oh, who gave you the rose? It's beautiful."

"READ THE CARD" I spelled out, trying to hold down my excitement.

"Oh, Bill, thank you. I love it."

I didn't anticipate her reaction. She spontaneously hugged me. It felt so good to be hugged by Wendy. When a guy is in an electronic wheelchair, has an electronic control system to operate all other electronic gadgets for him, and can open and shut his door via radio transmitter, he starts wondering whether, or when, his doctor will start taking his ampmeter reading instead of his blood pressure. But when my friend put her arms around me, I was reassured that I was human. I felt tenderness and warmth.

"So, this was your 'emergency,' huh?" she said.

"THATS RIGHT. THE ROSE WILL OPEN TOMORROW MORNING AND I THOUGHT THAT YOU SHOULD WAKE UP TO A BLOSSOMING ROSE." I was recovering nicely from her hug. "DID YOU KNOW THAT A YELLOW ROSE IS A SYMBOL OF. . ."

"Of friendship between a girl and a guy?" she completed my

question. "Yes, and that's why I love it." I resisted the temptation to ask her if she would have accepted a red rose from me as graciously.

The absence of any plants in my room bothered Wendy. One night she brought down a baby cactus.

"Hello there. I brought you something," she said and showed me the plant. "Your room is so lifeless. I thought it could use something green. I potted it myself."

"THANK YOU VERY MUCH, BUT IM AFRAID I HAVE A BROWN HEADSTICK"

"Oh, but a cactus can survive a desert. Surely it can survive your care," she teased.

"DONT BE SO SURE" We both chuckled. She set the little cactus down on the desk beside the typewriter.

"How was your day?"

"TERRIBLE," I spelled out. "IM FAILING MY COMPUTER PROGRAMING COURSE BUT FOR THE GRACE OF THE INSTRUCTOR I JUST DONT UNDERSTAND PROGRAMING"

I made a sweeping motion with my hand and knocked the potted cactus to the floor. The pot smashed into bits and pieces. I looked at the uprooted cactus. She looked the way I felt, sick at heart. We both looked like we were going to cry any second as we looked at the cactus' roots among the scattered pieces of its pot.

"SEE WHAT I MEAN ABOUT PLANTS NOT SURVIVING ME," I spelled out. "IM SORRY I DIDNT MEAN TO KNOCK IT OVER MY HAND JUST FLEW AROUND"

"It's my fault, dammit." It was the first time I had heard her swear. "If I hadn't put the cactus where I did, you wouldn't have knocked it over. You need to have something alive in your room. Now, please back up while I get the broom. If we can find a pot or something to put it in, I can save it. Open the door so I can get the broom from the storage closet. I'll be right back."

In twenty minutes she had the room, the cactus, and my ego back together, and she did it with care and love.

I wanted to share my happiness with my friend and my former aide, Roger. He was trying to make a living by producing and selling ice. Roger wasn't like my aide who monopolized the supertime conversation. That aide was perverted and cruel. Roger, on the

148   other hand, was sensual and compassionate. At the first opportunity
I told him that I had found a "special" friend.

"Oh really?" Roger said, as he lit a cigarette. "Maybe we can
double date when I get through at the ice factory in early December.
There's not much of a demand for ice in the wintertime. I'll bring
my girlfriend, and the four of us will drink and disco up a storm. In
fact, you'll have to drive me home because I'll be so damn drunk. I'll
be celebrating my release from the ice factory."

I asked Wendy.

"Sure," she said, "I've never danced with a guy in a wheelchair
before, but it sounds like fun."

It was a cold December night when Roger carefully threaded my
long body into his girlfriend's sports car. Our big night at the disco
had finally arrived.

Someday I'll buy you a damn van," he said when he bumped both
our heads on the roof of the car. Then he closed the door, checking
to see that flying hands were out of the way. He masterfully wedged
my manual wheelchair into the tiny trunk. The two women
clambered into the back seat.

At the disco we found a tiny table and ordered. I had a Coke
without ice as usual. I take Valium to control my muscle spasms.
Valium and alcohol don't mix.

When the drinks came, Roger stood up. "Here, I can give him his
Coke."

Wendy asked, "Why can't I give him his drink? Just show me
how."

"Oh, okay. You just pour it in his mouth, and try to pour it in the
left side. Otherwise he'll choke." Roger instructed.

She tried to give me a swallow, but her aim was slightly off and
the Coke went down the outside of my throat. Quickly she wiped it
with my napkin.

"What did I do wrong? Oh, I'm sorry." It was evident that she was
more upset than I.

"YOU FORGOT TO HIT MY MOUTH" I spelled out and threw
my head back and laughed.

Roger shouted above the loud din of rock-'n'-roll music, "We are
going to dance. I can get you down on the dance floor. Do you want
to dance?"

I looked at Wendy questioningly.

"Let's do it," she shouted.

People in the disco stared unbelievingly when Roger bounced my wheelchair down the three steps that led to the sunken dance floor. Wendy took my headstick off, stowed it, took my hand in hers, and proceeded to dance with me.

I made my wheelchair shake, rattle, and roll. This type of dancing has its advantages. Wild erratic movements, something that my body has all the time, are acceptable. Of course, when Elvis did it, it was called sexy and seductive. When I do it, people think I'm having a seizure.

As he was putting me to bed (my regular night attendant didn't want to wait up for me), Roger said, "I like your new friend. She seems really nice. Congratulations, buddy. I'm really happy for you. From what I saw you two have a special relationship going, and I think you're lucky. If I wasn't so drunk, I wouldn't be saying this."

I went home for Christmas break and Wendy and I went out by ourselves. It was the first time that a woman had the courage to take me out alone. My family was concerned. Suggestions included, "Don and his buddy could take you in our car and pick you up."

No. I didn't want to be escorted by my little brother and his friend.

"How about if Don and his friend followed you in their car? If you should get in trouble, they would be there to help. Sort of like passers-by."

It was tempting, but it made the outing too much like "Mission: Impossible."

"SHE THINKS SHE CAN HANDLE IT AND SO DO I," I spelled impatiently. "IF WE DIDNT THINK WE COULD HANDLE IT WE WOULDNT TRY IT"

But my family's concerns were justified. Wendy was short, and I was tall. The center of balance would make it easy for me to topple us. It was a risk, but I wanted badly to go out alone with Wendy.

My family let me do it my way. When Wendy came to get me, Mom carefully showed her how to transfer me. Mom then asked, "Are you sure you can handle his long lanky body?"

"I think so." Then, more firmly, Wendy said, "Yes, I can."

She had a little trouble getting me out of the car. My wheelchair

150   kept slipping away from us because its brakes were shot. But we somehow managed to get my body in the wheelchair and not on the cold, hard parking lot.

When we were in the small bar, the waitress asked Wendy, "And, what does he want to drink?"

"I don't know. Why don't you ask him?" she replied.

The waitress repeated her question to me.

"COKE" I slowly and carefully spelled.

Wendy helped the waitress by saying each letter aloud as I pointed to it. She added, "Without ice."

When the drinks came, we chatted.

We talked about things unrelated to school until the waitress told us the bar was closing.

"HOW ABOUT A CHRISTMAS HANDSHAKE" I asked Wendy as we were leaving.

"A Christmas handshake? Are you sure you want a handshake and that's all?"

"SURE," I lied.

As we walked through the bitter December night cold to her station wagon, she said, "Well, Bill, I don't give my handshakes to anybody, and I certainly don't shake hands where others can see."

When we got to her car, she shook my hand. Then, she said, "Close your mouth."

I did.

She gave me a Christmas kiss and a hug.

"There. Isn't that what you really wanted?" she asked softly.

I nodded. I wanted her to kiss me. She was special, and I was emotionally and sexually attracted to her, but I kept denying it, hoping my feelings would go away like a bad case of acne. Self-deception is the same as Russian roulette: sooner or later the game has to end. The kiss made me realize that I loved her.

Four days after Christmas an old friend came to my house. I was reading an exciting detective novel when my dad exclaimed, "Isn't that the girl Bill used to know coming up the ramp? Damned if it isn't! Lois, come quick and open the door. Never figured we'd see her again."

"Mrs. Rush, I don't know if you remember me," I heard Deanne saying. "It has been so long."

"Sure, I remember you," Mom replied, "Come in."

"Hi, Bill," Deanne said, "say something to me."

Although Deanne and I had been corresponding and exchanging birthday cards since May, this was the first time I had seen her in seven years. Her coming over to my house made me feel that the wounds of the past were completely healed.

"Give him a minute," Dad said, "He's keyed up. Bill, calm down."

My mom handed my clipping scrapbook to Deanne saying, "I thought you might like to take a look at what he has written during the past three years."

"Thank you. You know, I too have kept a scrapbook of his writing," Deanne said.

I was touched to hear that Deanne had done that. From that moment I thought of her as a part of my family because only family would take the time to compile a scrapbook about another person.

"Hey, Deanne," Dad said, "ask him how he likes computer programing. He got an incomplete in the course and was very upset. He would type in a whole screen of programing, accidently hit the erase button and zap what he had just typed."

"I know. I had a project involving computers for speech pathology, and I could not do the project," she sympathized.

"It really upset him, getting an incomplete for the first time. A lot of good people are behind him. During his first year down at UNL he kept saying, 'What if I blow it? What if I blow it?' So he's really stewing about this incomplete," Mom said.

"I can imagine," Deanne agreed.

"BUT I WILL COMPLETE THE COURSE NEXT SEMESTER FOR SURE," I spelled out.

Deanne glanced at the clock, and said, "Oh, dear, I should have picked up my husband ten minutes ago. He is probably wondering if our car has broken down."

"I WANT TO MEET YOUR HUSBAND" I spelled to her.

"And he wants to meet you too," Deanne assured me.

At the door Dad said to Deanne, "You have made Bill's day by stopping, you know that, don't you?"

CHAPTER 15

COMPUTERS AND HEARTACHES

When I went back to school in January, Mark Dahmke finally had enough of the needed parts to start building a prototype of my voice synthesizer. We spent many hours discussing what features I needed on the keyboard. We would suggest ideas to each other, modify, alter, change, refashion, and vary them. It seemed that every time that I presented Mark with a communication problem, he knew how to solve it.

Also, in January, I wanted to develop a different, nonplatonic relationship with Wendy.

I analyzed it from a jounalistic point of view. Six questions needed to be answered to make a story solid. One: Who? Wendy. Two: What? Sex. Three: Why? Love. Four: When? Now. Five: Where? I didn't care. Six: How? Unanswered.

So, I asked her if we could become more than just friends.

"Perhaps we shouldn't see so much of each other for awhile. I'm not running from you. I'll still be your friend, but not as close," Wendy said slowly.

My common sense told me that it was the beginning of the end. But what has common sense got to do with love?

How kept drumming in my brain. All my life, people had helped me to find the answer to that question: How? But, this time I had to find the answer myself.

One day in February Mark came up to me and said, "Dr. Schwab is coming to see the synthesizer. It would be neat if you could operate it for her, but I don't think I can bring it down to your room because I'm using my home-built computer to develop it. And you can't come up to my room, can you?"

Mark had never asked me any favors, but he was asking me one now. He was giving me a voice, so how could I refuse?

"YES I CAN COME UP IN THE MANUAL WHEEL CHAIR TWO FRIENDS CAN HAUL ME UP I DONT THINK THEY WOULD WANT TO MAKE IT A HABIT BUT THIS IS AN OCCASION THEY WILL WANT TO HEAR THE VOICE WHEN SHOULD I COME UP" I asked.

Then the answer to my problem with Wendy suddenly dawned on me. My new voice synthesizer.

On Valentine's Day I would tell her—not spell it, but tell her—that I loved her. I would put a poem on tape for her using my voice synthesizer.

I asked Mark if I could after showing the voice to Schwab, and he thought it was a classy idea.

For the demonstration I brought a book of quotations that had the poem. When I was wheeled into his room Mark was sitting at his home-built computer, demonstrating the system to her. He interrupted his chat with Schwab and said, "Well, this is your voice."

He indicated a big gray box with a keyboard that sat on his desk "Let's see. How's the easiest way to do this so that you can get to the keyboard? Did you bring your copy of the stuff about the voice synthesizer?"

My friends produced a sheet of phonetic spelling from my wheelchair knapsack. The paper listed words in English followed by their phonetic spelling.

Schwab looked up and asked, "Well, Bill, are you going to talk to us?"

I nodded yes and laughed nervously. I wished Mark had introduced me to the synthesizer before this. I could have practiced with it before demonstrating my lack of skill to the director of the Independent Living Center. I also wished I had Mark's confidence in me. I kept telling him that computers and I didn't get along, but he didn't seem to listen.

"All right, Bill, my keyboard is a little different than the ones where you have been doing your programming assignments," Mark said with a smile. Then he began to explain his keyboard.

After a quick shuffle of chairs, my buddies had me in front of

154   Mark's computer keyboard. I was facing a TV video screen. Mark typed in "GO."

"I have to enter this command to start the voice synthesizer. On the final version, you won't have to do anything because the program will come up automatically," Mark explained. "Also, we won't have this long a wait."

Mark's computer's disk drive made clicking noises for about a minute. I looked bewildered, and Mark pointed out, "It's loading the program from my computer to the new one I'm setting up for you. It takes a long time but the final version will load in about two seconds."

When the program for the synthesizer was loaded into the computer's memory, Mark began to explain his brain child. "As it is now, it has four modes, English, phonetic, spelling and direct.

"When you're in English mode, you can type everything in normal English. The phonetic mode is included so you can store words that aren't already in the machine's dictionary. That means that if a word isn't available, you can sound it out, store it, and it'll be in there forever."

I was reminded of the old television program "Get Smart," starring Don Addams. The Chief would explain a complicated mission saying, "Now, listen carefully Max. . ." After the explanation the Chief would ask Max, "Did you get all of that, Max?"

"All except one tiny part," Max would reply.

"Which part was that?" the Chief would ask patiently.

"The part after 'Now, listen carefully, Max.'"

I was beginning to empathize with Don Addams because Mark had lost me right after he said, "As it is now. . ." But I didn't really want to appear stupid in front of Schwab, so I prayed that what Mark was saying would fall in place soon.

"Before we start working on your poem, I want to show you all that this can do. For example, in the spelling mode it can be used just like your present letter board. Watch this." Mark touched a button and started to type out the alphabet on the keyboard. But instead of just printing the letters on the TV screen, the computer mechanically said, "A-B-C." I nearly went through Mark's ceiling. It could also say "One-two-three." It sounded like a Swedish Lawrence Welk.

"Calm down, Bill, there's more. You can type in a phrase in English and it will say it," Mark calmly said. "You can also store phrases and use a single key to say the phrase in the direct mode. It also has an unlimited vocabulary because when you're in the phonetic mode, you can create new words.

"Now," Mark said, "where's that poem you want to recite?"

The poem explained my feelings about Wendy precisely. Its first line was "I love you."

"Ah here it is." Mark said, looking through my knapsack. "See, the words 'I' and 'You' are already stored. All we have to do is enter 'Love' and we'll have the first line of the poem."

Mark gingerly typed LAHV into the computer and pushed the enter button. It was close to sounding like "love," but it had too little V sound. Mark tried again: LAHVV. Too much V sound. He tried LLAHVV. Sounded like a drunken Swedish sailor concentrating too much on making his L's and V's sound plain.

"MAY I TRY" I spelled to Mark who was slowly getting frustrated.

"Go ahead. The poem is your Valentine's Day gift."

Trying to piece together my fragmented knowledge of this computerized phonetic system, I tried LAH2V. (The 2 was a stress mark.) The voice synthesizer had pity. It said "love" very plainly. Schwab was on her feet, smiling with Mark.

"He catches on quickly. Good job, Bill," she enthusiastically said. "Just think. Your first spoken word was 'love.'"

Then, Schwab turned to Mark and said, "Call me in the morning with an estimated price list. I have to run. Good-bye, you guys."

"Quick, type in BAY3," Mark whispered. I did, and the computer shouted, "Bye" to Schwab as she was going out the door.

After Schwab left we worked on the poem. Both Mark and I are meticulous, so the project took longer than we had figured.

Two hours passed, and we were still working feverishly on the poem. My two friends came to Mark's room to take me back downstairs, and we were only half finished with the project. I looked at Mark panic-struck.

"I'll finish the poem. It'll still be your poem recited by your voice."

I had no choice but to accept Mark's help. I couldn't afford to take another night away from study, and I didn't have the heart to ask my buddies to haul me up to the third floor again.

156   When I returned to my room, I studied for about an hour. Then, as one of my aides was preparing me for bed, we heard a knock at the door. My friend-cum-aide answered it.

"Hi, is Bill still up? I have something for him. May I come in?" Mark asked.

After my friend had draped me, he reopened the door and Mark came in, looking crestfallen.

"It didn't come out as well as we had hoped. The voice didn't come across on the tape. Anyway, here the tape is and you can listen to it and decide whether you want to play it for your girlfriend."

The next morning I listened to the tape of my synthesized voice reciting the poem. Mark was right. The tape had damaged the quality of the voice. I could understand it, but anybody who didn't know the poem wouldn't.

Well, perhaps it was for the best. I didn't know exactly how Wendy would take a poem that had "I love you" in it. I thought about the unfairness of our friendship: She could hug and kiss me, but I didn't have the luxury of telling her that I loved her. What did she expect me to do? The problem boiled down to finding an answer to the sixth question: How? How? I supposed I could join the priesthood, but the same question popped into my head. How? I wasn't even Catholic.

Suddenly, I remembered that I had an appointment with my computer science professor to discuss how I was going to make up my incomplete in his lovely programming course. I didn't know how I was going to do that either. It seemed "How" was ruining my life these days.

"And how is my little robot today?" he asked as I wheeled into his office.

I resisted telling him that I needed to have my amps checked and that my heart was about to blow a fuse.

The reference to me being a robot was my electronic wheelchair, which intrigued him. His referring to me wasn't meant with any disrespect. It was sort of a private joke between us, but today I didn't find it funny.

He was, by nature, a mechanical fiddler. When I brought up the problem that the terminals didn't have a shift-lock so that I could enter my assignments into the computer, he designed something that would hold down the shift key that same night. Later, he designed a better shift key and put it on the terminal. From then on the modified terminal had a sign saying, "When Bill Rush comes in, please vacate this terminal."

"HI" I spelled. "IM ABOUT DONE WITH THE GRAPH PROJECT OR AT LEAST I THINK IM ABOUT DONE WITH IT BUT I DONT KNOW HOW TO BEGIN THAT LAST PROJECT"

"Ah, yes, you mean the project where you have to solve the algebraic equation. You have already told me that you weren't any good at algebra. And I have told you that I didn't expect you to do that assignment. I have another special assignment for you. Will you come to the terminal room with me?"

On the way to the terminal room, I thought of Wendy. She hadn't called me a robot, but she didn't regard me as a man either. I didn't know what she regarded me as. It was as frustrating as a terminal without a shift-lock key. Maybe the computer science professor could rewire her for me.

When we were settled at the terminal, which looks like a television set cross-bred with a typewriter, the professor said, "Now, what I want you to do instead of the last assignment is to write a story using the computer. I want to show you what a tremendously powerful tool a computer can be for you in your writing career. I have written a program that is for text editing and I'll give it to you to do this assignment."

"YOU MEAN I WONT HAVE TO WRITE A PROGRAM" I asked.

"That's right, Bill. All you need to do is to write a story, using my program. Now to show you how it works."

"WHAT DOES IT HAVE TO BE ABOUT" I asked the professor.

"Anything you wish. I'm primarily interested in getting you to use the computer as a tool. As far as I'm concerned, you can hand in five pages of nursery rhymes."

When the professor had left to help another student, I continued working on my graph program which had me pulling my hair out by the roots, and I thought how easy my other assignment would be compared to making a graph. The hardest part would be picking a subject that I wanted to write about.

My friendship with Wendy was deteriorating. We still saw each other because we took the same anthropology class. She walked with

158   me to class, set up my tape recorder and went through the motions of friendship, but the spontaneity and fun was gone.

I had decided to write our story as the computer course assignment. The voice synthesizer hadn't worked, but logically — or illogically—I thought a story about my current friend would put this friendship back together again like Humpty Dumpty. And it would make the computer science professor see that I wasn't a robot.

I had another reason for writing about Wendy. I wanted to give her something that was a part of me. A story was the only thing that I honestly could say was mine to give.

I overestimated my writing ability. I labored over my offering and kept up with my other course work.

My story, while technically perfect, lacked depth.

When my friend read my offering, she slowly asked, "Are you going to publish this?"

"IT WAS TO COMPLETE MY COMPUTER COURSE AND I THOUGHT MAYBE IF IT WAS PUBLISHED IT WOULD BE A SPECIAL GIFT FOR YOU"

"I don't want you to publish it. Why did you write it anyway? It has a lot of personal stuff in here, stuff I don't want to share with strangers," she said quietly.

A little voice in the back of my head said, "You have blown it again, Rush. Grab that story out of her hand and eat it quickly. Go back to the computer and write about Little Bo Peep or Jack and Jill."

Then the slow realization that it was April and the end of the semester was breathing down my back. I had to hand it in to complete my damn computer course. I was trapped. I should have tried the nursery rhymes. It seemed as though I was sort of a cross between Georgie Porgie and Humpty Dumpty.

I asked her to tell me what she didn't like, I would change it to her liking. She wouldn't, or couldn't, help me.

I didn't know why she objected to the story. Maybe she was just extremely shy and valued her privacy. Maybe she was ashamed to have others read about the affection she had shown me. Maybe she hugged and kissed me just out of pity. I wondered if she had used me to test her skills at rehabilitation counseling. I hated feeling like an experiment.

I asked a lot of people for advice on the story, and I got what I asked for: a lot of advice. Opinions ran from one extreme to the other, from "The story is a beautiful gift and she is immature" to "You have invaded her privacy and have betrayed her."

All of this advice was useless. The semester was drawing to a close. I had to hand in the story to my professor. The extra time and attention, not to mention the cost of the computer time, could not be thrown away. I had to finish the course as soon as possible.

I told Wendy I had no choice but to submit her story for my assignment.

"It's your story. Do what you want," she replied.

When I went to the professor's office, he was not there so I had somebody slip it under his office door with this note, "Here's my last assignment for the course. I can see how a computer can help me in my writing. But your program is a little bit time consuming for me. Please throw this assignment away after you have graded it. Sincerely, Bill."

That night I had one of my floormates help me call the computer science professor to make sure he had received the story.

"Yes, I got it. It was perfect. He has an A in the course."

"Thank you very much, Professor. I think Bill is in shock. Well, good-bye."

My dormmate hung up my phone and said, "Son of a gun, you pulled it out. Congratulations."

I looked at my little cactus next to my environmental control system. Wendy had given it in the fall along with her friendship. Both were dying. The A in the computer course had come at a high price.

Although Wendy's friendship was faltering, the voice synthesizer was proving to be a success. Everything worked, but several important parts were still on backorder so Mark couldn't give it to me permanently. Mark expected to have everything done by the end of the semester, but that was somewhat optimistic. Finals week came and went, but the parts still didn't come. Mark moved to the summer dorm, and I moved back to Omaha.

To our dismay, it ended up taking until July to get the parts. However, it seemed appropriate that I would get the synthesizer on the tenth-year anniversary of Neil Armstrong's trip to the moon, for the synthesizer would prove to be a giantic leap for me.

When Mark put everything together and drove to Omaha to give it

160   to me and show me how to use it, it didn't seem like a leap. The next day my mom called Mark to say that it had "broken." Mark questioned me through my mom and discovered that a minor programming error, one Mark had not noticed, caused the system to overwrite the dictionary of words on the diskette. After an extended phone conversation, we managed to solve the problem.

After the ordeal mom said, "I thought this thing would let you talk on the phone by yourself. I don't like it. It's too complicated for me."

Mark and I tried to explain that the system, as did all new systems, had a few bugs in it. But mom's reply was usually, "Fine. I will get bug spray and spray the stupid thing," or "Then why bother Mark? Shouldn't I call an exterminator?"

I couldn't blame her. This kind of thing went on for the rest of the summer. My mom would call Mark and say, "Bill's computer is buggy again."

My life was buggy that summer. I loved my new voice synthesizer and wanted to share my happiness with my parents. They were intimidated by this new electronical marvel. They didn't know how to fix it, and they felt obligated to fix my stuff as they did when I was a child.

When I was a boy, I thought Dad could fix anything with his magic pliers, and Mom could heal anything.

Now, Dad's fingers were too big for the delicate innards, and Mom couldn't handle my pain over Wendy.

Finally, I realized that I was growing up and leaving the nest emotionally as well as physically, which was normal, and natural.

In August, Mark and his sister took a vacation, a 10-day trip to the East Coast. It was his only chance to get away before classes began. We still had problems with the voice synthesizer that fall, but the problems decreased. Problems with Wendy increased.

Mark made minor improvements on the computer. Wendy moved off campus, causing major complications in our relationship.

I thought most of my communication problems were solved. The rest of my life would be duck soup. Sure it would.

PART FIVE

JOURNEY INTO AND OUT OF ACADEMIA

CHAPTER 16

RELUCTANT PROFESSOR

"'I'm afraid he can't take this course," I heard the journalism professor whisper to my male attendant.

"Why not? He's signed up for it," my aide pointed out.

"This is a professional school, and we must keep our high standards. The work is too demanding for him. I'm sorry," the professor said.

"Oh come on. You can't keep him out of this class. You have no right. It's the law," my aide countered.

"One of the requirements is a student type forty words a minute. Can he do that? And another thing, can he meet a weekly deadline?" the journalism professor asked my aide.

"I DON'T KNOW ABOUT THE 40 WORDS A MINUTE BUT I CAN MAKE THE WEEKLY DEADLINES," I spelled to the professor. I hated to interrupt the conversation.

"Can he stay for today at least? I have an appointment, and I can't take him back to the dorm," my aide asked the professor. (A January snow had forced me to use my manual wheelchair.)

"I suppose so, but he should drop this course as soon as possible," the professor reiterated.

My aide glared at him with contempt, and turned to me and said, "It's none of my damn business. You handle him. Goodbye. See you around five."

I wished my aide would have remembered that before he alienated the professor. But, he lacked tact and didn't believe in the old adage, "You catch more flies with honey than vinegar."

The journalism professor was of the old school of journalism, as I soon would learn. He looked past fifty-five. His voice had a trace of an

164   Oklahoma accent. He had used tried and proven methods and he didn't see any reason for changing his ways.

"Welcome to Newswriting and Reporting. This is a weekly class that meets three and a half hours a session. I urge you not to miss a class because if you do, it would be like missing a whole week of a one-hour class.

"Since this class is on writing, that's what you'll do. You will be expected to hand in one news story a week and to do some timed writing exercises in class because journalists have to write under pressure," the professor began mechanically.

Maybe it was my paranoid imagination, but I could have sworn that he glanced at me when he mentioned the timed writing. I shivered. Perhaps he was right. Maybe I should drop this course. I obviously couldn't handle the timed writing exercises. But, on the other hand, why couldn't he waive the time requirements like other professors had done?

"Now, I have these cards for you to fill out. They're for the office record and for my record," he said and passed out three census cards to every student except me.

"Since you're dropping this course, you won't have to fill out a card," he whispered.

I sat in on the rest of his introductory lecture. He stressed the importance of speed and accuracy in covering the news. He introduced the class to proofreaders' marks, carefully explained the correct way to head our papers, and showed the class good and bad examples of newswriting. Finally he gave the class an assignment.

"I want you to write me a letter about anything you want before you leave today," the professor instructed.

I saw my chance to persuade him to let me stay in his class. I motioned to the professor to put paper in the typewriter. He did reluctantly and said, "You don't have to write me a letter since you're dropping the class."

"LOOK MY AIDE WONT BE HERE FOR ANOTHER HOUR AND A HALF SO I MIGHT AS WELL DO SOMETHING RIGHT," I spelled.

"I suppose so," the journalism professor said. He rolled newsprint in the typewriter.

"I never could get used to these electric typewriters. I have a manual in my office, and it has served its purpose."

When the newsprint was in, I began the letter. I said that all I could do was write. I told him that I didn't expect to be a reporter for a daily paper. I reminded him that Arthur Hailey and Ernest Hemingway were journalists turned authors. I told him that I thought I could benefit from his class. I politely asked him to reconsider not letting me stay in his class.

I gave him the hurriedly written letter, and he went in his office to correct it. Ten minutes later he came out and handed the letter back. I got a C+ on it with a note that said he took off for incorrect spelling and then asked how I would do interviews.

After class I told him that I planned taping the interviews and playing the tapes back while writing the story.

"I hope you don't expect to have a job on a newspaper because the deadlines are too short. You can take my class if you promise to drop journalism. You'll be better off to major in something else like English," the professor said.

I nodded my head in agreement. I had seen the results of arguing with him.

"Damn, I thought I could be a journalist," I said to myself as I left the building.

That night I told Roger of my encounter with the journalism professor. Roger was concerned, but he, like me, didn't know what I should do. Both of us worked hard for two years for my goal of becoming employed as a journalist. Both of us felt as if the rug had been pulled out from under us.

"If you didn't take Valium, I'd offer to get you drunk, buddy," Roger joked.

A few days later I met a fellow journalism student who lived on my dorm floor.

"How's your journalism course coming?" he asked.

I told him what my newswriting professor had said.

"He can't do that. No professor can tell a student to drop his major. What did Dean Copple say? As the head of the J-school, he should have something to say about you enrolling in journalism."

"HE WAS VERY SUPPORTIVE WHEN I FIRST CAME TO UNL," I spelled.

"I'll be happy to call him for you," the journalism student offered.

I said he could use my speaker phone since I wanted to be in on the conversation.

166   "Hello, this is the Copple residence," a voice said flatly.

My friend asked for Dean Copple. After a few seconds a gruff no-nonsense voice came on and said, "Hello, Copple here. Who is this?"

"This is Bill and Tom—Bill Rush and Tom Anderson. Bill has a problem. His newswriting professor told him he couldn't major in journalism because of his physical handicap. We were wondering if you agreed with him," Tom said sincerely.

"Well, while it's true that some requirements are impossible for him to do, we can waive them for him," Dean Copple replied.

"Sir, you're on a speaker phone, so Bill can hear you," Tom told the head of journalism.

"Oh, excuse me. As I was saying, Bill, certain requirements for a journalism major can't be done by you. But I'll be glad to waive those for you or substitute something that you can do. For example, for a broadcasting course I might ask you to read books on broadcasting instead of doing a broadcast," the journalism director explained.

"DO YOU HAVE ANY IDEAS FOR EMPLOYMENT AFTER I GRADUATE?"I spelled to Tom, and he repeated my question to Dean Copple.

"Well, isn't your graduation a little bit off? We'll worry about that when the time comes," the director said.

I thanked him and hung up. At least I was reassured that the J-school wanted me. It was a good feeling to be wanted.

When I told Mark Dahmke that I was not being accepted by my journalism professor, Mark said, "I know how you feel. When I started grade school in 1962 in Osceola, I remember causing the kindergarten teacher trouble because I knew how to write—not print—my name before I had even started school. So when we had to print the letters of the alphabet, I did the printing and signed my name in the upper corner when I turned it in to be graded.

"I always seemed to cause problems for my teachers because I never was interested in what was going on in class, and I wanted to talk about Project Mercury."

"BUT MY PROFESSOR SAID THAT I WAS TOO SLOW TO BE A JOURNALIST" I said.

"Using the typewriter you probably are," Mark said flatly, "but we can fix that very easily. When I build your voice, I plan to stick in a word processing/text editing program. It won't be able to speak, but what you can do with this kind of program is write a story, save it in a file on disk, and then go back into the file to rewrite it without having to retype it. It works really slick. We can even interface it with your IBM Selectric. Since you can't write and talk at the same time anyway, when the voice program isn't being used, the text editing program can be."

The newswriting course was hard. The professor gave us students assignments such as covering a speech, conducting a man-on-the-street survey, using more than one source for a story, and writing a human interest story. I did all the assignments.

The most difficult one was the man-on-the-street poll, but where there's a will, there's a way, or so I heard.

I wrote my questions, which were:

"1. What is your name?

2. How old are you?

3. What is your occupation?

4. Are you superstitious about Friday the Thirteenth?

5. Why or why not?"

Mom taped the questions onto my tray along with a blank tablet and two pencils so people could write their answers and left me in the parking lot of our neighborhood 7-11 store. (I did this assignment on the weekend when I was home without the motorized wheelchair.) She told the store manager what I was doing, or trying to do, so he wouldn't think I had been abandoned.

Mom was reluctant to leave me over at the 7-11, so she suggested, "Why don't I call eight people and ask them your questions over the phone? It'll be faster and easier for you and less nerve-racking for me."

I shook my head "no" and spelled, "THAT WOULDNT BE HONEST ITS YOUR FAULT YOU ALWAYS TAUGHT US TO BE HONEST"

I remembered her offer as I sat in front of the store for two hours. Some ignored me. Some went out of their way not to stare. Some did stare. Some—God bless them—came to me and filled out my survey.

Around noon, Uncle Alan and Cousin Andy came to visit. Mom

168   told them where I was and what I was doing, so they came to check on
my progress. I showed Uncle Alan that I had gotten six people to
respond to my survey.

"That's terrific. But you need some kind of a sign to attract people.
Otherwise, some people won't understand what you're doing. They
might think you're selling pencils or something."

I laughed and nodded my agreement. I needed something to clarify
my sit-in.

"Tell you what. Why don't you take a break for lunch, and I'll make
the sign," my uncle, my childhood friend who was now an industrial
engineer for an computer company, suggested.

After lunch I resumed my post at the 7-11. Uncle Alan's sign said,
"I am a journalism student. I am doing a man-on-the-street interview.
Would you please let me interview you?"

The sign worked. More people stopped. By mid-afternoon I had
more than enough answers for the assignment.

When I handed in the story, the professor admitted, "When I gave
this lesson, I wondered how you were going to do it."

I told him how I did it, and he was impressed.

However, there were times when he wasn't impressed. He told us
to cover a speech of our choice. He gave the class pointers on covering
a speech.

"You can't record the whole speech, so pick out the major points of
the speech. Don't use a tape recorder to capture every word, but rather
use a pad and pencil to jot down ideas, paraphrases, and direct quotes.
Don't rely too heavily on direct quotes. Try to use an equal mixture of
your words and the speaker's words. Try to get an interview with the
lecturer before or after the speech to get his or her background."

I began to wonder if the professor hadn't been right in the first
place. I had to use a tape recorder because I couldn't jot down things,
and I didn't know how I was going to get an interview with the
speaker. It was going to be an interesting assignment.

That night in the cafeteria I explained the problem to Wendy, and
she said, "I'm giving a speech for my speech class Friday. You could
cover that if you want. I'll check with my instructor but I'm sure it'll be
okay if you sit in on my class Friday. I just hope my speech is good
enough for your paper."

Our plan was that I should meet her ten minutes before her class to set up my tape recorder and to get my body seated in an out-of-the-way location. Then, afterwards I would discretely disappear from the classroom with the help of my aide.

Unfortunately, my aide didn't cooperate with us. Wendy's class was right after lunch, so I wanted to skip lunch to insure I wouldn't be rushed. But, my aide wouldn't let me. He said, "As your aide, I'm responsible to see that you're fed three times a day. Besides, we'll have lots of time to make it to the speech class. Don't worry."

We didn't have enough time. I got to the speech class just as the instructor was making his opening remarks, and I didn't have the heart to ask Wendy to set up my tape recorder while he was talking. I would have to ask her for her notes later. I would have to rely on my memory.

Her speech was good but hardly newsworthy. She wasn't a recognized authority on her subject, so the general public wouldn't be interested in her opinion.

My journalism professor had a field day with this story. Before he read it to the class he said, "This is a perfect example of what not to do."

I blushed and typed to nobody in particular:

"I'm so glad I didn't hand in a mediocre example of what not to do."

When the professor read the note after class, he let the faintest of smiles pass his face.

A few days later Roger stopped by and asked, "How are you and your journalism professor getting along, buddy?"

"OK I GUESS IM GOING TO STAY IN JOURNALISM RE-GARDLESS OF WHAT HE SAYS" I spelled.

"Good. I went to see him the other day. I even dressed up and got my hair cut. Anyway, we talked. At first he was really defensive, but after awhile he relaxed. The problem, as I see it, was that you caught him off guard by showing up on the first day of class without anybody telling him about your physical handicap.

"When I was your aide, I used to talk to all your professors to ease the shock, but this professor wasn't told anything about you. Can you see why he was upset?" Roger asked and put out his cigarette.

I nodded but secretly wished that it didn't have to be that way.

"THANK YOU FOR TALKING TO HIM IM TOUCHED THAT YOU WENT TO THE TROUBLE"

170   "That's okay. I have two years of my life invested in you, and I was just protecting my investment," Roger joked.

On a story using more than one source, I proved to the reluctant professor, as well as to myself, Roger's two year investment wasn't wasted. The story was about a group of people who were disabled which professed to be an advocacy group for the disabled population. But the group was only helpful to its members. It had problems getting organized since three of its presidents resigned in a one year period. On the surface the organization seemed good and solid. But I had attended a few meetings and tired of them. I felt that its members concentrated too much on the proper parliamentary proceedings and not enough on issues such as attendant care, attitudinal barriers, and accessibility.

The organization thought it was doing a good job because it got the Lincoln mayor to ride one of the city vans for citizens with disabilities as a publicity gimmick.

I wrote the story and pointed out both the good and bad of the organization. The group did convince Lincoln to put in curb cuts and special parking in its downtown area, but on controversial matters regarding civil rights of people in institutions, it wouldn't take a stand.

The week after I handed in the story the professor came to me and said nonchanlantly, "If it's okay with you, I'm going to submit your story on the handicapped organization to our school paper. Every semester I get at least one human interest story on that group and what a good job it's doing, but your story took a different look at it. That's what makes your story good."

"HAVE YOU CHANGED YOUR MIND ABOUT ME BEING A JOURNALIST?" I asked.

"I don't know if you can or can't be a journalist. Not many people in your condition are journalists on a daily paper, but maybe you can work for a monthly or bimonthly publication. I just don't know anymore," was the instructor's reply.

CHAPTER 17

LIFE OF A PHOTOGRAPHER

" "You must redo this shot. It's not an action shot in the true sense of the word," my professor explained patiently.

"BUT" I argued, "ITS A PICTURE OF A WHEELCHAIR BASKETBALL GAME THERES ACTION SEE THE BALL GOING UP"

"Right, but there's no horizontal motion with the vertical movement. Therefore, it's not a stop action shot. Now, if I were you, I'd go down to some place like the track and shoot a jogger or the freshman football practice. I'm pretty sure the track's accessible," the instructor said.

I groaned.

"Remember, Bill, the slogan is: 'No guts, No glory,' " the photojournalism professor, who was also my advisor, chimed.

So, I took my Cannon AE-1 which was mounted to a special tray to the track. The camera had a motor drive, automatic shutter, and an automatic aperture. A retired camera dealer put a reflex viewer from a Brownie on top of the camera so that I could frame what I was shooting. Since the finder wasn't attached to the lens, I had to focus by judging distances, which was hard for me. Once I had judged—or guessed—the distance, I rotated the lens to the appropriate setting by using a ring that resembled a captain's wheel. I could move the camera mount up and down or left and right, but it required effort. I triggered the shutter by pushing the button on the hand grip of the motor drive. Then, in the lab, my professor developed the film and helped me make prints. I tried to remember my professor's slogan as I groped for a ramp onto the track-and-field section. I went around one fence post

172 and encountered steps. I backed up and tried the other branch of the Y-shaped fork. It looked promising. At least it sloped towards the field. I started down.

The incline was too steep. I lost control of my chair. I headed towards the end of the wide sidewalk. My right front wheel went off the side. Momentum and the sharp drop-off were enough to topple the 300 pound chair on its side. Like a good captain, I went down with my ship. What choice did I have?

"My name is Bill Rush. The year is 1979. I'm at UNL's track-and-field," I thought, to check for amnesia. "And I'll kill my professor. Should his death be slow or fast?"

A passer-by saw me on the ground and said the usual, "Oh my God!"

He knelt beside me and asked, "Are you all right?"

I nodded my head "yes" and laughed.

"Just a minute and I'll get help," the stranger said.

Then, he told another passer-by, "Get the campus police fast. He can't breathe."

I felt great until then.

One of the freshman football players made a beautiful catch.

"Damn, that would have made a nice shot for my assignment," I thought as I waited for the campus police. One wheel up, one wheel down, headstick sideways.

Two uniformed men came running, followed by the second passer-by. All four men pulled my electric wheelchair upright. The first passer-by made sure my torso followed the chair. I wondered how my chair and camera fared in the fiasco. My body would heal, but the expensive equipment would have to be repaired or replaced.

"Are you all right, sir?" asked the first officer.

I nodded my head "yes."

"Maybe we should call him an ambulance," the second officer suggested.

I shook my head "no."

I then spelled out, "CALL AAMCO (meaning AAMCO transmissions). I AM OK BUT I DONT KNOW ABOUT MY CHAIR HOWS MY CHAIR"

The policeman didn't understand, and started to speak into his walkie talkie, "We need an ambulance by the track. A quadriplegic tipped his chair off the sidewalk. He is conscious but unable to talk coherently. . . Over. . ."

I wanted to laugh and cry at once. I shook my head violently at the next mention of an ambulance. They got the message and talked to the dispatcher again, "Um, cancel the ambulance. The victim doesn't desire it."

"How does he talk to us?" the first officer asked the second.

"I think he talks by pointing to that letter chart beside his camera. Hey, I have to run. Sorry I can't be more help," the first passer-by said.

"Thanks," the first officer shouted to the departing passer-by. "Now, let's try again. Do you need an ambulance, sir?"

"NO I AM OK BUT I DONT KNOW ABOUT MY CAMERA AND CHAIR" I spelled slowly so the two officers could follow. MAYBE YOU SHOULD CALL AAMCO INSTEAD OF AN AMBULANCE"

The officers smiled. The first officer checked my camera and said it looked undamaged. The second officer checked the wheelchair and reported that the battery casing and the fuse holder had been broken.

"Who do we call now, sir?" asked the first officer.

"472-0733 OR THE SELLECK DESK 472-1075 MY AIDE SHOULD BE AT THE FIRST NUMBER IF HE ISNT CALL THE SELLECK DESK AND THEY WILL SEND A STUDENT ASSISTANT OUT TO GET ME" I spelled it slowly so that the officers could understand.

They did what I suggested over their two-way radios. I could hear the dispatcher five minutes later as she reported, "We didn't get anybody at the 472-0733 number, but the Selleck office is sending out somebody to get him. . . Over. . ."

When the Residence Director from Selleck arrived on the scene, so did my photojournalism professor.

"Rush," the prof greeted me light-heartedly, "you're going to have a police record as long as my arm if you don't watch it. Don't tell me your chair battery died again.

"A student who was monitoring the police calls came to my office and told me you were giving the cops a hard time, so I came to see if I could help."

"He didn't run out of juice. He tipped over," Doug, the Residence Director, or RD, said.

174   "Did you at least get some pictures before you tipped over, Bill?" joked the professor.

I shooked my head "no," and didn't laugh. I didn't feel like joking. I was cold, tired, and scared. I wanted to forget about the stop action shot. An "F" on this assignment suited me just fine.

"Now, Bill, you just took the wrong entrance," the professor soothed, "You'll have more luck if you go all the way around to the northwest entrance. I'm sure it's accessible. I'm also sure that as soon as your chair has recovered you will come back here and get a nice stop action shot. Notice how I said 'will.'"

What a day. Then a cheery thought popped into my mind. Wendy would stop by to listen to music and have a Coke with me. I would enjoy that and it would make up for my day at the track, I thought as Doug escorted me home.

When we got back to my dorm room, Paul was waiting with quiet calm and terrific humor.

"Hi strangers," he said as Doug wheeled me into the room. "A desk worker told me that you were experimenting taking vertical pictures at the track by tipping your chair over on its side. From the look on your face, I bet it didn't work too well. But the desk worker didn't give me much detail. She just told me you tipped over by the track."

The residence director related what happened as best he could. When he told Paul about the chair being broken, Paul immediately suggested, "Perhaps we should call the shop to see if we can get the chair in tonight. That way, Roger won't have to do it in the morning.

"Oh excuse us, Doug, we didn't mean to ignore you. It's just that the engineering shop closes in fifteen minutes, so . . ."

"I understand, Paul and Bill. I'll tell ya, he gets in more scrapes with the campus police than anybody I ever saw," the residence director teased. "I'll never forget when his battery died in the Avery parking lot. He totally baffled the cops. Well, I'll be seeing ya."

As soon as Doug left, Paul called the Engineering College and asked if he could bring the chair over to the shop. He explained what happened and that it was an emergency.

They told Paul he could bring it over, but it wouldn't be ready until the next afternoon.

"They also muttered something about a dirt bike," Paul reported when he hung up the phone.

Then, he quickly transferred me to my manual wheelchair and ran the disabled electric wheelchair over to the Nebraska Engineering Center.

"I'll be back in about ten minutes. Then I must get some typing done before we eat. What time did you say your female friend was coming?" Paul asked.

"NINE OCLOCK IM SORRY THAT THIS HAD TO HAPPEN WHEN YOU HAD A PAPER DUE THE NEXT DAY" I spelled.

"Forget it. If I had started on it sooner, I wouldn't be so crammed for time now," Paul said as he rushed out the door.

When Paul came back he said, "They said that we should call them tomorrow afternoon to see if the chair is done. Could you have somebody else do that? I must get this paper typed tomorrow."

I nodded "yes."

"Thanks," Paul said. He began typing.

He typed for half an hour, until my digital clock said 5:56. Then, he escorted me to the Selleck cafeteria, where I ate shoe leather roast beef, mashed potatoes that came out of a box, and canned fruit. It is hard to cook for over 150 people and still make the food palatable, let alone exciting.

When I was finished, Paul asked, "Is tonight the night for 'The Big Event'?"

"The Big Event" was our code word for a bowel movement. It was named so because of the work involved. My aide put a bed pan in my manual wheelchair, tied my ankles, thighs, and middle with surgical ties, and left me alone in the room for half an hour. A successful attempt meant another fifteen minutes to clean the bed pan.

I looked at the cafeteria clock. It said seven o'clock. We had two hours before Wendy came.

"YES LETS DO IT" I spelled.

After the bed pan and ties were in their proper places, Paul left to go down to the snack bar for a bite.

"I'll be back in twenty or thirty minutes," he said. He put a cassette tape in the player. He said "Good luck," and the door closed behind him.

Fifteen minutes later, I heard a knock at my door. (Fortunately, Paul had locked it.)

"Open up. It's me," Wendy's voice chimed. "What's the matter?

176   Doesn't your door opener work? Bill, I know you're in there. I can hear music."

I groaned behind the locked door.

"Bill, are you okay? Make a noise if you're okay," she said. Concern had replaced cheerfulness in her voice.

I tried to make a noise, but my throat was too tense. Nothing would come out—the eternal curse of a person with cerebral palsy: the more intense the effort, the more rebellious the body.

"Make a noise if I should get the RD to let me in. Oh, I'm worried. I'm going to get the RD. I'll be right back," Wendy said.

I panicked. I looked at my $3000 voice synthesizer across the room. It was useless to me now. Mark had wanted to equip it with a remote control, but I had discouraged him. I looked at my headstick lying on the bed and decided a remote control wouldn't have helped.

I'm usually a calm person. When the wheelchair tipped over, I was calm. I was calm even when the passer-by announced that I couldn't breathe. But the wheelchair tipping over had sapped my calm.

I felt like James Bond when Ian Fleming put him in a diabolical trap. But unlike good old 007, no author had written me a way out of this trap.

I looked around my dorm room that suddenly had turned into a prison cell. I saw the plaque that the Easter Seal Society had given me, "To William Rush for building a normal successful life," it said.

I saw the picture of the head football coach which I had taken. The whole Nebraska Journalism School had praised me for going to the coach and asking him to pose for it. I saw my plaques with expressions of courage. I saw the environmental control system which enabled me to control anything electrical in my room. I saw my night buzzer on the wall beside my bed. I saw my textbooks that had been recorded on cassette tapes. I saw the speaker phone by my voice synthesizer.

I was surrounded by over $5000 worth of sophisticated gadgetry. Yet, I was trapped. All these things didn't mean a damn thing at this moment. I had cut the back of my leg on the wheelchair. I was bleeding. I didn't care. I continued conducting *The Flight of the Bumble Bee* and doing the Twist. Adrenalin was surging through my veins. My heart was pounding wildly. I was naked from the waist to the knees, and any minute a young lady about whom I cared would come through my dorm door with my residence director. I felt as if somebody should flash a "TO BE CONTINUED" sign in front of me as in the movies or on television.

I started praying while tears of frustration poured down my face:

"God, help me. Having a female friend walk in on you while you're on the bed pan isn't healthy for the relationship. But, you know that, don't you? I'm begging you. Don't let it happen, please."

I could hear voices outside my locked door. It was my little friend and Doug.

"Well, he tipped his chair over, so I imagine that's why he couldn't open the door. . . Okay. . . I see. . . Well. . . " I could hear Doug saying.

I saw the door knob turn and heard a key jingle in the lock. I prepared myself to meet my company. Somehow I didn't think Emily Post would approve my attire.

"Hi, sailor. New in town?" said Paul; he was alone. "Your company is an hour early."

I went limp with relief and laughter.

"They were about five feet from the door when I came up from the snack bar. It's lucky I didn't have a second hamburger. Are you all right?"

I shook my head "no" and looked at my bloody leg.

"Oh, I'll put a Band Aid on that right away. Relax. Imagine that you have been run over by a semi. There, after that you are very relaxed. Dead, but relaxed." Paul worked as fast as he could to make me and my room presentable. As he worked, he said, "I sent your guest to the lounge. I think we should get her a watch and an appointment book."

In fifteen minutes Paul took me to the lounge to greet my company. Discretely he said, "Bill was busy doing something in his room. I'll let him tell you the details. Well, I think I'll go practice my flute."

The Engineering College had the chair repaired the next day.

"Any sane person would avoid the track after what happened yesterday," I told myself as I headed back to my Waterloo with the camera bolted onto my tray.

But, slowly and carefully, I crept along the narrow, bumpy sidewalk that led to the northwest gate of the track. It sloped down, so my chair might go out of control. I didn't know if this sidewalk had a curb cut. If it didn't, I would be in trouble.

Five minutes later I found out that I was in trouble. No curb cut. I

178 started to turn back. I hated to disappoint my photojournalism professor, but I didn't see any options.

Fortunately, a middle-aged jogger saw me and asked if I needed help. I explained my problem. He carefully held the front of my wheelchair as I drove my back wheels off the curb (with apologies to Everest and Jennings for abusing one of their children).

When we got inside the gate, I thanked the jogger.

"Forget it. What do you want to take a picture of?" the jogger asked.

"ANYTHING THAT HAS ACTION" I replied.

"You've come to the right place." the jogger reassured me. "Hey look, I have to get going. Do you think you can find somebody to help you out of here?" I nodded, and the jogger sprinted off to the fieldhouse.

I wandered around the track. I saw some football players practicing in the grass. They were too far away from me, so I tried to drive into the grass and got stuck. I remained stuck for half an hour until a football player saw me and helped me back onto the asphalt track.

"CAN I TAKE YOUR PICTURE DOING ANYTHING I AM A JOURNALISM STUDENT AND MY ASSIGNMENT IS TO GET A STOP ACTION SHOT" I explained.

"Sure. Wait here and I'll ask the coach if I can practice kicking field goals for you. Hey, don't you live in Selleck, on the first floor? I thought I recognized you," the football player said enthusiastically. His coach gave his okay as long as we did it away from the practice area. The coach didn't want me to get hit by a pass or by a blocker. I agreed with the coach.

I took five slightly-out-of-focus shots. Then the football player said, "Do you need help getting out of here? I know a quick way. C'mon, Pete, help me get this chair up some steps."

It took me two days to get into the track-and-field complex but only fifteen minutes to get out of it. The two football players pushed my chair up dangerously steep ramps, boosted it over steps, and carried it down steps until I was safely on familiar ground away from the track.

When I told the photojournalism professor about my experiences at the track, he chuckled and said, "Gee, Bill, since you had such a wonderful time at the track, I'll make the final exam to shoot something at the track. Don't you think that would make a good final?"

CHAPTER 18

LIFE IS COMING

My phone rang and rang while I hurried to get to it. But when I'm hurrying to do something, it takes me three times as long to do the task. Usually when I get my muscles relaxed enough to function, the line is dead when I answer. This wasn't the case this time because the phone kept on ringing.

When my headstick pressed the "on" button, a voice came over my speaker phone, "Hello, Bill. This is Dr. Schwab."

I scrambled to get my voice synthesizer turned on. I hit the "on" button and typed the command that would load up the program which enabled me to talk.

But in the meantime, Dr. Schwab had said, "Bill, how would you feel about some more publicity for you and Mark? The science editor from LIFE Magazine wants to do a story on new innovations for people who are disabled that resulted from the NASA space program. She would like you and Mark to be a part of the article. Perhaps I should come over to Selleck tonight instead of doing this on the phone. I'll stop by around 7:30. Have Mark call me back if that's not okay. Otherwise, I'll see you then. Bye."

The voice synthesizer loaded up the program just as Dr. Schwab hung up.

"Oh well, I'd better call Mark and tell him what's happening," I thought to myself as I turned the phone off and then back on again.

I dialed Mark's number and he answered on the third ring. "Hello? Oh hi, Bill, what's up?"

I switched to the number-letter mode, and began spelling quickly, "LIFE MAGAZINE WANTS TO DO A STORY ON US. . . DR SCH. . ."

180 "Hold on slow down. I'm sorry. I didn't get all of it. Who wants to do a story on us?"

"LIFE MAGAZINE," I spelled out slowly. Mark repeated the letters as they were said by his brain-child.

"Hmmm, interesting. Who told you about this?" Mark asked.

"DR SCWAB," I spelled out on the synthesizer. I was so excited I forgot the "H" in her name. "SHE IS COMING OVER TO GIVE US MORE INFORMATION AT 730"

"Okay, I'll be down in your room around 7:30. Tell me, who is doing the story? Did Dr. Schwab tell you who was doing the story?"

"THE SCIENCE EDITOR. . . I FORGOT HER NAME." I spelled out over the phone.

"Oh well, I'll see you at 7:30. Bye."

I pushed the "GOODBYE" button on the synthesizer and flipped off the speaker phone and the synthesizer.

I wasn't as excited as I should have been because I remembered other news stories about Mark and me and shuddered. They painted both Mark and me as supermen and concentrated too much on the mechanics of our lives. One such report ended with a picture of me heading across campus with the narrator saying: "Bill Rush, journalism student, extrordinaire," and Mark explaining his voice synthesizer like a scientist who never stepped out of his lab. It also had my photography professor saying how good I was at photography. I was having a hard time living up to that kind of press! (The same professor that bragged about me on television but had just given me a C on a test over the fundamentals of photography.) I would tell Dr. Schwab my concerns tonight. Maybe she could tell me what to do.

At 7:30 Mark came down to my room and asked, "Has Dr. Schwab come yet? Good. She hasn't. Do you believe this publicity?"

"I DONT LIKE BEING THE SUBJECT OF A SCIENCE ARTICLE I HOPE THIS ARTICLE TURNS OUT BETTER THAN THE THING ON TELEVISION." I spelled to Mark who was sitting on the bed.

"Yes, I know what you mean," Mark said as he shook his head. "That television spot was something else, but you must consider the source. It was produced by the University so it had to be super positive about you. Just the same, I know what you mean."

A light knock on the door interrupted our conversation. "Hi, Mark.

Hi, Bill," Dr. Schwab said cheerfully as she walked into my room.

"Did Bill tell you about Anne Fadiman of LIFE Magazine coming, Mark?"

"Only briefly. He didn't give me many details," Mark answered.

"Well, I met her at a rehabilitation conference this summer and she was looking for a person who uses electronic aids and Bill's name came up because I mentioned your work with the voice synthesizer. This intrigued Anne, and she asked me to talk to you about being the subjects of her article."

I moved to the voice synthesizer and began typing on the video display, "WILL THE ARTICLE BE JUST ABOUT MY TECH-NOLOGICAL AIDS OR CAN I BRING UP OTHER THINGS"

"It's primarily going to be about how technology has broadened your life, but I suppose other areas will be covered as well," Dr. Schwab replied.

"THERES ONE AREA OF MY LIFE THAT TECHNOLOGY HASNT IMPROVED AND I THINK THE ARTICLE SHOULD TOUCH ON THAT TOO SO PEOPLE WONT THINK TECH-NOLOGY IS A CURE ALL" I typed out.

"Yes," Mark said softly, "Should I tell her what you once said in a letter to me?"

I nodded and Mark began slowly, "Well, Bill said something like although technology has enabled him to get around, type, and now talk, girls still run from him when he tries to have a relationship with them that's more than just friends."

Dr. Schwab nodded and said, "You're not alone, Bill. Another woman who was supposed to die by the time she was eighteen years old told me, 'I didn't expect to live this long, but now that I am thirty-two I want a whole life. I want it all.' So I'm behind you, Bill. Tell me, who is your family doctor? Have you talked to him about this? Perhaps he can advise you in the physiological department. You know, the plumbing."

"THAT IS NOT WHAT BOTHERS ME THE PROBLEM IS TO DEVELOP A CARING RELATIONSHIP FIRST AND THEN WORRY ABOUT THE PLUMBING LATER"

While I was spelling this, I was thinking of saying, "Et tu, Brutus!" But I didn't.

"You're right, Bill. What about having Wendy in on this interview? I remember when you were up in Mark's room and trying to make the

182   voice synthesizer recite that little poem. You were trying to communicate something to her way back then. Were you successful?" Dr. Schwab said.

Mark interjected, "No, an artificial voice doesn't come across on tape like a human voice does. I felt really bad about that."

"I DONT KNOW ABOUT HAVING HER IN ON THE INTERVIEW SHES EXTREMELY SHY AND HATES PUBLICITY HER PRIVACY MEANS A LOT TO HER" I typed out.

"I could talk to her and see how she feels about being a part of this interview," Dr. Schwab offered.

"OK IT COULDNT HURT" I spelled out slowly.

"And," Mark said, "we could send LIFE some copies of your stories. I'm particularly thinking of your article on the voice synthesizer that appeared in the Omaha *World-Herald*. It's well written and points out the good and bad of technology."

"Good idea. One more thing, when they do come, kind of tidy up this room. Wash off the drool from the synthesizer. You know what I mean," Dr. Schwab politely said. Then, she looked at her watch and said, "I must be going shortly, but I'll tell Anne that you are both willing to do the story. And I'll send her copies of your articles. I'll set up a luncheon to talk to Wendy. Oh by the way, Anne reminds me of her. You'll like her."

With that, Dr. Schwab departed. Mark looked at me and said, "This is getting interesting."

When I told my parents the news Mom said, "You're kidding. Your occupational therapist is going to flip out. She already thinks your head is too big. Mrs. George has to hear this. She'll be happy for you." Mom sounded about as shocked as I was. We didn't believe this was happening. We thought only presidents and kings were in LIFE Magazine.

One night Mark came down to my room and said, "Dr. Schwab called and said she sent Anne Fadiman a letter with your article—I don't remember which articles she sent. Anyway she is trying to get football tickets, so we could take the reporter and photographer to a game and show them how you get good shots of the cheerleaders, if nothing else. Dr. Schwab mentioned the idea to the LIFE people as a possibility."

"I WANT SO BADLY TO GET MY POINT ACROSS ON   183
SEXUALITY" I told Mark.

"So I've noticed," Mark lightly said. "But you should kinda ease up a little bit. You have a tendency to—well—you interject the subject every chance you get and people might get tired of hearing about it," Mark said hesitatingly.

"OK, ILL TONE IT DOWN A LITTLE BIT I HAVE A TENDENCY TO OVER DO SOMETIMES SORRY" I spelled to Mark.

"Don't get me wrong. I'm all for what you're trying to do, and I think you should do it. Maybe it's because I have heard you talk about it to so many people that I am weary of hearing it. You know the old saying, 'Familiarity breeds contempt.' " Mark added quickly. Then he said, "When Anne Fadiman interviews me I will make sure she understands your point."

I could tell that he was as nervous as I about this interview and wanted everything to go smoothly.

A few days later I found a letter in my mailbox. Its return address was LIFE, Time & LIFE Building, Rockefeller Center, New York. The only other time I had seen that return address on a letter to me was when the magazine's computer sent me a subscription offer.

I asked a fellow student passing by to open the envelope for me. The letter was from Anne Fadiman. She said she would be arriving with a photographer late Friday, October 26th, and staying through Tuesday, October 30th. She asked me to think about my plans during those days and said that since I had a background in journalism and photography, I'd have a better idea than anyone else of what would prove interesting. She said that everyone at LIFE liked the football suggestion. She ended her note by saying that she would be back in touch around October 22nd to confirm her plans and that she looked forward to talking with me.

That night I wrote her a letter saying that I was looking forward to meeting her and that it blew my mind that a national magazine should have been interested in a college student like me. I thanked her for asking for my input for the article. Then I hit her with my idea. I told her that while space age technology had provided me with a means of getting around campus, opening doors, and talking, it

184 couldn't give me that certain warmth that two people share. I said it was frustrating because technology had opened so many other doors for me. I pointed out that the need to be loved was universal. I closed by saying that I was really honored that LIFE Magazine was doing a story on me and that I just hoped I could live up to it.

When I finished I reread it. I thought I'd better get Dr. Schwab's approval before I sent it. After all, LIFE Magazine's coming was her idea. I didn't want to do anything to spoil it. Besides, perhaps Mark was right. Maybe I was beating an exhausted drum.

So I got a friend who lived on my floor to read the letter to her over the phone. When my friend had finished it, Dr. Schwab said, "That's a good letter Bill. That says it all.

"Oh, by the way, I had lunch with Wendy, and she's willing to help out with the interview if you ask her to. You have a very good friend there. Let's leave it there for now. I'll give you more details when we can talk face-to-face."

"THANK YOU VERY MUCH AND HAVE A GOOD EVENING" I spelled out and had my dormmate repeat what I spelled to her, and she wished me a goodnight and hung up.

When I had a chance to talk to Wendy, I asked her how she felt about being interviewed by the reporter from LIFE, and she said, "Well, if it'll help you, I'll do it. But you know how I am when it comes to posing in front of cameras. It's not natural for me. But Dr. Schwab said it would help you if I did, so I guess I want to do it," Wendy said.

I couldn't help remembering another time when I put too much pressure on another friendship and lost it for three years. I didn't want to go through that again. Also, I remembered Wendy's reaction to my story about her and inwardly shuddered.

"FORGET IT" I spelled out to her.

"But if I can help, I want to," she insisted.

"YOU VALUE YOUR PRIVACY TOO MUCH YOU DONT LIKE PUBLICITY AND ALL THE REPORTER IS INTERESTED IN IS MY SPACE AGE TECHNOLOGY" I spelled.

She let out a little sigh of relief which made me feel good.

I wrote a letter to my new-found old friend, Deanne and told her that I was going to be featured in LIFE.

Her reaction was, "I told my husband, 'You know Bill has been in the Omaha *World Herald*, the *Exceptional Parent*, and on telethons. Guess what he's going to do now.'

"And Mark, my husband, guessed, '60 Minutes?'

"I said, 'You're close enough.'

"Really, I'm happy for you. It's about time your story was told. And when your fan club is formed, I'll be waving my banner. In fact, I might be president of it," Deanne joked.

I couldn't think of a better person to start a fan club for me.

On a warm fall day I met Anne Fadiman and the photographer, Brian Lanker. As Dad would say, I was as nervous as a whore in church. But both Anne and Brian were friendly and professional.

Anne started asking me questions the minute she stepped out of her rented car. While I understood why she did this it made me have to stop every two steps and spell out another answer since I couldn't walk and talk at the same time. I didn't mind answering her questions. I just wanted to get to my next class on time.

On her third question I spelled, "PATIENCE ANN"

"It's Anne with an E but okay. I just find both Mark and you incredibly fascinating. It's like waking up Christmas morning and finding a tree with a lot of packages under it. You want to start opening them right away," she said.

"By the way, out of curiosity, who else are you interviewing for this article on new innovations for people like Bill?" Mark asked.

"That story has been shelved for now. The editors read Bill's letter and sent me here to profile him and you. And yes, Bill, we will talk a lot about your problems with women," Anne said.

I thought, "Oh my God, what have I gotten myself into this time?"

Anne and Brian had planned to stay for four days but the four days stretched into seven days. They were like my shadows. My morning aide had to climb over them to get into my room in the mornings and my night aide had to escort them back to their hotel late at night. During the days they followed me to my classes, sat in on the classes, ate with me, watched me make prints in the photo lab, asked questions, and took pictures.

Once my night aide joked, "Brian should take a picture of you in the shower."

186   Brian said, "Sure. Good idea. I'll get my camera."

I looked at my aide and he said, "I'm sorry. I was just kidding."

Brian said, "Don't worry. I will crop it tastefully."

My only comment was, "IT WILL STILL BE OVER EXPOSED AND UNDER DEVELOPED"

Partly because she wanted to get a feel for my social life and partly because she wanted just to socialize with us, Anne took in a movie with Mark and me and went to a local bar with me.

Anne even went to Omaha to interview my parents. She would quote my dad as saying that I had gone beyond him. She would also quote my mom as saying that I could never stand to be ignored, even as a baby.

When Anne was leaving for New York she asked, "Do you have any last words?"

"YES TAKE OFF THE HALO MOST STORIES PAINT ME AS A SUPER MAN WHICH IS WRONG DONT DO THAT" I spelled.

The story appeared in the January 1980 issue. Anne took my suggestion. Most stories portrayed me as a disabled person who was courageously going to college but Anne's story painted a picture of two college chums: one was a computer science major who had made a voice synthesizer and the other was a journalism major who just happened to need a voice synthesizer.

When I finished reading her article I knew Mark and I made a friend in Anne because only a friend could have portrayed us in the way she did.

PART SIX

IN SEARCH OF
SEXUALITY

CHAPTER 19

EQUAL OPPORTUNITY EMPLOYER

"I hate to bring this up, but with Roger leaving and it being close to the second semester, we might have to seriously consider looking for a female aide to get you up in the morning," Paul said clinching his teeth. "I can't do it alone, and it doesn't look like a guy is going to come forth in time for second semester."

I grimaced and said, "LET ME THINK ABOUT IT"

"Sure," Paul said, "I just didn't want you to have to come back from Christmas break and have me tell you, 'Hi, meet Bill's Angels.'" But I hoped it wouldn't have to come to that. I remembered Mrs. George saying, "Our high school young men shouldn't have to be assisted in the bathroom by a female matron. It's embarrassing to them." My high school teacher had been right, of course. But my options were quitting school or having a female get me out of bed. Quitting school was impossible now with the LIFE article coming out in January.

"I'm going to the library," said Paul, "I'll be back around eleven. By the way, should we hire a woman, she'd be a nursing student so it wouldn't be like having a female off the street do it. I don't know if that is any consolation."

He left for the library without pressing the issue further. Paul knew he had given me a hard decision to make. He was also letting me know it was my decision.

A nursing student was living in Selleck. Her name was Kim and she had a brother who lived on my floor. I considered her for a possible aide. I remembered the first time we met. "Hi, I'm Kim. My roommate, Cathy, read one of your stories in her English class. I read it too, and it was good. Well, I had better get this vacuum up to her. See ya."

190   She was obviously scared to talk to me but at least she made the attempt. She had attractive eyes. They were brown and almond-shaped. Very unusual, because she showed no other signs of being oriental. Neither did her brother.

We had gone on walks around campus. The first walk was interesting because every time I had a muscle spasm Kim would panic and hold my hand saying, "Are you all right?" This continued until I finally said, "YOU WORRY TOO MUCH IM OK IF ANYTHING IS WRONG, ILL TELL YOU" Kim had a habit of doing something that attracted me even more than her almond-shaped eyes. When I spelled out the word "YOU," she'd automatically replace the word "I" for it. This made me feel as if I was having a conversation with her, not playing "Now repeat after me" with her.

"You're right. Excuse me. See I'm a nurse, so asking if somebody is all right is like a reflex with me. I'll try to tone down that reflex, okay?"

Once she told me that she had taken care of a quadriplegic 19-year-old boy in the hospital. She saw me frown and asked, "What's wrong? Something is definitely wrong this time. I can tell from your expression."

"ITS JUST THAT IT ISNT RIGHT FOR YOU TO HAVE TO TAKE CARE OF A NINETEEN YEAR OLD GUY IT MUST HAVE BEEN EMBARRASSING FOR HIM"

"I agree, but I used little tricks, like draping him with a towel. Plus, I did most of the personal care stuff when he was sleeping. I agree with you. There should be more male nurses, but there aren't." Kim said apologetically.

It was for these reasons that I thought of Kim when Paul had said, "We might have to seriously consider looking for a female aide to get you up in the mornings."

I rolled into the Selleck Hall office where Kim was on duty. She greeted me with a cheery, "Hi."

"What can I do for you tonight?"

I remembered that she was quitting her desk job because of conflicts in schedules—another point in my favor.

"IM IN TROUBLE," I began. "ROGER IS QUITTING TO GO TO COLORADO AND I CANT FIND ANOTHER GUY TO TAKE HIS PLACE."

"You are in trouble. That's terrible," Kim sympathized.

"Don't you have anybody at all?"

"NO, I WAS HOPING THAT YOU COULD" I lost my nerve, "SUGGEST SOMEBODY."

"I can't, not off-hand. I'll ask around." Kim hesitated. "You know that I'm a nurse, and I'm quitting this job, so I could help you, but you want a guy, right?"

"IM STARTING TO LOOK FOR GIRLS ITS EITHER THAT OR QUIT SCHOOL" I said and grimaced.

"Why don't you think about my offer and let me know," Kim said. "I wish there was a way I could change my sex."

I accepted her offer because no men applied, and it was mid-December. School would let out in a week, and it was next to impossible to round up help during the holidays. So I had Roger train Kim on how to get me up. Kim was a fast learner. When Roger came to the electric wheelchair's needs, Kim said, "I love this part. I'm no good with machines. Bill, do you mind if I electrocute you once or twice? I'm really lousy with machines, and this one boggles my mind, so go over this again please."

I didn't like the idea of having a female aide at all. Intellectually I knew Kim was a nurse, but Selleck wasn't a hospital. I wasn't sick. And I knew Kim on a social level, or at least wanted to know her on a social level.

During the holidays I went to visit my good friends Ed and Sally Henry in Waterville, Kansas. I confided my misgivings to them. Ed, in his characteristic calm manner said, "From what you tell me this gal is aware of your feelings. I don't quite see your problem. I can see how you feel, but you're not giving this gal much credit."

"And besides," Sally interjected, "she might be the best advocate for your sexuality crusade. A woman is more apt to talk about that than a man is. Ed and I know that you're scared because having a woman do the personal stuff for you is a new experience, but it's not the end of the world."

It was definitely not the end of the world. The appreciation of Kim began immediately when she didn't flip on the the harsh florescent overhead light when she came in the first Monday morning of the new semester.

"We'll keep that overhead light off in the mornings," Kim said

192   when she rolled me over. "I believe in the Lamaze method of child birth, bringing the baby out to face the world gradually without bright lights."

She wore a T-shirt and jeans. "I wore this outfit to look as asexual as possible. Sure did have a good vacation."

Before I knew what was happening, I was dressed. I was unaware that her conversation had been designed for just that.

It took us two hours to get me dressed, to eat, and to brush my teeth. Our time would improve as the semester progressed.

"I will be speedier, I promise," Kim chimed. "And, I'll give you about a week to get used to me. Don't worry. Look, I even bought a key chain shaped like a four leaf clover for good luck. Your room key will go on it."

Once I asked Kim to take my chair over to the Engineering College to get repaired. She said, "Okay. Will you type out directions for me like what room, what door to go in, and who to give it to?"

I did, and Kim set out boldly on her trek. When she got back to the room, she said, "Your Jerry Fritz wasn't there, so after I get you up, we'll call him to make sure he has your chair. I know how much it means to you."

"Hello, this is Jerry," the speaker phone said.

"Hi, Jerry. This is an aide for Bill Rush. Did you get his chair? I left it outside your room," Kim said cheerfully.

"No, there's no chair here. I checked."

"Is your room number 322 in Nebraska Hall," asked Kim.

"I'm in the Engineering Center right south of Nebraska Hall," replied Jerry.

"Oh, I see. I think I know what happened. I think I left it in the wrong building. See you in fifteen minutes with the chair, I hope," Kim turned off the speaker phone, quickly put her coat back on and said, "I wondered why everybody at that building was staring at me. Don't worry. Nobody will steal an electric wheelchair. That'd be like stealing crutches. Don't go away. I'll be right back. I'm sorry." Kim giggled.

In twenty minutes Kim came back and said, "The chair's in Jerry's hot little hands. I made sure of that. Now I must be going to class. Do you need anything else before I go?"

I shook my head "no."

"Okay, good-bye guy. I still don't believe I left the chair in the wrong building," Kim chuckled as she left for her class.

As I watched the nurse who was getting her Bachelor of Science leave, I remembered other aides that I had and considered myself lucky this semester. I could remember mornings when the harsh florescent light was flipped on waking me from a sound sleep. I was greeted with a not-so-cheerful, "We are going to war with China, and if it happens, you had better start looking for a new aide because this one is going to Canada. But what do you care?"

Other mornings I would be greeted with, "Oh, this stupid chair is busted again. And I don't have time to run over to Engineering this morning. I have a test that I have to study for. Why does this happen to me?"

Once while brushing my teeth, another aide asked me, "Why when you were at home didn't you get your hair cut this weekend like I suggested?"

"I DIDNT HAVE TIME," I replied.

"That's a poor excuse. Don't you care about your appearance? Because if you don't, I won't waste my time and yours by cleaning you up. . ." the aide said sarcastically.

"MY GRANDMA WAS IN THE HOSPITAL SHE WAS SICK MOM HAD TO BE WITH HER SO THE HAIRCUT HAD TO WAIT NEXT WEEKEND ILL GET IT OK"

I resented being bossed by my helper. The aide looked at me with cold eyes and said, "Your grandma sick, huh?" Then he turned his head and spat in the sink. "So much for your poor grandma."

Still another aide used to laugh at me when I had a cold and was trying to eat.

In contrast to these aides, Kim not only cared for my physical needs, but she also cared about my mental state. (Paul did too, and so did Roger.) Many a time both Kim and Paul would spend hours listening to my frustrations about girls. Kim, a woman herself, could naturally provide better insights into the female mind.

"Bill," she would say, "all guys are frustrated by girls. Look at my brother. He's a great looking guy. Broad shoulders, good facial features. No problem finding dates, right? Wrong. Girls are afraid of him. They are afraid of his size. He had to go back home to go out with a girl. The sad thing is that if a girl ever got to know my brother, she'll find out that he's nothing but a big teddy bear."

"YES BUT IM NOT BUILT LIKE YOUR BROTHER MY BODY

194 IS A WRECK. I LOOK LIKE AN ESCAPEE FROM A POW CAMP"
I spelled out.

She giggled and said, "Does a prisoner of war have bright shining
eyes? No. You have great hair and a lean figure. And most of all, you
have a good smile and some day a girl will notice it and be swept off
her feet. Well, maybe not quite the way you think, but don't give up
hope. I've seen too many so-called hopeless cases cured as a nurse. So I
never give up hope."

"MY BIGGEST PROBLEM IS THAT GIRLS KISS AND TOUCH
ME AND THEN WHEN I RESPOND LIKE ANY OTHER MAN
THEY FREAK OUT AND RUN AWAY"

"I can see where you might get a little more frustrated than my
brother. But you mustn't give up hope," Kim said firmly.

Somehow having an attractive 22 year-old woman tell me that my
love life wasn't hopeless almost made me believe it wasn't.

Once I asked Kim, "HOWS ABOUT GOING TO THE BAR FOR
A COKE MIDTERMS ARE OVER AND I COULDNT THINK OF
A BETTER PERSON TO RELAX WITH THAN YOU"

Kim, with toothbrush in hand, sat down on the bed and hesitated.
"Bill, when I think of going to bars, I think of guys coming on to girls
and picking them up."

I frowned and shook my head "THATS NOT WHAT I HAD IN
MIND"

"I know that," Kim leaned forward and touched my arm, "but that's
my impression of a bar, especially the ones in Lincoln. And Bill, do you
think it's a good idea for us to socialize when I'm getting you out of bed
and dressing you? I don't."

"YOU MEAN WE SHOULD REMAIN KIND OF REMOTE
SINCE YOU ARE DOING THE PERSONAL STUFF" I asked.

"You could say that. And another thing, see I love working with
you, but you take up so much of my time that I can't see my other
friends and I want to see them too. It's not your fault, I know. But do
you see where I'm coming from?" Her eyes were apologetic.

"I SEE" I spelled out. I then tried a compromise. "AFTER
SCHOOL LETS OUT FOR THE SUMMER CAN WE GO OUT ON
DATES OCCASSIONALLY"

"Yes, but I prefer 'outings' rather than 'dates' for us, okay guy?" I don't know how to transfer you to and from my car, but I guess I could learn."

I didn't press it further. I didn't want to scare her off.

Having Kim for an aide wasn't all fun and games. Kim was forbidden to go into the men's bathroom. This meant no hot water and that the urinal went unemptied until Paul came in the afternoon. Once I had an important editor from Washington, D.C., come before the afternoon emptying. I forgot to tell Kim to make a special effort to get the urinal emptied. But after she left for class, I spotted the full urinal on my chest of drawers and decided it would be unsightly, not to mention embarrassing.

So I wheeled into the hall to get somebody to empty the container. All my friends were at class. I saw a student-type stranger in the hall. I debated whether to ask him to empty the container. My watch made the decision for me. It said ten minutes 'til ten o'clock, and the editor from Washington was coming at ten. I didn't have much choice. Besides, it was easy to empty the urinal. Just dump it down the toilet. Anybody could do it, except me.

I wheeled up to the stranger in the hall and spelled out, "I NEED HELP IN MY ROOM WILL YOU HELP ME" "Sure," the stranger replied with uncertainty in his voice, "if I can."

I led him to my room and pointed to the problem and started to spell dump that down the toilet please. Unfortunately, the stranger stopped me at "D."

"Oh you want a drink?" he asked sincerely and started to put the urinal to my mouth.

I shook my head "no" violently.

Then the bewildered stranger realized what was in the container and sheepishly asked, "Do you want me to dump this down the toilet?"

I shook my head "yes."

When the urinal was safely emptied and tucked out of sight, the editor from Washington was duly impressed by Mark's bionic voice and my views on independent living.

"THERE ISNT ANY INDEPENDENT LIVING" I said on the synthesizer. "WE ARE ALL INTERDEPENDENT"

Once at breakfast I smashed into a table where two girls were

196   sitting. My hand caught between my wheelchair tray and the table.

"Oh my God!" one of the girls jumped up and said, "Bill, are you all right? Oh, your poor hand. You've crushed it."

Kim was coming out of the cafeteria line with a plate of French toast.

"Kim. Come and look at Bill's hand. He caught it between our table and his tray. I think it's broken," said the blonde girl, who was a second year nursing student. She also had a brother with cerebral palsy but he was profoundly mentally retarded. "Maybe we should get some ice."

Kim put the tray down on the table beside the girls and surprised the blonde nursing student. "I'm sure if Bill's hand was broken, he'd tell me himself. Bill, does the image of Cheryl Ladd in a bikini still excite you?"

I nodded "yes" and grinned. But I wondered what the connection was between a possible broken hand and Cheryl Ladd.

"His hand is okay. Now, guy, get over here and quit flirting with the girls," Kim teased.

While we were eating Kim whispered, "They don't understand you at all. Now I see why you get so frustrated. I'm sure if you broke your hand you'd find a way to tell me or somebody else."

"BUT YOU MUST EXCUSE THAT GIRL HER BROTHER HAS CP AND IS RETARDED SO I CAN SEE WHY SHE ACTS THE WAY SHE DOES SHE HAS IMPROVED LAST YEAR AND THE YEAR BEFORE LAST EVERY TIME SHE SAW ME SHE USED TO SAY 'YOU'RE SEXY BILL'" I spelled out while Kim was finishing her breakfast roll.

"Hmm, she's in my child development class. I think I'll have a very long chat with her about something or somebody who we both know. I remembered your telling me that she used to call you sexy. That's why I threw in that bit about Cheryl Ladd. I thought adding that would help their image of you. Don't worry. I'll definitely have a talk with her. Let's eat. I have a class at 9:30."

Sally Henry's spoken words over the holiday came back to me. "And besides, she might be the best advocate for your sexuality crusade. A woman is more apt to talk about that than a man is. . ."

I made a mental note to write Ed and Sally and tell them they were right about the benefits of having a female attendant.

CHAPTER 20

A   MEETING   AMONG   FRIENDS

A car's headlights whizzed by my electric wheelchair. I was momentarily blinded. I had left the safety of the sidewalk to cross some railroad tracks a few yards back, and now I couldn't find a curb cut to get back where I belonged.

As my chair hugged the curb on busy Sixteenth Street, I tried to sort out the past year and a half. Again, I couldn't find a solution to my problem with Wendy. I hoped my friend, John, could help me. I traveled on, lost in thought.

Although John and I had started out as a vocational rehabilitation professional helping his client, we had developed a close friendship. John had a knack of knowing when to be quiet and listen and when to say, "Bill, you're off base."

John understood my desire to develop a relationship with a woman. He had gone out with Wendy and me when the relationship was fresh and full of promise. He had taken a liking to her.

A chuckhole jarred me out of my reverie and reminded me that I was on a major thoroughfare. I slowly realized I was nearing the driveway that led to John's dorm. I drove carefully into the drive and onto the safe sidewalk.

"Hey, Rush, I'm glad you could make it over. Did you have any trouble? Why are you laughing?" John greeted me. "Why don't you come on into the lounge behind the office? I'll check the frig for something cold and wet—and non-alcoholic."

When he had given me a swallow of lemon pop to clear the mucous from my throat, John asked, "So how are you?" His brown eyes showed genuine concern. "When I saw you in the Selleck cafeteria the other day, you looked pretty strung out. Does it involve who I think it does? Wanna talk about it?"

198   "YES DAMNIT I GUESS ITS A COMBINATION OF THINGS WENDY IS DRIVING ME CRAZY SHE SAYS THAT SHES NOT RUNNING BUT OUR FRIENDSHIP IS DYING SLOWLY"

"Let me give you my gut-level reaction, okay?" John asked. He put his hand on my shoulder and began, "Your lady friend is a dynamic person, but she's a second year college student, which means she has a lot of problems—growing pains, you might say. From what you have told me on other occasions, she has been giving you some very mixed messages. She hugs you and holds your hand, but when you respond she pulls back, right? You, in turn, have some expectations that you don't want to admit just like she doesn't want to admit that she really wants to run from you, so you should have a long talk with Wendy, and get it all out in the open. It'll be painful, but it's the only way."

John was being no help. Pain was exactly what I wanted to avoid. Why did he expect the relationship to end? I resented his assumption, but knew that he was probably right. But damn it why did it have to be that way? But, another problem occurred to me. And, I told John, "I CANT DO THAT BECAUSE WHEN IM SPELLING ON MY BOARD I CANT ESTABLISH EYE CONTACT WITH HER AND MY CONVERSATIONS WITH HER USUALLY END UP LIKE IM LECTURING TO HER"

John looked off into space, "I never thought of that problem. Now I can see your point and where it might get frustrating."

"YOU KNOW I FEEL LIKE IM RUNNING A RACE THAT I KNOW I CANT WIN I KNOW ILL COME IN LAST BUT STILL I KEEP ON TRYING"

"I remember some people said that about you when you wanted to come to UNL, but you're proving them wrong, dammit, Bill," John said with his hand on my left shoulder and his right hand clenching my hand. Both his and my eyes had begun to tear.

"I KNOW THAT BUT THIS SEMESTER I HAVE A 22 YEAR OLD WOMAN WHO LIVES IN SELLECK COME IN AND GET ME UP IN THE MORNINGS SO EVERY DAY IM REMINDED THAT IM NOT SEXUALLY DESIRABLE TO WOMEN DONT GET ME WRONG THIS WOMAN IS A GOOD AIDE BUT SHE HAS MADE IT CLEAR THAT SHE DOESNT WANT TO SOC- IALIZE WITH ME AT LEAST NOT WHILE SCHOOL IS IN

SESSION BUT SHES A GOOD AIDE BUT I SURE WOULD LIKE   199
TO GET TO KNOW HER ON A SOCIAL BASIS ANYWAY BACK
TO THE IMMEDIATE PROBLEM HOW DO I AVOID ANOTHER
EPISODE LIKE I HAD WITH DEANNE"

"I hate to tell you this," John grimaced while he spoke, "but you already have it. The lady sounds like she really wants to run, but she feels guilty for wanting to run. Now the question is: Do you love her enough to let her go? Do you have enough guts to do that? You finally did it with Deanne, and I think she now respects you for it."

"I TRIED THAT BUT SHE DENIES THAT SHE WANTS TO RUN ITS A MESS COULD THE THREE OF US JUST SIT DOWN AND TALK ABOUT THE PROBLEM YOU ACTING LIKE A REFEREE"

"Good idea. Now all we have to do is to get ahold of Wendy, and we'll be all set."

"I HOPE YOULL DO ANOTHER THING PRAY"

"I always do. I always do."

We met on a rainy Wednesday. I climbed the zigzag ramp of the Union and entered through the electric sliding door. I made my way to the snack bar, which was a dimly lit lounge.

When all three of us located each other, John said calmly, "All year I have noticed something wrong between you two and I care too much about you both not to say something. I hope we can start the ball rolling and then I can disappear and let you two continue your discussion alone."

I wanted to restore what we once had. I even bought a red candle earlier in the day, hoping that after our meeting with John, Wendy and I could go back to my dorm room, listen to music by candlelight, share a Coke, and make a toast to a new beginning to our relationship.

"You want to hug and hold hands. And I don't want that. I know that I encouraged you in the beginning. That's why I don't like your story about me. It reminds me too much of a love story," she explained.

"I UNDERSTAND THAT BUT I WROTE IT TO SHOW THAT TECHNOLOGY CANT SOLVE ALL THE PROBLEMS OF A DISABLED PERSON SOMEWHERE THERE HAS TO BE

200   FRIENDS WILLING TO LOOK BEYOND THE DROOL AND MUSCLE SPASMS AND THE ELECTRONICS TO SEE THAT IM HUMAN"

"Yes, Bill I know, sexuality," the lady said wearily.

"No, not just that," John interjected, "I think Bill's talking about the ability to get to know a person who has a disability on a gut level. Most people shy away from that."

She nodded in agreement as if she could identify with what John had said.

"It's like last night," she said, "I had dinner with a guy. I thought we were just friends, but he acted like he had something else on his mind. So, now when he calls me up again, I'll tell him that I don't want to go out with him. But with you, I can't do that because of the bond that we feel for each other, or the bond that you feel towards me."

The slip was so slight that under other circumstances I would have missed it, but it was there. She didn't feel any bond toward me anymore. I wondered if I could get a refund on my red candle.

"And," she continued, "I think I have something to offer to those who are physically disabled or less fortunate than I am. But in your case you want more than I can offer. I don't know what to do about it."

"IF YOU DIDNT WANT ROMANCE FROM ME WHY IN THE HELL DID YOU HUG KISS AND TOUCH ME" I argued.

"I was proving that you *could* have a relationship with a woman, but that woman is not me. I know I led you on, and I'm sorry," Wendy said quietly.

Suddenly, I felt used. I wondered just who she was trying to fool, her or me? Then slowly I began to realize that Wendy had started practicing her skills as a rehabilitation counselor but got too emotionally involved with me.

It was John's turn, "Bill, I think what has happened here is that your relationship, just like a muscle, has been over-extended. And the only way for it to get better is to rest it."

I resisted pointing out that a person shouldn't exercise so much if she doesn't have the strength for it.

"I agree with John," the woman said softly.

"THEN YOU WANT TO STOP SEEING ME" I was tired all of a sudden. "IF THATS WHAT YOU WANT THEN THATS WHAT WE WILL DO"

"Yes, but I feel guilty because you need me." She looked at John for help and said, "But I'll feel guilt so I don't want to do it."

John sternly said, "You can't have everything. Bill is willing to do whatever you want, but you must decide what to do now."

She nodded slowly.

"Let me have a minute alone with him," John said.

She left the lounge area quickly and quietly.

"IM OK" I told John after she left, "WE DONE GOOD DIDNT WE BUT WHAT IN THE HELL DID SHE THINK SHE WAS PROVING"

"Oh, Bill," was all John could say. He had his arm around me trying to comfort me. "I'm sorry. I don't know what she thought."

"WELL AS WALTER CRONKITE WOULD SAY THATS THE WAY IT IS" I joked without humor.

"Here's another gut level feeling: she's looking for an easy way to leave here and you have to give it to her. It's the hardest thing you ever had to do. Are you ready to do it?"

I nodded. Wendy had used me, given me false hopes, bitten off more than she could chew, so now I was supposed to allow her to walk away from me. I wondered which one of us had the greater disability. But, damnit, I still loved her.

Anyway, John was wrong. Taking the stop action shot at the track was the hardest thing I ever did. This time I wouldn't even tip over. But I wished that the glass of pop in front of me would change into something stronger.

John went to find her. And a moment later she came back in sheepishly.

"WILL YOU GIVE ME THE REST OF THAT COKE" I asked. I tried to imagine it was whiskey. My imagination failed me.

"HEY LETS MAKE A TOAST" I spelled out after the first swallow.

"Sure, what should we drink to?" she asked.

"TO FRIENDS" I suggested wearily.

I drank two swallows of the Coke and she finished it off.

Then she put my coat back on. She put her hand in my sleeve to bring my arm through. I felt her hand for the last time. It felt good. I had to remind myself that in our family men don't cry.

"Can you get back to the dorm by yourself okay?" she asked me.

202   I nodded and tried to smile.

As she was leaving, Wendy said, "I'll write ya this summer. Bye."

I watched her go.

I was hurt. I was tired. I was disappointed. I had thought Wendy had perceived me as a man. She hadn't.

CHAPTER 21

REALIST OR PESSIMIST?

"Sorry I'm late, Bill. I got held up at another meeting," said the youthful professor. Glancing around at my dorm room, he remarked, "You sure have a lot of fascinating equipment here: environmental controls, voice synthesizer, electric typewriter, automatic door opener. I'm impressed."

"Yes," I typed out, "I'm UNL's answer to the bionic man. Unfortunately UNL hasn't invented a bionic woman for me yet, which brings me to why you have come."

"Clever lead in." The professor grinned a boyish grin. "Well, as I told you on the phone last Tuesday, the Human Development Department is offering a course on sexuality and the disabled which I will be teaching. I would like some insights from you on the topic. What should the nurses, special ed teachers and the rest know about your sexual desires? What should they be aware of?"

I considered and typed , "My biggest problem is that if women touch and kiss me, and if I respond as any man would, if I try to reciprocate their signs of affection, they freak and run away."

"In other words, women think you are safe. Yet, when they learn that you're like any other man, they are taken aback; they withdraw their friendship."

"Right," I typed and nodded.

"Tell me something," the professor said, "Have you ever had a date?"

I asked him to define what he meant by the word "date."

"By 'date' I mean have you ever gone out with a women, hoping to score with her?" he replied with all sincerity.

"No, that's not the kind of relationship I want." I continued typing. "I want to develop a relationship where I could get to know the woman and her family, then gradually develop a caring. . ."

"Excuse me for saying this but you sound like a prude, considering that this is the age of the sexual revolution and all," the professor interrupted. "I know you won't be offended if I speak frankly with you."

I wanted to laugh, for that was the first time anybody had ever called me a prude. Instead I typed, "Prudish or realistic? I could never seduce a woman to have a one-night stand."

"Why not? Who says you can't be seductive," he asked naively.

I quickly appraised myself physically. I couldn't walk, I couldn't use my hands, and I couldn't talk—excluding my voice synthesizer which hardly had a seductive tone to it. Maybe I could seduce R2D2's sister with it, but even that was improbable.

"OK, let's be practical," I responded. "Suppose I meet a woman, and suppose somehow we go out for a one-nighter. To get past the drinking would require me to tell her how to pour the drink down me. I have my jaw agape, head tilted back, and cough about every third swallow. Seductive?"

"Some people could find that seductive. Who's to say what's seductive to whom?" the professor replied. "Never sell yourself short."

This might be a good technique for counseling a person with a spinal cord injury, but it didn't work this time. Sorry about that, Doctor.

I continued, "Then suppose we're both slightly smashed and go to a motel. Transferring from the car and into the bed would take all the romance out of it. And once we're in bed neither of us would know what to do unless I took my headstick and language board to bed."

"I see your point, but I still say it could happen. You're too pessimistic," the idealistic professor answered.

"You're dreaming. And besides, I don't really want a one-night stand. I have a 22-year-old woman come in here and get me up every morning. We have a good friendship. If I even suggested having sex to her, it would ruin a nice relationship." I typed carefully. "Would you please get my yellow notebook? I'm taking a human sexuality class this semester, and the members of the class were supposed to write our views on sexuality. I want you to read my paper."

He did as he was told. He read, "I'm a 24-year-old male without any coital experience. I am a non-verbal quadriplegic as a result of cerebral palsy. Had I not been born with CP, I would have been married by now.

"Cerebral palsy has limited my sex life, but not my attitudes on sexuality. I don't believe in one-night stands or the fun romp in bed. I believe kissing and touching were made by God as communication aids for when feelings can't be expressed with words. I believe that if a couple have sex, or even touch, they are saying to each other, 'You're a very special person to me. I care about you.'

"I use girly magazines to 'satisfy' my sex drive. I put satisfy in quotes because the pornography only serves as a safety valve for me.

"My big sexual fantasy is to meet a woman who will look beyond the drool, beyond the electric wheelchair, and beyond the fact that every sign of caring would have to be initiated by her to see that I am a sexual person, not an asexual thing as well as loving me as a man. . . ."

After reading it, he said, "I see what you mean. Thank you for your input." He looked at his watch and said he had to go to another meeting.

After he went, I felt tired. He had cheapened expressions of love and caring between people. He was so damned clinical and analytical about it. Only one week had passed since John and I had met with Wendy at the Union, so I didn't feel like thinking or talking about personal relationships. Not yet anyway.

Suddenly, I remembered that my head control was scheduled to be fixed. I wearily dialed the engineering college, then asked Jerry via mechanical voice if my control was fixed. He said yes and that I could have one of my aides pick it up.

Paul was at home typing a paper. He didn't have time to pick it up. So I called Kim, my morning aide.

"HOW . . . BUSY . . . ARE . . . YOU" the voice synthesizer chimed.

"Why? What's up?" Kim asked.

"MY CONTROL IS DONE WOULD YOU GO GET IT" I asked.

She hesitated. "Okay, I'll be there in fifteen minutes. Goodbye."

She was obviously busy also, because she had hung up before I could press the "Goodbye" key on the synthesizer.

206   Twenty minutes later Kim rushed in and said, "I suppose you want me to put you in the electric wheelchair. Of course you could have just wanted to stare at the controls." She laughed.

It took several minutes to get all the plugs connected and me tied in securely.

"Well, guy, I have to get ready for dinner. We're roasting the faculty of the nursing school. Do you need anything else?"

I shook my head no.

"I'll see you later. Jerry said to be careful. I told him you always were. Cough-cough."

She gave me a warm, sisterly squeeze on the shoulder and a smile. "Goodbye, guy."

The choice between one-nighters and sisterly squeezes on the shoulders is like choosing between gluttony or starvation. I'm still waiting for a woman who is willing to share the hearty meal of marriage with me.

CONCLUSION

CHAPTER 22

INVISIBLE HEALING

"Did you know you could give glory to God if you only believed that He could heal you, brother?" my classmate, Stan, asked me after our interpersonal communication class. I ignored him for two reasons. My attendant was waiting to feed me lunch, and this was the second time Stan had asked me his question. The first time my answer was, "GOD HAS ALREADY HEALED ME" And it hadn't changed.

Somehow he didn't believe me. He just smiled at me and said, "I'll pray for you, brother," and walked away. As I steered my electric powered wheelchair into the open elevator and touched the first floor button with my headstick, I wished Stan would let me explain what I meant.

As I headed back to my dormitory, I reflected on how God had healed me via modern technology. I have an electric wheelchair that I can operate with the back of my head. I have a computerized voice synthesizer that enables me to talk over a special phone. I have the headstick and letter board. I have a family and friends who love and accept me for what I am.

At the dorm's cafeteria my attendant greeted me with, "Hi, I saw your column in today's paper. It was good. Here let me help you with your coat. You look angry. What's wrong?"

"THE GUY WHO THINKS I COULD WALK AND TALK STOPPED ME AGAIN AND TOLD ME THAT I COULD GIVE GLORY TO GOD IF I WOULD JUST HAVE FAITH THAT GOD COULD HEAL ME" I spelled out on my letter board.

"Good grief, not him again! Did you tell him to take off?" my aide asked. "Just a minute and I'll get your food before the cafeteria closes. The usual?"

210   I nodded.

"Oh, here's today's paper. You can read it while I'm getting your lunch."

As my aide went to get my lunch, I saw Stan come into the dining room with his friend. His friend was carrying a Bible. I watched the pair.

As I watched them, I remembered my mother had told me more than once that when I was little, she took me to a faith healer. He told her that God would heal me. But it wouldn't be in the way she expected and it would take a long time. The evangelist said God had conveyed that message to him while he had his hands on my head.

My attendant brought my food, which stopped my reflections.

While I was eating my lunch, the two came over to my table and Stan said, "We have undeniable proof that you are possessed by the devil. . ."

"What?" my aide shouted in astonishment. "He is not!"

". . . but can be cured by God if you would just have faith" Stan continued.

"I HAVE BRAIN DAMAGE NOT DEMONS" I spelled out angrily. "BESIDES I HAVE TOLD YOU THAT GOD HAS HEALED ME"

Stan's friend opened his Bible and read passages about how Jesus could cast out demons from people, how he could make a person who was blind see, and how he could make another person who was lame walk.

I started to tell how God had healed me, but Stan said, "Spelling things out isn't talking. I can't keep all those letters straight, so why don't you just let God cast out your demons?"

"Amen!" replied his friend. Then they left. But something told me that they would be back with more of their out-of-context Bible quotations.

Until now, they amused me in a way. But now I was angry. They wanted their will, not God's will, to be done. To them, being 'healed' meant having a perfect body. My point was that physical healing wasn't the only way to become a whole person.

Every day after class Stan stopped me, asked me when I would let Christ heal me to glorify God, and leave. One day after three weeks of this harrassment, I started to cry on my way back to the dorm. I was 26 years old and a journalism major at UNL, and all I could do was to cry.

I cried out of anger and frustration. I cried because I was tired of being regarded as either a saint or sinner. I cried because I couldn't take out my frustrations any other way. I cried because I was beginning to feel my faith fail. When you're constantly told something, no matter how ridiculous, again and again, you start to doubt your own convictions no matter how deep they are. Maybe Stan and his friend were right.

Then I decided to talk with Dwayne, a friend and a dormmate who was a Christian in word and deed and who respected me as a valid person.

When I told him about the harrassment, he said, "I don't believe it. You mean these guys have actually said that you're demon possessed? It's guys like those that give Christianity a bad name. They're wrong, of course."

"I WISH I COULD FIND A BIBLE QUOTATION TO GET HIM OFF MY BACK I FEEL I AM DOING GOD'S WORK JUST BY SPEAKING OUT FOR PEOPLE WITH DISABILITIES GOD HAS GIVEN ME A GOOD MIND AND THE ABILITY TO WRITE I DONT NEED TO BE SO CALLED NORMAL TO BE HEALED" I spelled out.

"That's very true. Let me consult my Bible and see what I can find," Dwayne said. "I seem to remember something about Paul."

When I was getting ready for bed that night, my aide and I heard a knock. When my attendant opened the door, Dwayne and his friend asked, "Can we come in for a second? We have something to show Bill."

Then, to me, he said, "We found what you need to show those guys. It's from 2 Corinthians Chapter 2: Verses 7-10. Listen to this:

I will say this: because these experiences I had were so tremendous, God was afraid I might be puffed up by them; so there was given me a sickness which has been a thorn in my flesh, a messenger from Satan to hurt and bother me, and prick my pride. Three different times I begged God to make me well again. Each time He said, 'No. But I am with you; that is all you need. My power shows up best in

212   weak people.' Now I am glad to boast about how weak I am; I am glad to be a living demonstration of Christ's power, instead of showing off my own power and abilities. Since I know it is all for Christ's good, I am quite happy about 'the thorn,' and about insults and hardships and persecutions; for when I am weak, then I am strong. The less I have, the more I depend on Him.

"There it is," Dwayne said. "If I were you, I would go to the campus minister. Don't let 'em get you down. You're okay."

I followed Dwayne's advice and went to the campus minister. I told her the story and ended with,"I BELIEVE THAT GOD HAS HEALED ME BY HELPING ME TO ACCEPT MY DISABILITY BESIDES ISNT THE FACT THAT I AM HERE AT UNL A MIRACLE IN ITSELF"

"You're absolutely right. How dare they tell you, or anyone, that. These characters sound like fanatic fundamentalists. They can twist the Scriptures every which way to meet their needs. You're not possessed. Don't worry about that."

We talked for an hour about how God had enabled me to get an education and use modern technology to become the best that I could be. Then we said a prayer.

"Now have I reinforced your faith enough? Is there anything else I can do for you?" she asked.

"YES WOULD YOU PLEASE TALK TO THE GUYS AND MAKE THEM STOP HARRASSING ME AND REMIND THEM THAT PAUL HAD A THORN"

"Certainly. It would be my pleasure. Can you give me their names? I'll take it from there. However, if they still persist in bothering you, you let me know about it," the minister said.

The next class period after my chat with the campus clergy, Stan ignored me except for an occasional hostile glance.

Stan still believes I'm possessed by demons. But more important, I still believe that God has healed me.

EPILOGUE

"WHAT WILL I NEED TO GRADUATE" I asked my J-School advisor who was carefully going over my record.

"Let's see. You need about 20 hours of nuclear physics and 40 hours of phys ed," my advisor said. "Twenty of which need to be spent at the track. Won't that be fun?"

I nodded and laughed.

"Seriously, you just need three more hours in English, three more hours in one of the social sciences, and three hours in geometry. That's it," my advisor said.

"I CANT TAKE GEOMETRY I CANT DRAW SHAPES" I spelled.

"Let's go and see the interim dean. Maybe something can be worked out. We could substitute those 20 hours of nuclear physics and 40 hours of phys ed," my advisor said.

The interim dean was merciful. She only made me take three hours of statistics.

"CAN I TAKE IT PASS FAIL" I spelled out.

"Yes you can," she said.

My reasoning for wanting to take the class pass/no pass was simple. I was tired and wanted to coast. I had a nice 3.66 grade point average, which I earned.

As one professor said, "You have proven yourself, so relax this semester. You've earned it."

In February, 1983, I was one of the 25 million people to watch the last episode of M*A*S*H. It seemed that it mirrored my life. The personnel of the good old 4077 had survived with their sanity. So had I. No one was a hero at the 4077. I wasn't a hero. They just did their best. So did I.

214   In March I sent out invitations. This time I sent one to Deanne and
her husband.

She joked, "But, Bill, how will we be able to spot you in the crowd?
We might miss you."

"DONT WORRY ILL WEAR A RED CARNATION" I shot
back.

I also invited Anne Fadiman. To my dismay she didn't send an
acknowledgement. I guessed that things at the Time-Life Building
were busy because after her story on Mark and myself had been
published Anne had become a close friend. It was unlike her not to
acknowledge the invitation.

In April, 1983, Roger invited me to his wedding. At the reception I
told him, "I GUESS THIS IS THE YEAR THAT HELL FREEZES
OVER YOUR MARRYING AND MY GRADUATING HAVE TO
FREEZE IT OVER£

"Yeah buddy," Roger said and laughed. "But I always knew you
would graduate."

"THANKS FOR HELPING ME I COULDNT HAVE DONE IT
WITHOUT YOU" I spelled.

"We helped each other, buddy," Roger said.

Three days before graduation, the affirmative action officer called
and said that the Omaha World Herald was going to do a story on my
graduation. He told me to prepare a statement to save time. He didn't
ask me if I wanted to do the interview.

I did what I was told. I didn't see any point in arguing. I had mixed
feelings about the publicity. On one hand, my ego loved it. On the
other, a lot of college students would graduate, but only I was singled
out for something unrelated to learning. It didn't seem fair. It seemed
akin to those barbaric circus sideshows—no matter how distant.

I told the reporter my feelings, and he said that he would take them
into account.

Then he asked me a startling question: "Do you feel that your
degree has the same value as the others?"

"WHAT DO YOU MEAN" I spelled, somewhat taken aback.

"I mean do you feel that the professors gave you the grades out of
pity," the reporter said. It was the first time the question had been
raised.

I answered it honestly. "I DONT KNOW I JUST DID THE
ASSIGNMENTS ASK MY PROFESSORS

"I did and the chairman of the News-Ed department said that you earned everything you got," the reporter said after consulting his notes. I breathed a sigh of relief. Then the photographer with the reporter took several pictures of me in my cap and gown.

A couple of days before the big day, Mom informed me that my graduation party would be delayed a week because she would be too tired to have it immediately following the ceremony.

On the night before the graduation I had plans to have drinks with Mark Dahmke and Roger. But before I did I had to goto graduation rehearsal.

The rehearsal was short, but not sweet. The head marshal informed me that I wasn't going to be in the processional or the recessional, rather I would be seated before the processional and leave the floor after the recessional. He also told me that I would be pushed up the ramp to the stage where I would get my degree. The tone of his voice made it clear that his decision was final.

I wanted to be in the processional, in the recessional, and my electric wheelchair, but graduation was only 16 hours away. I didn't want to complicate the home stretch.

When I got home, I was still angry. I was certain that the head marshal was wrong, but I didn't know what to do about it. Then, I discovered that my door didn't lock when I left. I took a quick inventory: Computer, printer, carnation, my special phone. . . Wait a second. Carnation? I didn't have a carnation when I left. I wheeled closer to the flower to read the scribbled note. "We wanted to make sure we could pick you out tomorrow. Love ya, Deanne."

I laughed and cried at once.

Soon, Roger and another male friend showed up to take me to meet Mark. When we got to the lounge, I was glad to see that Mark had a date and wished that I had a date. His date had her back to the door, but even from the back I could tell that she was good-looking. "Good for you, friend," I thought.

I was preparing for an introduction, but got a warm hug. It was Anne Fadiman.

"You didn't really think I would miss your graduation, did you?" Anne said softly still hugging me.

"She wanted to surprise you. Your family and I were in on it. Were we successful?" Mark asked.

I nodded, still in shock.

216   "I'm staying the weekend," Anne said. "I asked your folks to delay any parties because I want to spend as much time with you as possible. Is that okay with you?"

I nodded. "THANK YOU ANNE FOR COMING ALL THE WAY FROM NEW YORK I CANT BELIEVE YOU DID IT£

"Actually, I came from San Francisco where I was doing a story," Anne said. "We should figure out all the places people are coming from just to be here for your graduation."

I thought for a minute. Mom, Dad, brother Jim, brother Don, two sets of aunts and uncles, Mrs. George, and Deanne and, Mark, her husband, were coming from Omaha. Brother Bob, now a student at Kearney State, and John McGill, now out of the rehab business, were coming from Kearney, Nebraska. Ed Henry (leaving Sally behind to nurse their three sons who had the chicken pox) was coming from Waterville, Kansas.

The next day, May 7, 1983, Ed came and took me to the ceremony. I needed a ride. He needed directions.

"I CANT BELIEVE IM GRADUATING" I spelled out.

"I can," Ed said. "I always knew you could do it."

When we arrived at the graduation, we were greeted by my dad, who was trying not to let his pride show but failing.

He and Ed put me in my cap and gown. The head marshal put a medallion around my neck. I waited for dad to tease me about wearing jewelry. He didn't because he knew the medallion meant that I was an honor graduate. I was one out of seven graduates with a bachelor's degree in journalism to graduate with distinction. Then, the head marshal wheeled me in to the arena of empty seats.

As I sat there trying to be inconspicuous. I thought of how ironic it was that after seven years of trying to blend in I was sticking out like a sore thumb.

To add insult to injury, I saw Anne holding up the Omaha World Herald. I was on the front page, but the headline was: "CEREBRAL PALSY VICTIM. . ."

"Damn," I thought, "I'm graduating from an accredited Big Eight school, but still I'm regarded as a victim."

Then, I heard the music and saw my fellow graduates filing into the auditorium. Slowly I melted into the crowd.

As the ceremony progressed, my mind went back to my high school graduation. I remembered the very idealistic songs that a very naive boy picked: "The Impossible Dream," "You'll never Walk Alone," and "Climb Every Mountain." While they weren't realistic and didn't prepare me for the hard times, they were prophetic. I realized my impossible dream, a college education. I never walked alone. There was always somebody standing by to help me. God made sure of that. And my college experiences taught me that I could climb every mountain.

My reverie was broken by a marshal's voice saying, "You're next to go up. Ready?" He pushed me to the foot of the ramp.

"I present the College of Journalism's graduates of 1983," Dean Copple said.

"I accept them," the chancellor said.

As I was going up the ramp, I remembered Martin Luther King's last speech, "I have been to the mountain top, and I have seen the promised land. . ."

I saw my promised land—the people who accepted me. Mom was snapping pictures. Dad was watching proudly. My brothers were applauding along with Mark Dahmke, Ed Henry, Mark Caughey, (Deanne's husband) and my uncles. My aunts, Anne, and Deanne were crying.

". . . .We as a people will get there. . ." King continued.

I know that people with disabilities will get to the promised land. All it takes is becoming educated enough to educate others that we're merely humans.